Winning Richmond

How a Progressive Alliance Won City Hall

Gayle McLaughlin

HARDBALL PRESS

Dedication

This book is dedicated to the richly diverse people of Richmond, California, whose strength, heart, and resilience created a remarkable transformation against all odds!

If we could win a progressive agenda in Richmond under the money might of Chevron's major oil refinery, it can be done anywhere!

Library of Congress Cataloging-in-Publication Data
Winning for Richmond: How a Progressive Alliance Won City Hall
1.Richmond, CA—Nonfiction. 2. American political history. 3.
Progressive Politics. 4. Gayle McLaughlin.

Contents

Introduction

Richmond's story is a tale of transformation and political upheaval. A company town long ruled by the Chevron Oil
Company and their corporate-owned political insiders saw in the
first decade of the 21st century a new approach to progressive politics. With this new approach, an organized movement of local
activists seized power in City Hall and held it, ushering in a bold
new agenda focused on social good and climate activism.

This book chronicles the story of that progressive alliance as
we dove into the shifting political currents of this mid-size San
Francisco Bay Area city. It describes how in a little over a decade
we transformed City Hall, with the help of many grassroots and
union organizations. It tells how we prevailed against the multi-
national billion-dollar oil industry that had long gripped the city
government in a stranglehold.

I am a founding member of the Richmond Progressive Alliance
(RPA). As a group of community activists, we came together to
address economic, social, and environmental issues facing the
city. Many of these problems were the direct result of Chevron's
pollution and its political power—its colossal refinery operating
in Richmond producing a morass of negative conditions.

But there is power in people who organize for a higher purpose. That is exactly what we have done, and continue to do as
we hold onto City Hall and the cause of economic and climate
justice.

My election as city councilmember and then mayor, along
with the election of other progressive councilmembers, allowed
us to set a new direction that led to numerous projects benefiting
our diverse community and the environment. Through continued
work and reorganization of the alliance and the city, we offer both
a model of progressive politics and a challenge to others to take
action to realize democratic ideals.

1

Our story begins with a description of the geography and brief history of Richmond as a way to introduce you to the city through my eyes. And since this book is my vision, I tell you a little bit about myself—my working-class roots, my foray into political activism, and how I arrived at this West Coast city that would become my home. I share my motivations for getting involved in local politics, and I discuss how I stood with other activists in our community against the abuses of a giant oil refinery and in support of good, healthy, and just initiatives for the benefit of our diverse and a largely low-income population.

I relate how our progressive alliance formed and burst onto the local political scene in a city known for its corrupt politics. I speak of how we defied the conventional wisdom with my winning a seat on the City Council while taking no corporate donations, and how this victory placed us in a new setting for creating the kind of change our community needed.

But as a lone RPA voice on the Council, I soon realized I needed a higher-level job to accomplish the goals we had set out, so I ran for mayor. Our struggle soon lent itself to seeking fairness in local taxation and ultimately led to Chevron paying more taxes into the city coffers. This was really as much about justice and fairness as about the money they owed the city. This episode illustrates a powerful example of people acting in their own interest and making local industry accountable to the city in which they operate.

We waged a political fight over the course of several years in order to save a scenic piece of land in our city, formerly a Navy Fuel Depot, from becoming a Las-Vegas style casino. This would lead to more environmental health and justice work, including preventing a refinery expansion, stopping an irresponsible developer who sought to build on contaminated land, and the protection of an intact wetland on our shoreline.

My re-election as mayor and the campaign against me demonstrated new lows from our adversaries in the form of a vicious personal smear campaign. There would be more drama ahead for me in the following years. I give some of the inside story working on the City Council, particularly with one councilmember's continually destructive behavior that wreaked havoc over the course of his four years in office. This is a saga about the disgraceful and contemptible shenanigans of an elected official, abetted by a handful of followers, and how they had hobbled our local democracy, hindering participation by the rest of our community. It is also the story of how we endured and survived as a progressive community in the face of continuous and outrageous attempts to undermine us.

I detail many of our successes, and I provide some examples of how our local political work intersected with the arts and with international political efforts. Richmond is not an island; our aspirations as a working-class community are evidenced universally in the arts, as well as in our solidarity with global struggles.

My hope in this book is to give a glimpse of community strength in action and what an organized movement can do. In Richmond, we have taken our rightful place on the map as a leader in progressive change. We have shown that principled commitment and perseverance can create phenomenal transformation.

We are committed to continuing our progressive work not only for the benefit of our own city, but to inspire others to do likewise. Every community can create political and social change from below—in fact, it is only through bottom-up, grassroots democracy that we will become strong enough to create a more civilized society and a sustainable planet.

Local organizing efforts are driven by a city's particular issues and dynamics. You may see your community's problems or ones like them in this book—an epic tale that shines new light on what is politically and personally possible. As you peer through the keyhole of our Richmond experience, you may also glimpse a bit of yourself and your own values and dreams. I hope my journey of leading a working-class city in northern California will awaken in you, wherever you live, the desire to act boldly and create a better future for your community as well.

Richmond: A Window to Our Nation

In 1998 I made a pivotal shift in my life and moved to the San Francisco Bay Area, making the journey westward, like so many others before me, in search of new beginnings. Back in the mid-nineteenth century, when settlers migrated across the U.S., there was a romanticism about starting a new life in the West. I held this same sentiment as I made my way across the country over a century later. I was following a call to "go west" as much as anyone. That migration of the 1800s stretched the geographic boundaries of the U.S. For me in 1998, a single woman in mid-life, I was stretching my boundaries and starting a new adventure.

Having spent four years living in Massachusetts furthering my college education, I contemplated a couple of choices. While considering a move back to my hometown of Chicago, I also gave thought to a bolder move that would take me all the way to the Bay Area. I had made trips there in past years to visit one of my sisters and to attend political conferences. While Chicago held familiarity for me, San Francisco's cultural environment had a unique appeal. It embodied what was left of a revolutionary spirit emerging from the 1960s, including activism centered in Berkeley.

In the end, my decision was about searching for an atmosphere rich in many cultural expressions—art, politics, and activism. Setting aside my nervousness and uncertainty, I ventured out in my compact car with only essential possessions and began my solitary drive across country. I added to the experience by listening to my artist and political friend Frank Garvey's compelling music, "Seasons of the Veil" and "Rapture of the Deep"—prophetic sounds that reminded me of the convergence of progress, the arts, and history. Fixing my sights on a far horizon, I made my way westward across the many plains, valleys, deserts, and mountains that grace our country's natural beauty.

Encountering Richmond

During my first couple of years in the Bay Area, I rented rooms in homes while I learned the lay of the land before settling into a place I would call home. In those early years, I didn't know much about Richmond, except for the general impressions I had garnered through word of mouth and mainstream media. What I heard was that Richmond was known for high levels of street violence. It was reputed to be one of the most dangerous cities in the region. Yet there was another image of the city that would soon come into my purview.

Two years after my arrival, I grew to know a more intricate, complex, and poignant Richmond. It started with a budding romance with my now husband Paul, who had lived in Richmond for about seven years. Once we moved in together, a more in-depth view of my new city began to reveal itself. I had lived in inner city Chicago neighborhoods in the 1980s and early 90s, so was familiar with the two faces of despair and desperation, combined with that corresponding determination and perseverance present in so many neighborhoods.

As my life in Richmond took hold, I recognized a sense of American life that looked like many other urban settings across our nation. I saw Richmond as a snapshot of that same urban America. It is a captivating recognition; one in which I felt an immediate affinity and familiarity. I saw people as vibrant, active participants in their community, even amid their pain and suffering. I recognized a vitality that was generated day after day, as people let in the freshness of each new morning and recommitted to their struggles for a better life.

It wasn't long before I saw that Richmond's notoriety as a high-crime city was but a slice of a more intricate city. Those sensationalistic and one-dimensional portrayals of Richmond were inaccurate distortions of the city I was coming to know. When I pulled away the veil of this limited representation, what came into view was poetic and stunning. The splendor of the San Francisco Bay, its surrounding landscape and the beauty of the city's diverse working-class population in the Richmond landscape came into better focus. As I came to know Richmond further, I saw a resilient community with the courage to persist in the face of daunting challenges. Whether walking along the bay at Point Isabel or hiking the hills, I saw my city with new eyes. Nestled between thirty-two miles of exquisite shoreline and the vast beauty of the Richmond hills, a varied city emerges. A walk on the water's edge in Richmond, with Mount Tamalpais in Marin Country to the west and a view of the glimmering skyline of San Francisco across the bay, would give anyone a vastly different appreciation of Richmond than the previous night's televised sound bite. The view of the hills Paul and I enjoyed from our second floor apartment was especially captivating at night, as lights came on and illuminated the hillside. To me it was a surreal vision, looking much like candles in the dark, conveying a visual metaphor of hope at this new juncture in my life.

Contradictions and Unfulfilled Promises

Richmond's natural beauty is something to behold, but that wasn't the only vision that stands out on the landscape. On the bay at the city's northern limits, a giant oil refinery with smokestacks belching toxins protrudes into view. Not visible from a distance was the impact of these emissions on land, water, air, and the people living within the refinery's periphery. With the refinery's legacy of one hundred plus years of fossil fuel development, the Chevron Richmond Refinery has despoiled the environment. While Richmond beholds vast natural grandeur, the land and its people also endure the effects of environmental degradation.

I tried to make sense of this disjointed and contradictory picture: a city with such beautiful natural landscape that simultaneously struggled with serious pollution that was unsightly as well as a serious public health hazard for its residents. I observed a strong, determined community of activists pursuing rights to a quality existence. I also saw a downward spiral in quality of life for those people living near the refinery, not to mention the street crime and other urban problems they faced. Richmond's contradictions pointed to much larger systemic failures and unfulfilled promises. The unkept assurances were not just endemic to Richmond, they were a window into our nation's failed American Dream; one that has befallen many cities across our nation. Like many other cities, Richmond's history is a microcosm of America, lined with tales both beautiful and ugly, promising and tragic, filled with despair.

And hope.

Chevron refinery

Beautiful Richmond

First Inhabitants—The Huichin Ohlone Tribe

Going back 5,000 years, the Huichin Ohlone Tribe, our city's original settlers, made their way to what is now Richmond. Finding the region rich in food, they made it their home, and over the course of those many centuries left massive piles of clam and mussel shells along our creeks and bay shoreline. The Native Americans, though faced with the harsh reality of basic survival, had a sustainable connection with nature and each other. They fished and gathered food they needed for survival and respected the earth's need for replenishment. Foraging for food and finding living accommodations has changed since the Ohlones lived in harmony with the environment in this place we call Richmond. Yet the indigenous people that remain here today still hold strong to a cultural identity that has demonstrated a resilience to their past and to centuries of abuse by other settlers.

Post-European Settlement and Early Industrialization

Fast-forward to the nineteenth century, when European voyagers came to America and conquered the land from the indigenous people who were living here. For the Native Americans, the land was sacred; they felt connected to it. There was no concept of land "ownership." Instead, they revered the land that gave them sustenance. As stewardship of the territory was wrested from the hands of indigenous people, the foundation was laid for a different relationship to the land. By the mid-1800s Richmond became part of a larger area used mainly for grazing called Rancho San Pablo. This harkens back to the time when Mexico had control of California, having won independence from Spain. The Mexican government encouraged settlement by giving land grants to its citizens for ranches (ranchos). These ranchos would later disappear when the U.S. took control of California.

Looking back, one can imagine what we now know as Richmond draped in moist grasslands and meadows with towering trees, flourishing native plants, and a vast diversity of animal species. This largely unspoiled ecosystem contributed to a balanced planet. The Mexican land grants fostered lifestyles that were largely non-damaging to the land, such as herding and grazing, and the people maintained a healthy relationship to the land. Later, this crucial connection to the environment would be sacrificed, as industries moved to Richmond, bringing soil, air, and water pollution that contaminated and desecrated the land while considering this part and parcel of doing business.

By the turn of the next century, a new industrial future was taking shape, prompting Richmond to incorporate as a city in 1905. Since then, the city has taken many twists and turns, taking on various characterizations amid the backdrop of a changing nation. Richmond's history pulls back the curtains on the workings and subsequent failings of the 20th-century industrial era. By virtue of its geography and location, the landmass that came to be known as Richmond was poised to become an industrial center, even before the city's incorporation. Edgar Cervano-Soto explored Richmond's early industrial history and development.

There is a commonly held misperception that Chevron, once known as Standard Oil, built Richmond. However, Richmond's formation and eventual emergence as an industrial powerhouse in the mid-twentieth century predates Standard Oil....In 1900, Augustin S. Macdonald, an Oakland real estate developer, purchased the eastern flatlands of Richmond after he convinced the Santa Fe Railroad Company to establish a terminal here. Macdonald subdivided the land into lots and sold them. The subdivision created a block plan and a new thoroughfare, Macdonald Avenue. Because of their proximity to the railroad terminal and the accessibility of Macdonald Avenue, the for-sale lots became desirable. It was at this time, in 1901, that John D. Rockefeller brought Standard Oil to Richmond. Rockefeller's company was already embroiled in controversy, over accusations that it had monopolized the oil industry in violation of the Sherman Antitrust Act. The refinery in Richmond was just one of thousands operated by Standard Oil across the country.[1]

As the industrial growth of the city grew, it was given the nickname "The Wonder City." Media started promoting Richmond as on its way to being a great city, advertising at as "The Pittsburgh of the West." A congressional delegation visited Richmond before the opening of the Panama-Pacific International Exposition in 1915. On August 7, 1915, nearly 3,000 Richmond residents boarded a ferry to San Francisco for "Richmond Day," commemorating the tenth-year anniversary of the city's incorporation, and drawing attention to Richmond as an up-and-coming city.

In the early 1900s, as industrialists were solidifying their influence throughout the San Francisco Bay Area, all eyes were on Richmond. The July 1912 issue of the *San Francisco Chamber of Commerce Journal* announced it this way: "Richmond was well surveyed from a business point of view and astonishing in its development—a worthy daughter of San Francisco." Wealthy manufacturers from the city of San Francisco dominated the land use in the Richmond area. These businessmen were tired of complaints from neighbors and liability issues they encountered in San Francisco, so they moved their operations to places less populated, like Richmond, where they were welcomed by city officials and industrial leaders.

As California Spanish *ranchos* gave way to industry, working people soon populated Richmond to work in industry. Over several decades, the city was shaped into a vital urban industrial center, with a population reaching nearly 24,000 in 1940.[2] This growth of industry was widespread throughout the 20th century, with profits expanding exponentially, while generations of working people faced a host of new challenges. Members of the community did not experience the benefit of such industries, but they did suffer from the spills, fires, leaks, and the daily health impact of polluting industries that put profits before people. Today, many industries have abandoned Richmond, leaving their toxins behind. For the remaining industries, including Chevron, the money continues to roll in, as the relentless search for greater and greater profits leads the way. From those early days, when the first industrialists saw Richmond as no more than a way to enrich themselves, it would take nearly a century before the community began to push back against those powerful forces.

The Shipyards of World War II

In mid-century Richmond was headed toward a new era. In the 1940s the city saw its greatest population growth, and it was driven not by private industry, but by the U.S. government. The population soared from under 24,000 to over 100,000, with people flocking to Richmond for jobs in war-related industries. Large numbers of African-American families migrating from the South came to work in the Richmond shipyards. With this influx of a diversified workforce—unimaginable prior to the war— Richmond shipyards built and launched 747 ships, more than any other shipyard in the country. Although Blacks who made their home in Richmond and other Bay Area cities had more economic opportunity than in the South, they were still subjected to racial discrimination. They faced segregated housing, assignment to menial jobs, and were not permitted full membership in trade unions. Women, both black and white, came into the workforce in unprecedented numbers during this era as well, with "Rosie the Riveter" becoming the iconic image of working women during the war.

After World War II, the military packed up and left Richmond, eliminating jobs for the many people who had moved here. The city felt the grave economic impact of systemic racism, where prosperity passed over the many Black families who had provided their labor in support of the home front efforts. Politicians made empty promises to open doors for new opportunities and create new jobs that never materialized.

Postwar Era

As jobs were disappearing during the postwar period, little known to most people, Richmond sustained a vibrant blues culture that brought together several great musicians. Notable talent included North Richmond's Jimmy McCracklin, T. Bone Walker, Ivory Joe Hunter, Amos Milburn, Big Mama Thornton, and Big Joe Turner. During the 1950s and 60s they played at the Club Savoy and the Brown Derby, hosting such luminaries as Lowell Fulson, Etta James, and Ray Charles. Richmond was a happening place for many well-known musicians. It was also home to family-centered neighborhoods where people maintained a close connection to one another, preserving generational and cultural roots. This was a thriving culture, reflecting the spirit of a community with strong ties to one another.

But preservation of culture wasn't the only thing afoot in the city in the postwar era. In the 1950s, the African-American struggle for civil rights began to take off in Richmond with the fight against segregated housing. African-American former shipyard worker Wilbur Gary and his family courageously took on that struggle, demanding their rights and taking a stand against bigotry and racism. The Gary family bought a house in the all-white Rollingwood neighborhood in 1952. When they moved in, a mob of 300 whites shouted racist epithets, hurled bricks at the house, and left a white wooden cross on the lawn.

Calling on the NAACP for help, the Gary's stood firm, in spite of intimidation and offers to buy them out. Gary decried, "I'm not afraid and I will not be forced out...We've got to whip this thing sometime, and it might as well be now!"[3] Soon the tide began to turn, with more than 800 people showing up to defend the Gary's rights, including supporters from the NAACP, East Bay Civil Rights Congress, trade unions, the white progressive community, and a few of the Gary's white neighbors. In 2009, Jovanka Beckles, Richmond Progressive Alliance (RPA) community leader, brought attention to this story, reporting it as a "proud moment of local African American affirmation" and a success "achieved by an amazing formula: Standing up for our rights and sticking it out, defending the principles, seeking and receiving the support of decent people of all races and income levels."[4]

The Sixties and Civil Rights

Throughout the 1960s the Richmond community continued standing up for civil rights, including playing an early role in the development of the Black Panther Party. On April 1, 1967, Denzil Dowell, age 22, was shot and killed by law enforcement in North Richmond, leaving many unanswered questions for his family and neighbors. Details of the shooting didn't add up. Testimony and reports of the killing by neighbors, newspapers, and law enforcement were vastly different and called for an investigation. The family reached out to the Panthers for protection from police harassment. The Panthers responded valiantly, making their presence known first by organizing a rally of 400 people. Within two weeks, and after just thirty minutes of deliberation, a jury of ten white and two black citizens ruled the shooting as justifiable homicide. By the end of that month, the Panthers published their first issue of the *Black Panther Party Black Community News Service* with this case as their headline story. Although the case was not resolved satisfactorily, the incident catapulted the Panthers to the national stage and marked the beginning of their fight against harassment, brutality, and unjustified police killings.

The Black Panthers continued to thrive in Richmond. While

the Panthers kept the spotlight on local police brutality, they also successfully ran a breakfast program in North Richmond, giving many African-American children a healthy start to their school days. Individuals who would later join the progressive movement made, packed, and distributed those meals for children. One key member was Bobby Bowens, whose efforts with the Black Panthers, among other key groups, helped raise political consciousness and activism in Richmond. He tirelessly advocated for public health, and he educated the community on the fight against racism. Bowens died in 2010, but his memory lives on as the name of RPA's office building in Richmond—the Bobby Bowens Progressive Center.

Immigration

Richmond's African-American history is just one part of the city's diverse past. In the last decades of the 20th century, waves of immigrants came to our city, bringing a large demographic shift. In the post-Vietnam War era, Laotians, Cambodians, Hmong, Vietnamese, and other Asian populations came as refugees of war and other regional conflicts. Large numbers of Latinos also came to Richmond in the 1980s and 90s fleeing war, poverty, and disastrous U.S. trade policies, such as NAFTA. Our large Mexican-American community has enriched Richmond for many decades. Since the 1980s, Latin American immigrants have come from Mexico, El Salvador, Guatemala, Honduras, and various South American countries. These newly arrived residents had witnessed grave injustices in their countries of origin. Many of them had been active in organized resistance. Consequently, many of them brought those leadership skills with them to Richmond and have helped advance Richmond's progressive movement.

Our population as of the 2010 census records is comprised of just over a hundred thousand residents, with 40% Latinos, 27% African-Americans, 17% White, 14% Asian-American, and smaller portions of Native Americans and Pacific Islanders. [5] With a majority people of color and one-third of our residents foreign-born, as well as a working-class identity that cuts across all demographics, Richmond serves as a porthole to modern day America.

Gayle McLaughlin

Poverty, Violence, and the Need for Solutions

Even as people came to Richmond with dreams and determination, the social problems facing our city intensified in the latter decades of the last century. In the 1980s Richmond, like many urban communities, was hit hard by the crack cocaine epidemic. By the mid-1980s, the widespread availability of crack cocaine in inner city neighborhoods created an alarming situation. Crack was cheap, plentiful, and addictive, and the effects were tragic. Already suffering from racial and economic inequalities, Richmond was the setting of a failed national approach to this drug epidemic, and for years the city's poor and Black communities fell victim to that travesty. Draconian, zero-tolerance drug policies under the Reagan administration led to overcrowded prisons and blocked expansion of needle exchange programs that could have saved hundreds of thousands of lives from the HIV and AIDS epidemics. Throughout the 1990s, rather than face these problems with drug treatment, harm reduction programs, and poverty abatement, prisons filled up with Richmond's poor, Black, disenfranchised youth, who found themselves staring into a void with no future in sight. Simultaneously, hospitals were caring for "crack babies" with critical health challenges. Local school districts offered little help, as funding for education was also in steep decline. Nor did local government prioritize addressing this issue.

The suffering of poor, non-White people in Richmond mirrored similar industrialized cities across our nation. The military had abandoned a large swath of African American shipyard workers after World War II, leaving them unemployed and scrambling for poverty wage jobs in a city with few opportunities for advancement. Companies like Chevron, with their money and power in local government, were unaffected by the decline of communities surrounding them. They kept running their refineries, spewing toxins in the air and offering few jobs to local residents. For countless Richmond families, hardship intensified.

The onslaught of drug addictions accelerated nationwide. Rather than treat the causes and conditions as a public health problem, the response was mass incarceration, resulting in a revolving door of poverty and recidivism. Richmond's community, low-income, largely people of color with few resources to fight back against abuses, was an easy population to cast aside with little concern. Reagan's trickle-down economics had *not* trickled down to those most in need, but it had expanded the gap between the rich and the poor. A comparison of Richmond's economic, social, and environmental trajectory with surrounding cities in the Bay Area demonstrates the wide disparity of wealth. People who had already been suffering from oppression and impoverishment were further marginalized by inadequate and cruel responses to serious problems, leaving families divided, broken, and in pain. As the 20th century drew to a close, the problems of the urban poor in Richmond loomed large, with no end in sight.

This was the state of Richmond when I came to this community in 2001. In the coming years, I would dive deep into the causes and conditions facing our people, and to the best of my ability would confront the good, the bad, and the ugly.

Initially, I settled into life in Richmond, a place with other working-class people, and joined others who simply wanted to search for a better future. Yet even as I began to feel a sense of identification with my new city, the knowledge that Richmond remained a dangerous place was never far from my mind. What the media saw and wrote about was real. The trauma, anger, and fear were pervasive. At the same time, the reporters and camera people didn't stick around long enough after each story on "another Richmond homicide" to see how people coped and kept on going. They didn't see neighborhoods go quiet, with kids kept inside over the coming weeks and months after an eruption of street violence. They also didn't see how little by little city blocks would fill once again with the laughter of children and a community's warmth and love for one another, as neighbors shared frustration and anger amid their searches for viable solutions.

With changing our city's reputation in real and concrete ways ahead of us, I saw a working-class community that knew how to endure harsh and tragic circumstances and re-emerge with a nurturing support for one another. I saw a Richmond that understood the power of community. Richmond's story is the story of growing that power by coming together broadly as a working-class community, building a grassroots democracy, and uniting in our common interest.

My personal history shares a common thread with many working-class people. Each of us was socialized as children into a society without a level playing field, without the security bestowed on those born into money. Later in life as an elected official I would champion remedies for these inequities and take on thorny political battles to implement a social justice platform in my city of Richmond. Much in my earlier life prepared me for this challenge.

I was born in the 1950s in Chicago into a blue-collar family. My parents, four sisters, and I lived in the upstairs apartment of the house built by my maternal grandfather, an Italian immigrant, who lived downstairs with my grandmother. The neighborhood was an industrial area, with factories situated directly across the street and throughout the vicinity. There were strong, noxious smells coming out of these places, especially from soybeans manufactured a few blocks away. My first-hand experience living in the shadow of heavy industry helped shape my awareness and understanding of environmental justice. Both my grandmother and mother worked in these settings, often under harsh conditions.

My mother shared stories about working in those factories. One of the tales she recounted was about how my grandmother fought Chicago City Hall when she and her co-workers were being forced to work in a flooded factory with water up to their ankles. This petite, 4-ft 11-inch, Italian woman, with broken English, made her way to the government offices, on her own, making it clear to officials that this situation was unacceptable. My grandmother's feistiness showed me that you can fight City Hall and win.

Just before my sixth birthday, my family moved to Norridge, a township adjacent to the northwest corner of Chicago. Our house was situated right on the border of the busy city, with a bus line a half block away from our home. It was one of many newly built small brick homes occupied by working families.

Like many who grew up in blue-collar households, my childhood was filled with rich and positive experiences, along with difficult times. My family life was filled with deep love and deep pain.

My dad was a good provider, even in times when he was laid off from his construction jobs. He worked outdoors in the hot summers and cold winters of Chicago. I have enormous respect for his willingness to keep our family afloat harsh season after harsh season. He only finished the eighth grade, but was self-educated over the course of his life and had a keen intellectual appetite. He had a love for new adventures, good and bad. At one point in his youth, he landed in jail for "joy-riding," which was at the center of a growing car culture, popular among young men of his day (joy-riding is an old-fashioned term for driving around in a temporarily stolen car for fun—they would always return the car after riding in it—it was akin to a teenage antic). My dad wrote a poem when he was in jail that he shared with me later in life. Though I don't remember the exact text, I remember my dad conveying his desire to live an honest life. That was when I came to realize that like my dad, we are more than our mistakes. Though he committed a small but illegal act, he was not a bad person due to this error in judgment in his youth.

During the years while I was growing up, my dad worked as a union carpenter. With pride he often took me on drives to see his construction sites. Once I was old enough to form my own political opinions, our relationship evolved into a series of deep conversations about how to change things in our society. Over many a cup of coffee, we talked about the plight of civilization and how society needed to be fixed. These discussions helped shape my politics and hopes and dreams for a better world. At the same time, my personal relationship with my dad was emotionally distant. As I became a young woman, I saw in him a level of sexism that was hurtful—whether through occasional off-color jokes or flirting with women in the presence of my mom. It wasn't until I reached adolescence that I came to understand the pain my father's behavior must have caused my mother. Later in life, my dad acknowledged these shortcomings.

My mom was born of Italian immigrant parents. As the only daughter with three brothers, she rebelled against the old-school thinking that boxed her into a traditional role of women from that culture. She often told the story of how she refused to learn how to make homemade spaghetti noodles, telling her father: "Why do I have to learn this? I'm not going to marry an Italian." That turned out to be true when she married my dad, an Irishman. Yet it was the Italian culture that permeated through our family life growing up, mainly because of the close relationship we all had with my grandmother. Everyone in my family, including my dad, had an unshakable bond of affection for my grandmother, whose kindness was only matched by her strength. My mother's deep relationship with her mother gave me an up close example of how women's solidarity can be passed from generation to generation.

My mom, like my dad, had a limited education, finishing only a couple years of high school. While she worked in factories and as a cashier during some of my childhood, for the most part she worked as a housewife and mother. Like most women of her time, she was the key disciplinarian.

Mom made sure our childhood was filled with fun-packed times, stretching the money my dad earned as far as it could go. She took us on summer outings to amusement parks and visits to the zoo, and made sure we had a yearly pass to the neighborhood pool. She also made sure every Christmas there were lots of gifts under the tree. She made us feel special, even though most of the presents were sale items from discount stores and sidewalk sales. Mom clearly wanted us to have good childhood memories, even as she struggled herself with her own stress and personal issues.

No doubt my mother wanted the best for her daughters, though she didn't necessarily want us to rise up the ladder of success. She sought a deeper experience of life for us. I learned from her that there is a more poignant side to being human than elevating one's economic status. This poignancy emanates from an appreciation of culture and the aesthetic experience. She often talked about how she had been chosen to play lead roles in school plays. That seemed to be a place where she felt both pride and joy. She had a theatrical side to her personality that came out it in various ways. For example, she would hold us children spellbound when she read to us or told us stories, moving us in a dramatic and awe-inspiring way beyond the words themselves. I recall her recounting for me later in life that she liked observing the expressions on the faces of actors—illuminating the intricate way emotions are often conveyed. I found it interesting that more than the storyline, it was the artistry of the actor, not the surface performance, that intrigued her. My mother's craving for artistic endeavor was etched in me and has remained a constant thread throughout my life.

My mother also influenced me in the realm of politics. One day during the week of the 1968 Democratic Convention in Chicago, I watched my mom fixated on the television in a state of shock and anger. She was watching live coverage of demonstrators against the war in Vietnam being clubbed, beaten, and arrested by the police. Stunned, my mom kept repeating, "Look at what they're doing" over and over again, as if she couldn't believe what she was seeing. The brutality against those young protestors totally unnerved her. She felt the pain and injustice as if the blows were falling on her own teenage children. I don't know if my mother realized how much of an impact she had on me that day, but her outrage gave me a new view of the world.

Both my parents were impassioned, loving individuals, but like most adults, they had their flaws. They fought a lot. I remember often waking up in the pre-dawn hours to their intense arguments. Money was often a problem, but it was more than that. Neither of my parents ever really fit into the middle class society to which they aspired, and their frustrations boiled over time and time again.

And the fighting wasn't just between them. My mother would lash out at my younger sisters and me out of proportion for little things, like not hanging up our clothes or other typical kid's chores. Although my mom doted on my sisters and me in our early childhood, as we got older she was at times unable to control her temper. She would hit us in fits of anger. While the physical impact of her hitting was not extreme, her angry tantrums were frightening. My mom would turn into a different person, and it was hard for me to process what was going on. Here I had a mother whom I loved and knew that she loved me, but who could turn into an angry person that I feared. Soon after each tirade, my mom would feel a deep sense of regret, and she would follow those episodes by trying to cheer me up in the midst of my tears.

It wasn't until later in life that I understood that her behavior was what today we call an anger management problem. With some therapy or education from a local mental health clinic my mother would have learned how to cope with her feelings or get to the root of her anger, and my sisters and I would have been spared a lot of grief. Those angry outbursts left psychological scars that lingered into my adulthood. Yet I was also fortunate that my mother and I cultivated trust in later years. As a young adult, I was able to confront her about some of that trauma. I had worried she would be overly defensive, but instead she looked me straight in the eye and in a voice weighted heavy in emotion, she assured me with the words: "Don't you know how much I love you?" I knew implicitly that she did not want to risk losing her relationship with me. I also knew I had the power to forgive her. And from that day forward, our relationship took on a healthier course.

Many of our conversations were political in nature. I found my mom receptive to new views. Among the topics we discussed was legislation in Sweden that prohibited parental use of physical punishment. Both my mother and I agreed with this policy, and we became outspoken about this issue with others. Today Sweden is an example that has been embraced by forty-nine countries. They have shown a marked decrease in youth crime, drug, alcohol abuse, and mental health issues.[6] My mom and I both came to understand that creating peace begins in part with less violence in the home.

As I grew older, I realized that both my parents carried a lot of pain with them, as they were both victims of physical abuse in their families. We now know that psychological cycles of anger are often passed from one generation to the next. I also came to realize that these cycles are not only family-related, they are systemic, emerging from unjust socio-economic systems. Inequalities in our society create conditions of instability and despair for many people that often result in personal and societal violence. I was fortunate to have parents who, in spite of their own difficult emotional circumstances, were also open-minded enough to grow over the course of their lives. They gave more than they received from this world and instilled in me the desire and yearning to embrace life for all it has to offer, and fight like hell for something better.

Each of my sisters looked for that something better in their ways as well. Although we were raised Catholic, my parents were not devout. On the few occasions we all attended Sunday Mass, my parents would be critical of how the parish priest was always asking for money. There was a period of time when the priest, in an attempt to get more money from parishioners, would print in the Sunday bulletin how much each family contributed. Thinking this was in poor taste, my parents complained that it was belittling to families who couldn't contribute much, which of course included our family.

My sisters and I were sent to Catholic elementary schools, followed by public high school. While the catechism I learned stayed with me for a while, I soon abandoned organized religion as I came to believe that our society's injustices were put into play by human beings and as such, it was the human person's obligation to become agents of change for the better. I came to appreciate what renowned abolitionist Frederick Douglass said in regard to his escape from slavery: "I prayed for twenty years but received no answer until I prayed with my legs."[7] His life only began to change when he acted on his own behalf. Social and political activism became, for me, the way to make change.

My own view of the world is not religious per se, rather it is based on humanistic values. Religion never seemed to have the answers for me. My philosophy of life and how to live well comes more from reflecting on historical struggles and the issues facing us where we live. From where I stand, I believe we are all part of something much greater than ourselves, and that greater vision does not emerge from any creationist or pre-determined design. I believe as a human species we have the ability to alter the course of civilization. I am optimistic about changing our direction when we make bad choices and that by our own efforts we can bring forward justice and peace, once we face our problems and realize we need to act in the present time, not wait for Divine intervention or pray for an afterlife where everything will work out.

My path has been one of activism and working in the political arena. I respect people of all faith traditions and those who hold different worldviews as they seek the comfort, joy, and guidance offered by their religious practices. I feel that it is up to us to build our own future in the here and now as active participants in creating change in our world.

A Child of the Sixties

I grew up in the 1960s and 70s at a time when cultures were clashing. It was a time when politics and social conventions were changing rapidly. As I entered adolescence, my generation of women experienced a new sense of identity and promise. Through the Women's Movement I learned about reproductive rights, equal pay for equal work, and the right to be leaders in politics, science, and other fields largely dominated by men. I was influenced by authors like Evelyn Reed, who offered fresh insights into our struggle as women against oppression. Reed's *Women's Evolution: From Matriarchal Clan to Patriarchal Family* and *Is Biology Women's Destiny?* intrigued me.[8] She disputed the "hunting theory" promoted by patriarchal anthropologists that postulated males as the superior sex, due to their greater involvement in "the hunt" to provide subsistence for the tribe. I was inspired by Reed's portrayal that it was more likely women, given the greater amount of time they spent at campsites and dwelling places for child-bearing, who made breakthroughs in agriculture, leading to early advances in civilization. This understanding has given me confidence when taking up new ideas and thinking as a political leader that go beyond traditional limitations often presented as eternal truths. When I hear phrases like, "There will always be war" or "There will always be poverty," I remember our female ancestors picking up the digging stick and cultivating the soil, thus assuring the survival of the tribe, when the men came back to camp after an unsuccessful hunt.

Understanding our history as women is essential to gaining the dignity and respect that we deserve and need. Feminists have had to fight for the revision of history books that espoused patriarchal views, not unlike African-Americans who have had to correct their history. And just as the Civil Rights Movement provided the impetus for academic inclusion of Black History and African-American studies, the Women's Movement provided a similar impetus. Having access to those writings led me to resolve that my life would not be defined by those who frame women in stereotypical and limiting ways.

Yet the more prominent movement that had an impact on me in my college days was the youth antiwar movement opposing the Vietnam War. I took a stand with those who wanted our country to reverse course and make peace rather than escalate the war. I was part of the generation of young people who stepped away from tradition and looked at political situations with a new lens. The youth movement had a phenomenal effect on me as a budding activist. It breathed hope in me. My generation asked different questions that were not merely a search for intellectual answers. We came from a place of the heart, as well as the mind.

One day, standing on the periphery of an antiwar vigil, I felt the first glimmerings of an activist movement drawing me to it. Many in my generation were coming together as people of conscience, saying we need peace, not war. Becoming part of something bigger than me, I felt a sense of inclusion and empowerment. Standing with my peers that evening, I felt the beauty of solidarity.

College Years

My parents did not encourage me to go to college. They held the perspective that a girl didn't need college, since raising a family would likely become my vocation, a worthy vocation for sure, but not necessarily for me. A good student, I won a full scholarship, working full-time in the summers and part-time during the school year, and saving money on top of that.

After about three years in college, it become clear that I didn't want to just fit into society in the ways that the academy was advocating. I dropped out of school, returning later to earn my Bachelor's degree. For the time, I knew some major changes were needed in our society, and I wanted to find a place for myself in those political struggles. The Vietnam War was winding down, but I was just winding up in terms of finding my role as a change agent in the political arena. I was still living near the university when I dropped out; many of my friends were doing the same, seeking lifestyles outside the mainstream and trying new ways to live. Those were counterculture days filled with incredible music that spoke to our youthful yearnings for a better world. Music dominated my life and spoke to me politically, especially new experimental and non-traditional sounds, like the Grateful Dead and Jimi Hendrix. I believed in my heart of hearts that breaking with tradition, both politically and culturally, was necessary to convey new feelings and ideas, and ultimately to create a better world.

A Pivotal Year

In 1974, though no longer a student and still living in the university town of Champaign-Urbana, I was working at a hippie deli and coffeehouse called Bubby's and Zadies. The war in Vietnam had ended and President Nixon had resigned. "What now?" was a question for many of us who had been swept into the youth movement. I found myself confronting two currents of thought taking shape in the culture around me. There was an upsurge in the early seventies of New Age religions that attracted many who held a global belief in the "good karma" espoused by my generation. Following a guru or New Age religion, however, seemed a detour away from what I was seeking. Some of my friends tried to convince me that this was the way to live out one's idealism and hopes. But such pathways were out of step with my desire to affect a real transformation of people's living conditions. I was more aligned with one of our founding fathers, Thomas Paine, who said "My country is the world, and my religion is to do good."[9] To me, being active in the world was more compelling than what appeared to me as navel-gazing.

I was coming to understand that we live in a society defined by class hierarchy in which the rich get richer and the poor get poorer. That understanding gave me a new window on the world. I was inspired by the power of mass movements to propel social change, including the antiwar movement. I started exploring the concept of class-consciousness in conversations at Bubby's and Zadie's, especially with artist Frank Garvey. I was impressed with Frank's revolutionary artistic vision, conveying the predicament of the urban working class under siege within capitalism. His surrealist style of art portrays nightmares of our times alongside beautiful manifestations of humanity and our potential. Frank and I remain friends to this day and collaborate in political and cultural work. We recognize that art and politics are interconnected; both are essential for communicating with our working class brothers and sisters the importance of fighting for our rights.

Prior to my understanding of how we all are affected by living in a class society, I had never quite fit-in, even among the countercultural ethos of my day. I tended to blame myself for not feeling a part of the social milieu around me. My thinking changed after I connected with local activist groups and coalitions supporting working-class peoples' struggles. We were committed to charting out a transition to a better society based on human needs rather than the gargantuan profits for the few and privileged class. These movements offered me a starting place for beginning to wade into political waters.

That early foray into understanding how the cycle of production in our system revolves around big business's bottom line was liberating for me. I realized that class forces were at play in our social landscape, and that I was not alone in my feelings of alienation and oppression. There was an isolation and subjugation confronting the working class as a whole. Knowing I was not alone may not have eased the pain, but it set me on a course to making change collectively. It was liberating to stand shoulder-to-shoulder building a powerful movement guided by shared needs and desires.

This period of my life, though heartening in a political sense, was also marred by a traumatic event. Like many young people of that era, I occasionally hitch hiked; something that was not considered uncommon or dangerous. It was about midnight in the college town where I lived. Since I didn't have to work that night, I spent time reading in the student union. Hitching a ride back to my apartment, I was picked up by a man. We hadn't gone further than a few blocks when he thrust a large knife at my throat and said: "Stay put, woman." I'll never forget those words. For a split second, I felt like I was in the middle of a horror movie. But then I reached for the door handle, swung the door open, and jumped out of the moving car. I hit the asphalt, picked myself up, and ran to the all-night coffeehouse where I was employed. Though in pain from hitting the roadside from a moving car, I never regretted having the presence of mind to find that doorknob and move so swiftly. I reported the incident to the police, but no arrest was ever made. There had been a couple of similar times in my young adult life at that point when I narrowly escaped sexual assault and rape. Many women have not been so lucky. That episode was the last time I hitch hiked.

After that awful confrontation I relinquished any naïve notion that "good karma" would keep me safe. I felt a vacuum both culturally and politically. Those radicalizing years of the late 60s and early 70s, where so many had rallied against the Vietnam War, were dissipating, and I was still searching for ways to participate in justice work.

I came to understand that racism and sexism are symptoms of our capitalist system. Even as our system needs to be fundamentally changed, racism and sexism need to be exposed and defeated as we denounce the deformed, unjust society that spawns them. I volunteered with popular coalition efforts that were standing up against these social ills, and stood in solidarity at marches and demonstrations with other activists who knew we needed to keep activating for justice, even at a time after Vietnam when the momentum was at a low point.

Political Activism Part II

I became involved in the solidarity movements of the 1980s, working to end unjust wars in Central America. It was highly inspiring to connect internationally with a movement that was making great strides in overcoming the injustices of our global society by standing against U.S. interventions. This took my window of experience to new and different levels. Being in solidarity with national struggles abroad, where people were fighting for their self-determination under an imperialist domination, gave me hope for a truly higher and better civilization.

As I was doing solidarity work, I was also visiting my mother, who had been diagnosed with Alzheimer's. For ten years, she struggled with this debilitating disease. My dad took care of her at home until she died in 1988. I am deeply grateful that prior to my mom showing symptoms of the disease, I was able to spend many deep and enriching times with her, as part of a positive and loving adult relationship—learning, growing, and sharing support for one another in the face of ongoing struggles in each of our lives. My adult bond with my mother allowed me to appreciate the intergenerational strength that is evident in so many Richmond families, predominately in African-American families who have lived here for generations.

After my mom died, I worked at various full-time jobs. In the mid-1990s I earned my bachelor's degree in psychology, graduating Summa Cum Laude from Bridgewater University in Massachusetts. I went on to do graduate work in psychology at Rhode Island College. After graduate study, I was drawn to the Bay Area, in part because of my friend Frank Garvey, who ran a theater in San Francisco. I felt his work had much social and political relevance. But I also wanted a new start in life, and it seemed that California was as good a place as any to start again. So I packed up my car and drove cross-country to California.

My sister Kathy, who lives in the East Bay, generously provided me a launching pad for my new venture. Living in the Bay Area proved far more difficult than I had imagined, mostly because of the extraordinary high rents, even back in the late 1990s. Yet I managed—living in rooms and rental spaces from San Francisco to Oakland to Vallejo—excited and motivated to make the Bay Area, with its vibrant culture and progressive politics, my home.

Coming to Richmond

I came to Richmond in 2001 after meeting Paul Kilkenny, who already lived here, and whom I would later marry. I saw in Paul someone who, like me, was ready for a real partnership. We had both been through hard times in our earlier years with both family issues and unhappy relationships. Yet we both came through still believing that love could be possible for each of us. I was seeking real intimacy with someone who was thoughtful, kind-hearted, and open-minded.

Paul has a quiet social demeanor, more introverted to my more social side. At the same time he is insightful and deeply reflective about life and politics. He is not out to impress anyone, but rather looks to connect with people on a down-to-earth, equal level. Those qualities drew me to him.

It probably goes without saying that it was important to me that a partner be open to my political views. I soon learned that Paul was not only open to my politics, but he heightened my consciousness with his knowledge of and commitment to environmental protection. Paul and I also share a love of music and the arts, and how the creative experience has the power to uplift and enhance our understanding of humanity. Personal compatibility, love, shared values, and collective visions give our relationship purpose and beauty.

Birth of A Movement

I had been curious about the Green Party and known and admired Peter Camejo's work for years. Peter was a leader in the Green Party who ran for governor of California as a Green Party candidate three times. He also ran as Ralph Nader's running mate for the 2004 independent presidential campaign. I learned about the Green Party as it was gaining ascendancy during Nader's earlier presidential run in 2000. While watching Peter's first gubernatorial campaign, I found that the Green Party's ten key values mirrored mine completely. (See the ten values listed in Appendix 1.)

One of the Party's values is grassroots democracy, which is central to my political philosophy. I believe that democracy is an active process that must be practiced in every facet of life, from neighborhoods to workplaces to city halls. The Green Party's belief that people should be able to participate in the decisions that affect their lives offers a healthy route for expanding our democracy from the bottom up. This value spirited in me the decision to start taking stands on local issues and to advance change from the grassroots.

Richmond, on a smaller scale, was not unlike Chicago with its diversity of population and the host of problems that working-class, urban communities face. I found the Richmond Greens website, and from there met many wonderful local people who were involved in projects near and dear to me. The Richmond Greens were accomplishing important things, such as stopping a 500-Megawatt polluting power plant in Richmond and standing up to Chevron, demanding pollution reduction, as well as calling for a responsible transition to renewable energy. I registered Green and started attending local meetings, working with other activists on local efforts, such as the Homelessness is not a Crime Coalition, which was working to reverse an ordinance that made it illegal for people without any other means of shelter to sleep in their cars or on public property. This ordinance would eventually be overturned a few years later when I was on the City Council.

As a local group, Richmond Greens were becoming better known in the community based on our activism and willingness to join with other groups to advance our community's needs. I took on more responsibility, like representing the group speaking at press conferences and addressing issues publicly. I was finding my voice and speaking my values, and in the coming years I would also serve as a representative of Richmond on the Contra Costa Green Party County Council.

My involvement with Richmond Greens led me to join with other activists of various political affiliations to create the Richmond Progressive Alliance (RPA). From there I took another new step, running for a City Council seat. Being a candidate placed me in the public eye in a way that was foreign to my past experiences. As someone who saw herself as introspective, I added a new layer to my self-understanding. Both of my parents were deceased by this time, but I felt certain they would have cheered me on, knowing I was reaching further in my life with my principles in hand. As I stretched myself into this new arena, I took with me my working-class identity and have never veered from that core place. It is from those roots that all my values and yearnings have emerged, and it is through my solidarity with working people everywhere that I began my work as a public figure.

The RPA and Initiation as a Candidate

Richmond used to be known as a "company town." Living in the shadow of an oil refinery that has spewed its toxins into our air for over one hundred years has not been easy for generations who have called Richmond their home. While the impacts of this oil giant haven't been the only source of Richmond's problems, they played a major role in shaping a problematic image of our city.

At the time I entered Richmond politics in the early 21st century, the Chevron Corporation had dominated City Hall for decades. Chevron operates its colossal oil refinery—Northern California's largest—atop 2,900 acres of land in Richmond, taking up 13.5% of the city's land. It is the most productive and profitable refinery in California, the largest polluter in the region, and the top stationary greenhouse gas emitter in the State of California. Looking back on the refinery's one hundred plus years of operation, we see the stark contrast between a major oil refinery that burgeoned into a multi-billion-dollar-a-year operation raking in healthy profits existing side by side with a community just outside the refinery's fence line experiencing extreme poverty and grievous health effects. When I began my involvement in local politics, these contrasting views were hard to behold.

I soon became aware of some startling realities about Chevron's relationship with the city in which it does business, some of which remain the case today:

• Few Richmond residents are actually employed at the refinery. Chevron has refused to divulge the data, but many have estimated that only 5–10% of the refinery's 1,200 employees are Richmond residents, and Chevron has not disputed that. [10]

• The refinery never paid its fair share of taxes, while over the years city councilmembers for the most part neither questioned nor addressed this issue.

• Chevron ran its refinery with years of neglect and lax oversight, which would have a negative impact on the health and safety of their workers and the residents living in close proximity to the refinery. Periodic spills, leaks, heavy flaring, toxic gas releases, and fires have been familiar emergencies in our community.

Chevron was able to operate with impunity for decades because it had the majority of city councilmembers in its pocket. For years, councilmembers minimized problems, apologized for the oil giant, and referred to highly preventable incidents at the refinery as if they were unavoidable acts of nature. While councilmembers made excuses for Chevron, not wanting to risk financial support for their campaigns, the people of Richmond continued to wait for their local government to address their priorities and not kowtow to the big business bully running the show.

It was in this context, in a city largely run by corporate-beholden politicians, that I joined with other Richmond progressives to co-found the RPA. We were brought together by the political climate of the times—Chevron was one key figure but there were other issues as well.

Earlier that year, in March 2003, the U.S. occupation of Iraq had begun. Prior to our country's invasion and occupation, many RPA members had been involved in the antiwar movement happening all over the world. Some of us had been involved in earlier antiwar movements, while others were new activists, coming into their own sense of political awareness for the first time. We joined together to stop the madness that we saw unfolding from our government's retaliatory approach to 9/11, forging new relationships and gaining a new sense of civic responsibility on the ground at local levels.

It was horrifying to watch our nation ignore the will of millions of people demonstrating for peace. As we moved into the new era of war without end, our government was following a foreign policy that resulted in overwhelming and tragic loss of human life, along with untold mental and physical harm inflicted upon countless individuals and families both abroad and here at home. We were also being dragged domestically into a war economy, leaving cities and counties with an ever-decreasing number of social programs. The poorest among us were being forced to bear the greatest burden of the war economy on top of our nation's failed economic policies.

Our nation's foreign policy was disproportionately harming our already struggling community in Richmond. In 2003, Richmond was known for its high crime rates, especially violent crime. Poverty had left many of our youth in states of anger and despair. Too often this anger erupted in violence on our city streets. Now, a war economy was sapping national aid from rural communities and cities like Richmond, already in difficult straits.

Before the RPA came onto the scene, city councils had proved unable to provide any real solutions for Richmond, precisely because they lacked the political independence required to put the interests of the community first. The councils instead built up a financial dependency on Chevron over decades. Things were only getting worse under the status quo political leadership, with some elected officials having served on the city council for far too many years.

It was time for a new political formation. Community activism, on its own, could not turn Richmond around. Without support from local elected leaders, grassroots organizations were destined to have continual uphill battles. How much more effective could local activism be if we had principled and progressive decision-makers sitting at the table as city councilmembers? And what if we had candidates running for office who pledged not to take a dime of corporate money in their campaigns? Wouldn't that resonate with the people of Richmond and help set the stage for a true grassroots democratic governance, as opposed to the corporate governance for which Richmond had become known? With death and destruction dominating the national scene and a domestic agenda in peril, this group of activists believed there was no more perfect place to start than right in our own city. Thus began the RPA.

The RPA came together as a group of progressive activists proposing new elected leadership in the city. We came from various sectors of progressive work: homeless and youth advocacy, citizens who demanded accountability of Chevron and the Richmond Police Department, and activists across other arenas—labor, environment and health, education and student rights, antiwar, and racial, social, and economic justice. We led with our values and visions. We chose to look past party affiliation and be unified under one group. Some of us were registered with the Green Party, some were progressive Democrats, and others were non-aligned. We knew we needed solidarity with a focus on our local problems and issues. Each of us who formed the RPA had a history of activism, and each of us had been locally active in Richmond. We felt a kindred spirit in each other and believed we were stronger together.

While releasing Chevron's stranglehold on the city was important for us, we were also calling for an end to police brutality, stopping gun violence, supporting immigrant rights, and supporting rights of the homeless—all issues crying out for new solutions. We wanted to chart a new course in our city based on shared values of peace, grassroots democracy, social justice, equity, and ecological wisdom, beginning with the following vision:

> Our mission is to create a space for public discussion of issues affecting Richmond; to propose solutions and ideas to address Richmond's problems (or create an alternative platform); to expand grassroots organizing in Richmond to demand change; and to endorse progressive candidates running for city council (see RPA candidate endorsement process in Appendix 2).[11]

Election 2004: A Better Richmond is Possible!

The first among our local group of progressives to decide to run as a city council candidate was Andres Soto. Andres had grown up in Richmond. He is a Latino advocate and had previously worked on violence prevention efforts with Contra Costa County and the State of California. In 2002, he and his sons were attacked by the Richmond police during a Cinco de Mayo celebration and he filed a lawsuit against the City. He saw and experienced Richmond's inner-city problems and was ready to take on the existing state of affairs by running for local elected office.

Andres is an outgoing person who likes conversing about politics and relating about his family. He is also an accomplished musician who plays a mean saxophone, as well as flute and other instruments, and has graced many an RPA event with his musical talent.

Andres' activist enthusiasm and energy made him a viable candidate; he was eagerly embraced by RPA. Once he agreed to run, we then set course to seek even more candidates since there were still five open council seats. I was taken by surprise when Juan Reardon asked me to run. Juan, like me, was a member of Richmond Greens.

While Juan eventually became my campaign manager and guided my campaign, his value to our early efforts went far beyond that.

Andres has referred to Juan as "the engine of the RPA," a fitting description indeed. The idea of forming an alliance and running local candidates initially came from Juan, and he has worked at it tirelessly.

Born and raised in Argentina, Juan is a survivor of the dirty war in his country.[12] He has three adult children from his first marriage, Gabby, Eileen, and Juan Jr., and with his current wife,

Kay, a daughter, Lucy. Juan holds an M.D. and an MPH. He worked as a Public Health epidemiologist for Contra Costa County for twenty-five years.

Juan is strong-willed, determined, and incredibly hard working. He is outspoken and unafraid to speak his mind, especially on issues for the underserved and undocumented. As a key founder of the RPA, he has brought a strategic outlook and principled determination that laid the foundation for our progressive direction for Richmond.

As I considered running for a city council seat, I realized this was a chance to spread the progressive message, to share with others that they are not alone in their struggle, and to be a voice of the people in the community. If I put myself out there on the campaign trail with everything I had, it seemed possible that I could touch some hearts and minds. Even as I reflected on this, I didn't think I might actually win. But instinctively I knew this undertaking was important. I also had to weigh the implications of this endeavor and possible new life style with Paul.

In conversation with Paul, I highlighted the positive impact of this candidacy for our overall movement, and downplayed the challenges. Looking back, I see how I was already beginning to make my decision, unconsciously knowing this was a choice of my heart and more than a rational one that was simply going to result in a new job. Paul supported my determination to run, while we both knew it would have a significant impact on our life together.

Paul's support deepened our relationship. His love and emotional backing provided the foundation for many of the challenges I would endure as a candidate and later as an elected official. He also became a dedicated RPA campaign volunteer and a strong participant in building our progressive movement. While some relationships might not have survived the rigors of public life, I was privileged to have someone beside me with the strength, sensitivity, and independence to reach higher and dream bigger at each critical juncture, regardless of the challenge.

Once Andres and I made our decisions to run, the RPA formalized our efforts as an alliance with our official name and goals. We were local activists who had come together to increase our political action in local government. Although we were unable to find additional candidates to join our slate, Andres and I were committed to pledge mutual support for one another, to not take corporate donations, and to support RPA's values. Andres and I each signed a statement entitled "Richmond Progressive Alliance Platform Ideas, Policies and Intended Directions" (as of 1/12/04). The pledge included goals that built on RPA's mission statement:

Restore democracy and efficiency
Restore community safety
Restore the city's financial health
Restore basic justice
Restore the joy of living in Richmond

There were specifics outlined under each goal, such as promoting participation in city government, advancing community policing, requiring the oil industry to pay its fair share of taxes, an Industrial Pollution Prevention Ordinance, a Rent Control and Just Cause Protection Ordinance, empowering the Police Commission, promoting home ownership, among other ideas. We acknowledged these ideas needed further work, research, and refinement, but they were all reflective of the RPA's thinking and policy ideas for a better Richmond.

Our newfound group held regular meetings, which started out with about fifteen people gathering in Juan and Kay's living room. It wasn't long before we doubled in size. We set about growing our base of supporters and brought in new volunteers to help build progressive political power throughout the city. Soon we had about thirty core activists working on various projects (see Appendix 3 for the list of early RPA members with brief backgrounds).

Juan and Kay's home was always welcoming, and they made sure we all felt comfortable. Lucy, Juan and Kay's toddler, would often make an appearance. The chubby little girl gave us all a chance to take a break from political talk and experience the joy of a child's laughter and wide-eyed wonder. Those breaks helped us cultivate a good mix of working and playing together.

Juan took copious notes as we brainstormed how to shape our campaigns. From our suggestions, Juan would come up with ideas for fliers and set up email updates on a regular basis. In addition, each week he would feature one of us activists articulating positive visions and stories about our individual work. We each had a turn to be featured and that was uplifting. This fostered community and helped us get to know each other better.

We also put our collective heads together to seek out other activists in the community who might be willing to join our group. Beyond that we set up tasks that included outreach to groups, researching campaign tasks and tools, and planning forums and events. We had many passionate discussions about how to work together. Andres pushed for autonomy, while I leaned more toward coordinated efforts. Eventually we compromised and decided that campaigns would maintain a level of autonomy but run mutually supportive campaigns.

In future elections, RPA campaigns have formed a coordinating committee made up of representatives from each candidate's committee to integrate our efforts. We put out joint mailers and host house parties together. This kind of campaigning is both more economical and efficient. But more importantly, we make the case that we do not just put forth individual candidates as if to portray a lone hero approach to serving in elected office, we are in this together.

The Making of a Candidate

More than anything else, as a candidate I wanted to reach people at a level of our commonality as ordinary people looking for better ways to live and govern our city. Like so many in our community, I was struggling to make ends meet. As a working-class person, I understood the suffering of hard-working people who were just trying to survive. I also understood that hard work alone does not guarantee success. Where you begin your life and under what circumstances are significant factors in determining whether you will build a secure and stable life. Keenly aware that there is no level playing field in our economic structure, I wanted to reach out to people to demonstrate that I understood this, sharing my belief in a better reality, as well as be a leader who forges a better way of doing politics.

The working-class people in Richmond, both employed and

unemployed, were accustomed to candidates promising more jobs, and that certainly must be a priority for any serious-minded candidate in a low- to moderate-income community like Richmond. But our communities needed so much more. They needed to hear from a candidate who embraced a sense of wonder in the possibilities people could attain. One of my main goals was shifting the political dialogue in Richmond. I wanted to open up the discussion, tap into people's hopes and dreams, and bring forth those values. Too many people have resigned themselves to the hardships of life and have let their expectations and visions languish. I earnestly believe that we must get back to dreaming big. Langston Hughes said it well in his poem:[3]

What Happens to a Dream Deferred?

Does it dry up
Like a raisin in the sun?
Or fester like a sore —
And then run?
Does it stink like rotten meat?
Or crust and sugar over—
Like a syrupy sweet?

Maybe it just sags
Like a heavy load.

Or does it explode?

When I was young and started expressing lofty dreams of changing the world, my mother, a pragmatist by nature, would say: "You know, Gayle, life is not a bowl of cherries." Or my dad would often say, while shaking his head: "It's a dog-eat-dog world out there." They gave me a glimpse of their lived reality, but also wanted to caution me from being overly optimistic. In time, my personal experiences led me to realize that they were right, yet I didn't waver from wanting to be part of something different; something that would encourage me to go after higher pursuits. All this was in the back of my mind as I stepped into this new challenging role.

I learned quickly that playing such a role for the greater good also meant growing and stretching personally as an individual. In order to do what I wanted to do as a candidate, I had to step out of my comfort zone. A lot of people—regular working people like myself—were counting on me to be their voice. While I was honored to do that, it was a new and daunting journey. I needed constant inspiration if I was going to provide that to others. So I looked to other political figures, like Peter Camejo, who had been a role model for me. I read speeches and books he had written over the years and watched videos of him where his voice would ring out as a clarion call in building a mass movement for real social and environmental change. I was deeply moved by his work and his easy speaking style. Camejo had a way of drawing in his audience with a down-to-earth style of oratory, building up the excitement of the crowd to a crescendo whenever he wanted to impassion them with a sense of urgency to halt the downward spiral of our civilization and take charge of changing the direction of our society.

I wanted to reach out and influence others as Camejo had done for me. I knew he had different qualities than me, and simply copying him was not the point. Leaders like Camejo don't necessarily leave blueprints for making change, they inspire us to find our own pathways to deepen our work for a better world, and so I was stirred within to find my voice, learning from what he did. In Richmond, win or lose, there was new ground to cover that would allow me to put into action what I had found so moving and encouraging in other leaders.

On the Campaign Trail

One of our first campaign activities was to hold an RPA forum in January 2004, introducing Andres and myself as RPA candidates. We called the forum "A Dialogue on Richmond." San Francisco Supervisor Matt Gonzalez joined us. In his recent campaign for mayor of San Francisco Matt had come incredibly close to breaking through the two-party machine by winning 47% of the vote as a registered Green Party member.

I was nervous about introducing myself publicly as a candidate at this first forum. Public speaking would require new skills for me. I had spoken at some conferences in the past and at various Richmond events. Yet stepping forward as a candidate put me in the spotlight in a pronounced and sustained way. I had the good fortune of getting help from Kay Wallis, who taught public speaking at a nearby adult school. She, Juan and Paul, were my closest confidants and advisors. With some basic guidance from Kay, I embraced the art of public speaking. I remember the delivery of my first candidate speech. I spoke every word with deliberation, making it clear that we were on our way to something new and exciting. We were going to break through the corrupt, corporate-dominated politics for which Richmond was known, and put the people's priorities front and center. Conveying a message of unity and confidence, I stated with conviction:

Speaking at first RPA forum

We, the people of Richmond, with our full array of cultural diversity, have the capacity to weave a beautiful tapestry together. So I'm not running for cover from the mess created by the current city council. I'm staying put and telling them with all my determination: *it is time for change.* It's time for progressive values and ideas to govern in Richmond. We need to end the ineptitude and the chaos. And allow me to tell you, with all humility: I can do far better than many of the people currently sitting on the council. Giving that speech gave me a feeling I had never known before. When my words resonated on a human level with the people, I felt as if I had made a precious connection with an audience. That audience was made up of individuals whose own principles and personal yearnings were in unison with mine. None of us are complete without each other. To be given the opportunity to share my values and vision with others as a public figure is something I cherish. Others have often told me I was just "too sensitive," but when I gave that first speech, my sensitivity was definitely working for me. Howard Sodja, one of our key RPA activists, once told me he thought my sensitivity was both my greatest strength as well as my greatest weakness. In later years, I would certainly have to learn to toughen up, as the harsh criticisms of adversaries came my way, but I also made sure to keep my sensitivity intact with how I spoke with the public at-large, valuing that vital connection I had experienced with others at the first forum.

We held a second forum the next month in conjunction with the Dennis Kucinich for President campaign. I was doubtful about holding a forum that linked the RPA to the Kucinich campaign, believing that the change we need has to come from independent organizing outside the two-party system. Kucinich was a Democrat who believed progressive goals could be accomplished within the establishment party. Many of us disagreed. So we considered a panel discussion between Representative Kucinich and Peter Camejo, who had just thrown his hat in the race. It was clear, however, that the Kucinich campaign did not want another well-known public speaker in the forum. Eventually I agreed that this joint forum between RPA and the Kucinich campaign could have worth, but only as long as I could speak about the problems with our two-party system (for full text of that speech see Appendix 4).

This turned out to be a well-attended forum, with hundreds of people packed into the foyer of the Richmond Auditorium. I delivered my speech in the manner I saw fit and stayed true to RPA's mission and values as well as what our Richmond residents needed to hear.

Waging a People's Campaign

We campaigned on the heels of the forum, getting out our message of cleaning up the city's governing style and promoting substantive changes. One of the major issues of the campaign season came to light in late 2003 when we learned that Richmond's budget had a $35 million deficit. This propelled the city into a full-blown crisis. In a desperate attempt to stabilize financial inflows and outflows, the Council approved nearly 300 layoffs and cut essential services. The unions were up in arms. Although fire and police bore some layoffs, they were largely spared. The budget crisis most severely affected the general service employees of the city, who were covered by SEIU (Service Employees International Union), lost hundreds of jobs. They were outraged to bear the brunt of the debacle.

As layoffs took place, elected officials justified the cuts, claiming they were needed to prevent bankruptcy. In response, the SEIU bargaining unit put forward job-sharing and reduction of executive staff salary proposals until the city got back on its feet. Those suggestions got little traction. While local government needs to find solutions to repair financial deficits regardless of what contributed to it, those solutions need to be fair to all parties. This Richmond city financial crisis was caused by executive level mismanagement. The decision-makers expected rank and file service employees to pay the price. In order to right the city's financial ship, the City Council imposed severe terms on SEIU and forced hundreds of layoffs. By doing so, the City Council created an adversarial relationship between the city government and its public service employees, undermining any sense that their government served the common good.

I come from a union family and was a union member myself, so it came easy for me to stand up for these employees. I also firmly believed this was in the interest of our community.

Fighting these early battles alongside unions and workers brought me new insights and memorable relationships. I learned how much dedication many municipal service employees bring to their work. During that first campaign I built lasting relationships with many city employees. I remember Kathy Myers who worked as a coordinator at the Richmond Annex Senior Center. She was loved by the seniors and dearly cared for her clients. She was laid off in 2004, and even volunteered to keep the Center open until her job was eventually restored. Over the years, I came to know her and through my visits to the senior center I saw why so many people adored her. She had a heart of gold. For sure she left an imprint on the Center, yet it was heart-breaking to see her lose her job and the impact that she had on both the people she served as well as the loss of income that resulted for her and her family during her unemployment.

I also recall Lynda McPhee, a former President of SEIU 790. Lynda was a fierce fighter for both the rights of city employees as well as the needs of our community. I remember the struggle to keep the Disabled People's Recreation Center (DPRC) open. This is a unique center for young people and adults with disabilities where they learn life skills and experience enhanced communication through art, music therapy, and sports. I fought side by side with Lynda and the many families who depended on that center. It was an agonizing battle to keep the Center open but we succeeded because of people like Lynda. Over the years, amazing things have taken root through the DPRC, like its partnership with Maya's Music Therapy Fund, a Bay Area non-profit that has enriched many people who live with disabilities[14]. As mayor, I would attend the annual Maya's Spring Music Festival and felt deep gratitude that we had saved DPRC.

These battles took time to bring to successful resolution. For years afterward, there was a certain amount of back slapping and self-congratulation among members of the council who had made those so-called "hard decisions." They celebrated their collective ability to navigate through hard times and produce a balanced budget, in effect justifying the hardships they created. It always struck me as odd that people would congratulate themselves for imposing layoffs and service cuts that were a tragedy for our city.

For me, this was not a time to celebrate, it was a call to action to chart out a new direction.

The community showed their indignation as services were cut back or discontinued. As library branches and community centers were closed and festivals were cancelled, the RPA was always there, uniting with those who were outraged, always standing on the side of the community and the workers in our city. We demonstrated by our actions that we were not only interested in presenting alternative candidates, we were dedicated to building an independent movement. We didn't just put out a campaign platform and talk about it. We knew that change comes by uniting people. We fostered a new political culture with a community movement inserting itself as a new political force, seeking to prevent our city from imploding. No longer waiting on the sidelines, we were taking the reins to better our own lives. Our slogan became "A Better Richmond is Possible!"

Richmond had long been in crisis. Prior to this financial disaster, as our city carried the stigma of crime, violence, and danger, the community continually confronted the City Council to find solutions. The RPA made violence prevention one of our key focal points, and the way forward was to address the roots of the violence. Our youth needed opportunities that would provide a future for them. We proposed developing a small business economy with jobs for our youth, given that small businesses provide 80% of all new jobs. We also called for after-school programs, reopening library branches and community centers, and setting up mentoring programs to guide young people into healthy lifestyles, away from guns. While acknowledging the importance of a responsive police force, we wanted a shift toward community-involved policing. Beyond proposing police reform, we kept the focus on giving our youth opportunities through city services, like recreation and job training, and providing them with the guidance they needed to make good decisions in their lives.

Given the complexity of our urban problems and knowing that we (the RPA) had a significant monetary disadvantage compared to the corporate funded candidates, we wasted no time in getting out on the streets to walk the precincts. We knew we had to get started early because our strength was in reaching out to

47

the people. Since big business candidates had big money backing them, they could get their message across with expensive mailers, signs, and other campaign materials, while we depended on ordinary people building relationships with other common folks. So we canvassed door to door to publicize our message.

Andres and I, along with dozens of volunteers, knocked on doors every weekend, sharing the message "A Better Richmond is Possible." We encouraged residents to vote for Andres and me as the candidates who could break through the decades of injustice that Richmond had experienced. The great thing about canvassing is the opportunity to interact with neighbors and residents one-on-one. In our modern world, too often we have erected unnecessary boundaries between each other; canvassing can reach beyond this. I have found time and again from these simple door-to-door encounters that people have similar needs, hopes, and dreams.

As a candidate committed to movement building, I recognized that it was important that I speak to our community at every opportunity that presented itself. I attended community events, parades and festivals, union gatherings, and neighborhood council meetings, introducing myself and sharing my views. I actively engaged in community-led marches, rallies, and protests, and spoke at the public podium at City Council meetings which often overflowed with public attendees sharing their growing concerns about the city. I used my role as a candidate to encourage and build support for community mobilizations. But the campaign wasn't only about movement-building—people were searching for better political leadership. The RPA, with Andres and me as its candidates, stepped up to fill that political vacuum.

Andres and I joined with every effort rising up that demanded fairness and quality of life for Richmond residents. We built relationships with groups all over the city involved in a multitude of issues. Together we promoted all the goals and initial platform ideas the RPA had stipulated, including the preservation of our shorelines and hillsides, infill development (that is, build in the inner core of the city where development already exists and where people have access to public transit), comprehensive cleanup of toxic land, immigrant rights, and better education. We called for an end to the corporate-beholden elected leadership and management in the city that had led to the financial fiasco, and we insisted on full transparency so the people could hold their government accountable. We called for environmental health and sustainability by promoting renewable energy and holding Chevron accountable for pollution reduction. We called for an end to tax perks, like the utility users tax cap that benefitted only one taxpayer in our city—Chevron.

As the campaign year moved through the summer, we grew as a coalition of groups networked together by the RPA and our candidates' efforts. Other candidates entered the electoral arena as well. There were a total of fifteen candidates who filed papers for the five open City Council seats in 2004. We felt it was time for a convention to fully disclose where we stood on the issues and to hear from the community at large.

The Richmond People's Convention

With the fiscal crisis stirring up public outrage, we knew we needed something big to elevate the campaign citywide. We chose a convention to further introduce ourselves and publicize our platforms.

The convention was sponsored by several grassroots organizations in addition to the RPA: Just Cause Richmond, ACORN (Association of Community Organizations for Reform Now), Richmond Improvement Association, Contra Costa Central Labor Council, SEIU 790, IFPTE Local 21, and Richmond Vision, among others. More than 300 people attended the forum. To clarify our vision and mission, we created and adopted a Richmond Residents' Bill of Rights at the conference.

All Richmond residents have the right to fair and affordable housing.

All Richmond residents have the right to equal access to quality education.

All Richmond residents have the right to a representative and accountable city government, and to equal rights under the law.

All Richmond residents have the right to live in a safe environment free from the threat of physical and mental harm.

All Richmond residents have the right to live in a community that promotes health, defined as a state of physical, mental, social, and cultural well-being and not merely the absence of disease.

All Richmond residents have the right to live in a city in which the plan for economic development has as its priority the economic needs of working people.

People's Convention with Henry Clark

Community participants at the convention had an opportunity to add more rights and vote on specific RPA initiatives, as well as their own. We heard presentations throughout the day that included Juan Reardon's presentation: "A Long, Long Journey into the Crisis: What the Hell Happened in Richmond?" His slideshow spelled out examples of corruption in Richmond over decades and the injustices that had been left to fester.

Candidates were presented with both the RPA and other community initiatives and asked to vote on them. Eleven of the fifteen candidates came to the convention, with ten candidates publicly turning in their questionnaires and indicating where they stood on the issues. The tabulated results showed that in addition to Andres and me, candidates Eddrick Osbourne and Tony Thurmond supported all of the initiatives recommended by the Convention. Other candidates indicated support for many of the ideas. To me, this showed how far the RPA had come and what an impact we had already demonstrated. Even Chevron-sponsored candidates attended—recognizing that we were developing a strong base they could not afford to ignore—even as they opposed key initiatives, such as removing Chevron's tax perk and fines for industrial pollution.

The people of Richmond came alive in the political arena that year, grasping the fundamental understanding that it was up to all of us to define our city's destiny. While the People's Convention was just one part of a dynamic campaign year, it also represented what RPA was about: electing representatives who will govern with and for the people and furthering the power of grassroots democracy. The RPA was the vehicle for that vision with candidates willing, able, and eager to do the work.

A Win and a Loss

There had been so many great campaign events and activities that took place in Juan and Kay's backyard. There we were again on that memorable election night in November 2004, awaiting the election news.

Among the campaign volunteers at the election-night gathering were Juan, Kay, Tarnel, Tony Sustak, Evan Blickenstaff, Howard Sodja, Marilyn, Paul, Soula Culver, and Mary Oshima. Some of the folks at this backyard event had been there from the very beginning of the campaign: Tarnel Abbott, Marilyn Langlois and my husband Paul They had braved spring downpours in door-to-door outreach, and in early October, heavy rain washed out many yard signs that had to be replaced. Many came to that election-night celebration wearing worn out shoes, having traversed many long, soggy miles.

For many, it was their first election watch. Waiting for the returns to come in was intense. I was nervous, not knowing what to expect. We had fully and completely thrown ourselves into the campaign. We put forth new ideas, and stretched ourselves to go that extra mile in the final weeks to reach as many people as possible. Some of this was fun, like the caravans we formed, decorating our cars with signs supporting Andres and me. We were also pretty damn tired.

Juan and Kay made that election evening special. They made a poster sign with photos from the campaign activities with the word "Imagine" in big letters referencing John Lennon's popular song, intersecting it with our campaign message to "imagine" a better Richmond and working to make it happen. A campfire burned in the center of their yard with chairs in a circle around it—we felt like family.

When the first results came by way of absentee ballots, Juan jubilantly announced that I was in first place. I was taken by surprise. I felt good having been a progressive voice for making change, but didn't expect to win. Then I told myself, just because I was winning with the absentee voters, it didn't mean I would *win*. Since we had started campaigning early in the year, something the mainstream candidates had not done, it made sense that we were succeeding among those voters who paid attention to our local politics and cast their votes early. The last weeks of the electoral season often changes the outcome once all the votes at the polling centers are counted.

I wondered how I would do when all the votes were counted. If I was going to win, my other hope was that Andres would also win, so I wouldn't be alone on the council. I knew Andres had been a strong candidate and he would be a good friend and ally for me on the city council.

The final votes came in later that night, and though I had dropped to third place, I had won one of the five open council seats. Andres, however, though the better-known progressive candidate, had been attacked with hit-pieces from the Police and Fire unions, likely due to his lawsuit against the city. It is likely that that fueled the fires against him. The establishment did not want Andres to win, painting him as an ultra-left radical who used confrontational politics to challenge the law. Those attack ads did the job and Andres lost his race, coming in a close sixth place among the five open seats.

I was sad for Andres, who deserved to win, and disappointed for the many voters and community members who would have had a great representative in him. I was also unhappy for myself, as I would have to take a seat on the city council without the support and camaraderie of a like-minded political colleague.

Despite Andres' loss, the prevailing feeling on the night of our first RPA win was one of great accomplishment and joy. So many people had worked so hard to make a crack in the Richmond establishment. We had a foot in the door; it would be my job to keep that door open to address all the issues for which we had stood during the campaign.

Later that election night we had more drama. Most folks had gone home, with just a few of us still milling around in the aftermath of a full evening of excitement. Seemingly out of nowhere, someone came waltzing into the backyard—it was none other than currently sitting Councilmember Jim Rogers. Rogers was not a candidate for reelection at this point, but suffice it to say he was not close to the RPA. Rogers' political positions drifted with the political winds of the moment—he was not a person of firm vision and direction. In contrast, the RPA had solid positions and values, and we stood firm regardless of political climate.

Councilmember Rogers apparently felt a need to approach me that election night. Those of us remaining at the celebration were quite taken aback by this uninvited guest, since this was after all a private affair. But we remained cordial. I had never met Rogers personally but he proceeded to sit down next to me as if he knew me, and he congratulated me on my win. He said something to effect, "Now there will be three of us progressives on the City Council—you, me and Tom Butt." While the RPA had had some friendly alliance with Tom Butt at that time, we never imagined the same in Jim Rogers. His voting record wavered from one end of the spectrum to the other—rarely in line with RPA's positions. But suddenly that night, Rogers was ready to cozy up to me and the RPA, now that he realized an RPA member would be sitting on the dais with him. Of course I was suspect and this new gesture led me to trust him even less than before.

That very night Rogers started to pressure me to support some of his stances on issues— even as my electoral victory was just beginning to sink in. Thankfully, Juan joined me and Rogers to lighten the tension. He said, "Come on, Jim, she hasn't even been sworn in yet. Don't you think she deserves a break and you can hold off on the lobbying for now?" That night was my first introduction to one of my new "fellow" councilmembers.

Following that first RPA win, we had our ups and downs. We

needed to reaffirm our principles and guidelines now that the election was over as we moved forward to advance the work of transforming our city. We also wanted to make sure we were all on the same page as we looked toward the next electoral season. A few RPA members weren't as solidly committed to the principle of taking no corporate donations, but in the end, after heated discussions, it became clear that this was central to our principles and our local movement. There was no debating the fact that my 2004 corporate-free campaign had beat the odds. The RPA had challenged the political establishment and won. Together we had shown that a scrappy group of activists with a kitchen-table campaign could win an election against candidates heavily funded by big business. With a different way of doing politics, we learned everything from scratch, with no campaign consultants. Nor did we follow any party guidelines.

We never stopped believing in our progressive mission, even with discouraging naysayers who persisted to voice their negativity into the post-election period. There were even some among our own ranks who feared I wouldn't survive a hostile council. This pessimism from a few in our progressive circles was hard to take, but I fought the reflex to take it personally. I knew better. For sure, I harbored my own trepidations and knew I was about to enter unfamiliar waters. But stronger than my fear was my determination to keep my head above water and swim as hard as I could. I had confidence that I would land on solid ground that would allow me to lead our community with new progressive ideas. I took comfort knowing that the current of our local movement would help me navigate that new territory.

And yet internally something completely different was going on inside of me. I had been focused throughout the campaign on having my candidacy help raise the progressive voice in the city. Even as I started feeling a significant shift of the political winds in the latter stage of the campaign, victory still seemed a long shot to me. After all, the entrenched local Democratic Party was supporting corporate-backed candidates, while I was running as a registered Green. So when I actually won, I felt both a sense of amazement and caution. As a newly elected official, I was entering new terrain on my own, without my RPA colleagues, and that brought with it some disquieting feelings. But I knew my values and principles were far stronger than any internal uneasiness, so I prepared myself for the road ahead.

There was no doubt in my mind that my life was about to change drastically, as I instinctively knew that making inroads with a progressive agenda would require completely throwing myself into the work. Mediocrity was not what I was after. Our progressive movement deserved more from its first elected official, and I felt a strong commitment to use my council position to do all I could to put those values into action. So during the two-month period between the election and being sworn into office, I steeled my political will for this new challenge.

Our victory had breathed life into a new effort, with progressive leadership now existing both on and off the dais. It was up to each of us to continuously motivate each other to go further. The RPA had brought to the surface what people already knew—the people's interests had not been served. The RPA came along to serve the community and change the direction of our city government. RPA was now known as a strong political current in the community and we had a city council member in office.

We had just begun.

Shaking Things Up: New Governance

When I was sworn in as a councilmember in January 2005, I entered a political culture that was vastly different from anything I had ever encountered. I had been a political activist throughout my adult life, but serving in public office was different, especially given the make-up of the Richmond City Council. As an elected official, I was propelled into public service with people who had a radically different vision for Richmond's future. Coming into office to challenge the way things worked in our city, I had no desire to be integrated politically into the status quo culture that existed; a culture that lacked the political will to put the priorities of the people first, since that meant standing up to big bullies in the city, like Chevron.

I was the new kid on the block. In order to effectively serve and implement progressive ideas, it was important to have a full grasp of the proper rules and procedures that our municipality utilized. Two different sets of emotions churned inside of me. First, I was clinging tightly and passionately to the strength of my convictions. And two, I was embracing an earnest desire to learn the more process-oriented side of city government. With both these sets of goals guiding me, I cautiously stepped into my new role.

There were eight other members on the Council, including Mayor Irma Anderson. I was the only newcomer, as all the other winners had already served on the Council. The Council was made up of four African-Americans, Mayor Irma Anderson and Councilmembers Mindell Penn, Nat Bates, and Richard Griffin, and two Latino members, Councilmembers Maria Viramontes and John Marquez. These six were tied to establishment politics and all had been supported by Chevron. None of them understood that it was essential to separate the people's interests from those of the oil giant. There were two white men, Councilmembers Tom Butt and Jim Rogers. Tom Butt was one councilmember the RPA saw as amicable to many of our causes. Like me, Tom was not a favorite of the Richmond political establishment, we were both vocal proponents of renewable energy, and he was another voice willing to fight against Chevron (he had battled Chevron in previous times but had given up the fight before I joined the Council). The second white male was Jim Rogers, a lawyer who would later resign from the California bar due to scandals in his practice. Jim would be forever unwilling to take clear-cut stands, as mentioned previously, always trying to work both sides of any issue, and he steered clear of anything that might ruffle Chevron's feathers. I was the lone white woman and was opposed to most policies supported by the others on the Council.

In mid-2005, Mindell Penn would resign from her seat and subsequently moved to Detroit for personal reasons. Her vacant seat became filled by another African American, Tony Thurmond, who had run in the recent election. The RPA supported Andres for the vacant seat, since he was next highest vote getter, but the majority on the Council went with Tony. We had actually tried to get Tony to join RPA in early 2004, but he did not share our commitment to not take corporate money. Still, though, we appreciated Tony's positions on many issues, so we were not completely disappointed.

Walking into my first closed session and sitting behind closed doors with other elected officials who blatantly lobbied for Chevron's interests or tip-toed around making sure they didn't upset Chevron's agendas was unsettling. I had already informally met with a couple councilmembers. Casual small talk came just fine, but as soon as discussions shifted to policies and issues, a huge divide became apparent. Being the lone voice was not going to be easy. Standing up for progressive issues while surrounded by oppositional people would require courage. I felt alienated. But there was no turning back.

Sitting on the Council would remain uncomfortable. Mayor Anderson did not appreciate my voice on matters when I differed with others. In fact, she would call me out of order if I started to share my views when she recognized me to speak. She would often declare that my speaking time could only be used for questions to staff. This was really frustrating, especially since my comments were never long-winded, and I felt they were important. She seemed inflexible with me. Still, I respected her role as chair. I knew I had a unique and weighty responsibility. I needed to lead people in thoughtful dialogue and engagement on issues we deemed important, so I reached out to RPA and others. Juan continued to be a key advisor for me, but I also needed a committee of activists to help me pour over Council agenda items. The agenda and supporting documents (all hard copy in those days, and sometimes a full eighteen inches thick, no less) were delivered to my home each Friday night prior to the Tuesday meetings.

I formed a "packet reading" group with a few RPA folks: Tarnel Abbott, Soula Culver, Mary Oshima, Devin O'Keefe, Debbi Landshoff, and Paul. Each Sunday afternoon we assembled in Paul's and my living room to go over the agenda items. At that time the city was in shambles—many employees were still laid off, $35 million was unaccounted for, and an initial green light had been given for a casino amid much outrage, to name just a few crises. It was hard to prioritize. At the same time we knew we had to seize my new bully pulpit and put into action all we had talked about in the heady early days of RPA. This was new territory for all of us in our activist community, one we happily embraced.

Still Stirring Up Some Dust

I observed tension among some councilmembers starting with my first Council meetings. One of the councilmembers requested that the Mayor change her seat on the dais. I suggested a lottery for seating—saying it might not hurt to "shake things up a bit." I received a sarcastic: "*Haven't you shaken things up enough!*" The comment elicited laughter, and yet everyone knew what was behind the sentiment.

Things were different now that a new political player had burst onto the scene. Even before I set about bringing new policies and ideas to the table, I brought unfamiliar dynamics to the elected body just by my presence. And while my Council colleagues were getting acquainted with me as a person, they also knew they were interacting with a new local movement they had not given much credence to in the past.

I felt a mixture of feelings. I was honored to represent our local movement, but at the same time felt a heavy responsibility. The work was about to begin, and to some extent it was about resisting those who felt they had a better understanding of how to serve and set agendas. I stirred people up, not due to some strategic plan, but simply by asking new questions and drawing from a different set of solutions. I made others on the Council uneasy. But I couldn't and wouldn't fit into their social strata or political club, nor was I seeking membership with them. I liked my place and the people I represented. I was a working-class person consciously representing the voices of many people living in a system dominated of, by, and for the rich. Call me idealistic, but I wanted that domination to end.

Sifting through the Morass

One of the first things I realized once in office was that I wasn't going to get anything done without an organizing campaign on each issue. Quite often I was a solitary voice on the Council on controversial issues. This was difficult, but I wasn't deterred.

Possibilities open up when progressives get elected, as opportunities for new analyses emerge for solving problems. I proposed that we tackle Richmond's problems at their source, which meant correcting systemic injustices. The long-standing status quo thinking in Richmond had failed. Trickle-down economics had not brought the prosperity to Richmond residents that other Bay Area communities had enjoyed. The City Council needed to critically examine the poverty and lack of opportunity in our city.

In mid-year 2005, just months into my first year on the Council, there were eight homicides in two weeks, including the shooting death of a man in front of his seven-year-old daughter. People were overwhelmed with grief and their patience with the Council's failure for years to stem violent crime had worn thin. Nearly 600 people packed the Council Chambers on June 21st to voice their concerns. With so many people in attendance we had to set up a tent outside the meeting with closed circuit cameras so people could watch what was going on. Emotions were high. People came carrying signs with pictures and names of their loved ones who had been killed.

Many on the Council responded to the cries of the people with the old answers to violence, proposing it could be ended primarily through police suppression, as if this tragic cycle of violence could be broken without presenting pathways out of poverty. Some councilmembers wanted to declare a "state of emergency." I spoke strongly against this approach, saying it wouldn't resolve the violence. Things would calm down temporarily until the declaration was lifted, and then the crime would return at another street corner. This wasn't a hard prediction to make, it was happening in urban environments everywhere and had been happening in Richmond for years.

The Council attempted various strategies, including the "Broken Window Theory," which maintains that a disordered environment (broken windows, graffiti, litter, etc.) signals that an area is not monitored and suggests that criminal behavior has little risk of being detected. The answer then is to clean up the mess. This was the City Council's solution. But to me, that was just the beginning.

I was frustrated that the entire Council seemed uninterested in discussing the causes of street violence. I wrote an editorial in the *Contra Costa Times* titled "The Roots of Richmond Violence Runs Deep" debunking the state of emergency line of attack. I made the argument that we need to prioritize giving people real and consistent opportunities by investing in substantial youth employment, recreation, and education-strengthening services in order to see a long-lasting reduction in crime. My article was an attempt to highlight and shift the conversation of addressing crime with root cause solutions. (See Appendix 5 for the full article.) Throughout my elected years in Richmond, I held to this approach to stem the tide of violence.

Toxic Turbulence

Another dire situation in the city that had been left unresolved was the toxic legacy of industrial manufacturing in Richmond. One of my first successes as a councilmember in early 2005 was passage of a resolution calling for proper state oversight of some highly toxic properties on our southeast bay shoreline, including a call for comprehensive cleanup of the area. The Redevelopment Department was pitching a development that would build multi-story condominiums on an eighty-six-acre property, commonly known as the Zeneca site, which had been owned by AstraZeneca, the world's second-largest pharmaceutical company, and before that by Stauffer Chemical. With over a hundred years of chemical, pesticide, and fertilizer manufacturing, what remained on the site was a toxic brew made up of a long list of extremely harmful chemicals, including benzene, arsenic and polychlorinated biphenyls (PCBs)⬜chemicals known to cause cancer, birth defects, and reproductive harm.

Because of the magnitude of the contamination, it had been classified as a Superfund site. James D. Levine, a principal with LFR Levine-Fricke, an environmental management and consulting firm specializing in toxic waste cleanups, proposed a woefully inadequate cleanup of the site, offering Zeneca a far less expensive plan that would simply cap these extremely dangerous toxins on site rather than responsibly trucking them away. Soon after this plan was under construction, a developer, Simeon-Cherokee, wanted to erect high density high rise towers on the site. They sent Levine to attend the community meeting when they pitched their case for the new development. Community members wanted answers as to why these dangerous toxins remained on the site.

Levine, with encouragement from the Richmond Redevelopment Agency, approached the community with a devil-may-care attitude. His comportment was casual, but he had an air of entitlement and acted as if his superior status rendered him unchallengeable. He was quick to argue and would deny culpability of contamination responsibility. When the presenter asked Levine to address the cleanup, he spoke with great agitation and dismissiveness to the concerned neighbors. He sidestepped the questions and instead said arrogantly something along the lines of˙ "I don't even have to be at this presentation. I'm just here as a favor to the developer."

Levine will go to his grave denying involvement with the botched cleanup even though the "bury and cap" scenario was designed by LFR while he was the principal, and later implemented by the same firm, even as Levine would later leave his post. The whole idea of capping those dangerous toxins at the site made the community furious. To this day Jim Levine has not taken responsibility for setting that insufficient design plan into motion.

Today 350,000 cubic yards of toxic soil are buried under a cap that wears with the wind and rain. The proposed development, slated to be built on top of the cap, would have had fans blowing twenty-four hours a day, seven days a week, whisking away hazardous soil gas that would accumulate underneath the 1,400 proposed residential units. The community was incredulous and rightly stood up in protest.

The entire Zeneca site needed the proper state agency to oversee the complexities of cleanup, as did the neighboring University of California Richmond Field Station, with its own slew of toxins from past manufacturing. The whole area needed to be transferred to California's Department of Toxic Substances Control (DTSC) from the Regional Water Quality Control Board (RWQCB), which was inappropriately placed in charge when Zeneca ceased to operate in 1997. DTSC, unlike RWQCB, has protection of the public health as one of its mandates. DTSC also has staff toxicologists and a public process, both which RWQCB lacked.

Sherry Padgett, a Richmond community member, led the advocacy for a comprehensive cleanup. She had worked directly across the street from the site for years, and she was present from 1998 through 2002 when the manufacturing site was demolished with little government oversight, followed by the failed and inadequate cleanup. AstraZeneca systematically dug up, moved, diluted, and buried hundreds of thousands of toxins onsite in an effort to save $80 million. At times the entire area was cloaked in clouds of toxic dust, with none of the neighboring businesses or residents aware of the hazardous nature of the dust they were wiping off their cars and sweeping out of their driveways and parking lots. A year later Sherry was diagnosed with a rare form of cancer. Many people suspect she had been exposed to carcinogenic chemicals. Though it is impossible to link her cancer to any one chemical, this led Sherry—even while battling her illness—to spend years researching and leading the fight for protection of public health and for a responsible, comprehensive cleanup of the site.

We all knew it would take a community-building effort to overcome the bureaucratic resistance of the city and the state to get DTSC to take over the site remediation. In response to the outcry of the Richmond community, then-Assembly member Loni Hancock held a hearing, which led to DTSC taking over control of the part of the site. But we all knew that proper oversight on just part of this toxic area was not sufficient.

With the help of the RPA and others, I proposed a City Council resolution and worked with other groups to assure its passage. We worked with Bay Area Residents for Responsible Development (led by Padgett), Richmond Greens, Richmond Annex Neighborhood Council, Marina Bay Neighborhood Council, Physicians for Social Responsibility, and even residents from the nearby city of El Cerrito. We kept the momentum going by organizing rallies, demonstrations, and press events, as well as encouraging neighbors to speak out at Council meetings. Eventually, after two City Council meetings—and around thirty-five impassioned public speakers—the Council unanimously approved my resolution. As a result of the council action and pressure from the community, the entire Zeneca site and the UC Richmond Field Station were transferred to DTSC, the proper regulatory agency. A Community Advisory Group (CAG) was also formed to provide advice to DTSC, initiated by Ethel Dotson, a long-time African-American community member who grew up in wartime housing, right next door to this toxic area. One of our core RPA leaders, Tarnel Abbott, has served as a member of the CAG since its inception. Tarnel lives close to the site and has consistently taken a leadership role in holding DTSC accountable to the people of Richmond, advocating for the rights of our community to live free from the health risks associated with toxic land. I also served on the CAG, as a local government representative.

Heavy industries of the past and their leftover toxins have caused many problems in Richmond. Elected officials were not giving those situations their due. It was a major accomplishment to have shifted the council's attention to protecting Richmond's public health. With years of hard work and community pressure, we were able to stop a harmful development from happening. But even today we continue to wrangle with the manufacturers responsible for the contamination, as they continue to thwart a comprehensive cleanup. It had taken a community mobilization, with the Community Advisory Group's leadership to shift course and keep a watchful eye on the work ahead. This was an early victory for a new approach to governance. It felt good to have presented the first concrete example of how my sitting on the Richmond City Council could help the community.

Rattling Political Cages

But this was just the beginning. Every time one of our progressive issues needed City Council attention, it required people to organize and mobilize to make sure all the elected officials heard and understood the community's concerns. While I was a conduit for the aspirations of these Richmond residents, their direct participation was needed as well.

Even with the support of the community, being a minority on a city council that was bought and paid for by Chevron was not easy. Too often we see individuals with good intentions get into elected office and simply follow the crowd, proving themselves ineffective in carrying out a progressive agenda. When progressives have few or no allies on a city council—especially in this political climate, where politics are heavily dominated by moneyed interests—there are really only a couple of ways to proceed. One is to compromise one's values and vote with the majority. A second way is to work closely with the grassroots, whose values you share, to put pressure on those elected officials who lack the political will to approve good policy and programs.

Many first-time elected officials, seeking a sense of group identity and cohesiveness, identify with incumbents, ignoring the control that corporations exert over these officials who have lost all capacity to think independently in the political arena. These newly elected officials also then become part of the problem. I chose instead to immerse myself in community struggle, linking up with community activists whose values were similar to mine. That is how I maintained my political integrity during these early breakthrough years, even while surrounded by political opponents on the City Council dais. That is also how we took positive steps forward as the RPA.

Looking back, Richmond's challenges were overwhelming. New thinking and new solutions were needed in so many areas. I strongly believed that better solutions would be inevitable. And yet I had more than practical challenges, I had internal political Council battles brewing.

Debating issues of violent crime and Chevron's undue influence revealed major differences between me and my Council colleagues. I felt they were unwilling to look more deeply at the root causes of our persistent urban problems. My view was that we had to think outside of a political system and culture that had failed our community. Fellow councilmembers seemed more inclined to adhere to conventional wisdom, beliefs, and, from my perspective, inactions of the past.

With Richmond's big, systemic problems flowing from corrupt policies on all levels of government, I often thought about Martin Luther King's words when he said: "The bombs in Vietnam explode at home; they destroy the hopes and possibilities for a decent America." He was commenting on the fact that the federal government was using tax dollars on a bloated military budget, wreaking destruction in other lands, and leaving our own cities devoid of funds for growth and development. Dr. King's words were as true in 2005 as they had been in the 1960s. While national politics needed (and still needs) to change, we could not wait for the federal government to step in and help. We needed to present solutions now.

Creating a more peaceful city, always at the forefront of my agenda, wasn't the only thing I needed to contend with. I was eager to share my perspective on all the issues facing the city. Unfortunately, getting my point of view heard became challenging. I would be called out of order whenever I started explaining my positions on various agenda items. And it wasn't just the mayor; others on the council would repeatedly call for a vote before I had a chance to speak on issues. The progressive viewpoint that I was longing to express was often thwarted.

As a person working in the electoral arena, I needed to hold onto my ideals to envision better governance while remaining pragmatic in order to get those ideas enacted. My relationships with my colleagues would have likely been less confrontational if I had simply been an idealist talking the talk, and not been intent on making things happen. But I had shown early on that I could get things done with a tool none of them had: grassroots organizing. Grassroots organizing is the way we move each other to action, developing skills, and confidence along the way. We do this by building relationships of trust with one another, bringing forward a sense of purpose and mission that allows the organizing effort to flourish. While winning any particular issue is important, it is shifting the relations of power to the grassroots that is crucial. People begin to feel a sense of their own power as they join with others and from there sprout significant accomplishments.

As an elected official, I was building my relationship with the community. Constituents frequently told me what they liked about me was that I was a regular person and that they could relate to me like an ordinary person, which was something I also value in myself. Being a public servant to me means working *with* those you are serving, and not from afar. I would never jeopardize those lines of trust that were materializing. However, this new experience of being an elected official was taking me to a place I hadn't known before. I was now operating in two different political cultures. On one side were the residents of the community who shared their stories with me and with whom I felt an affinity, and on the other stood the largely pro-big business City Council, where my voice became more and more squelched by those who had no stakes in a new approach toward governance. This presented me a barrier to getting my voice heard.

I was learning that the mayor's voice set the tone for the city. The mayor at the time had a different perspective, blocking my RPA outlook from the attention it deserved. I had been elected on a new set of ideas and values, and I wasn't going to let people down. I needed to find a way to advance political issues in a new direction. So I soon found myself, with support from the RPA, contemplating a new electoral run—Mayor of Richmond. This seemed the only way forward. From the highest elected seat in the city, I could amplify our message and reach more people. And reaching more people was essential for building the local transformation we desperately needed. My decision was made. I would run for Mayor and I would "reach for a better Richmond."

Win or Lose: Fighting for Richmond

The 2006 mayoral race was surely my hardest race to date. It was one thing to seek a seat at the table two years earlier, but now I was pursuing the top political leadership position. This fueled opposition by many powerful city forces, including the oil industry and the local Democratic Party. From the onset of my mayoral campaign, I feared if I didn't win, our movement would lose the momentum we had gained, and the seeds of progressive change we had planted would not bear fruit. There was no telling how long it would take to reenergize from the bottom up once again if that happened.

So much time had already been lost because of ineffective and corrupt city leadership. Ever since the U.S. military left after World War II, Richmond politicians had looked to big business, especially Chevron, to lead Richmond into a better economic future. The politicos were still looking to them, even after decades of decay. Leaving those relationships intact would continue to inflict more suffering and poverty on the community. I wanted to offer new leadership that would steer city government toward serving the people's interests and releasing the grip of private industries that held so much sway in City Hall. Bringing forward the message that we could navigate our own local governance would be a defining moment in our local politics.

But even as I prepared for a new electoral challenge, I was still a sitting councilmember working with the RPA to bring forward new policies and projects. Actually, it wasn't so much preparing rather improving, expanding, and driving home issues with the values that I and the community shared. As both an activist and a councilmember, I found the greatest satisfaction in the solidarity relationships I was building. Such associations weren't hard to build because of the interlinking identities we share as working-class people. It was important to help unify and empower the people. The political and practical challenges we faced in Richmond demanded that we work together to achieve our collective aims. I was elated with the feedback I received from many residents who conveyed that I was living up to their expectations, yet I also knew I had to keep earning and deepening their trust. I was still considered a newcomer, having served only one year. So in order to further my communication with the public at large, I needed people to know what work I had done on their behalf and what I had in mind for the future. Staying focused and engaged vigorously on the issues that had won me my council seat kept me accessing more and more of the people's trust.

I kept track of all my Council votes and gave full explanations for them on my website so everyone could see them. Paul helped me by staying on top of all the issues, closely watching every Council meeting, and providing me with the votes, including short summaries of the debates. Juan and Kay would later prepare a compilation of that first year in office.

In late 2005, my City Council campaign committee sent out my "2005 Report to Richmond Voters and Residents," a four-page full color mailer listing some of the achievements. This was the first time that people had received a hard-copy year-end report in their mailboxes from a councilmember. My message was simple and straightforward:

One year of hard work for the people of Richmond.
One year of standing against special interests.
One year of integrity. One year building a better Richmond.

To the people of Richmond who elected me, and to all the people of Richmond I represent—I am accountable to you. You are entitled to this report because you, and only you, placed me in this office. Not a single dollar for my campaign came from a corporation. I work for you, the people of Richmond, and this is my year 2005 annual work report.

Although some positive steps have been taken, the city of Richmond continues to be in serious trouble. Street violence continues to decimate our neighborhoods, tearing Richmond apart.

The city keeps rolling up its sleeves, creating the appearance of taking action with summits and meetings. However, our city [government] has lacked the political will to obtain the funds needed to implement the programs known to prevent violence. In the meantime, the community itself has taken the lead and is already embracing our youth. The city of Richmond must follow the example of the community and start leading. Violence has been endemic in Richmond for over twenty years and it will take all our efforts and concentrated resources to eradicate it.

A Better Richmond is Possible!

My report tapped people's imaginations, reminding them of accomplishments and reaffirming the vision for a better future. I listed goals for taking more positive steps in the upcoming year:

Defend Richmond's public assets
Preserve Richmond's open space shorelines
Make the shorelines clean and accessible to the public
Monitor the forces who put profits before people and are rushing to re-zone Richmond's shoreline area
Facilitate increased public participation in the review of the general plan
Promote and support concrete short- and long-term solutions to Richmond's endemic violence
Invigorate the City's general fund by ending tax loopholes, perks, and favoritism to big industry
Defend and promote Richmond's small businesses
Continue to learn more about and from Richmond communities through neighborhood councils, grassroots organizations, and individuals willing to share their experiences and knowledge
Restore Richmond libraries and community centers to full operational capacity
Promote solar energy utilization in Richmond by the city, local businesses, and residents
Promote justice and fairness for tenants and landlords

After wrapping up a year, I began to strategize for the mayoral race. I was surrounded by a talented and dedicated team of friends and progressive colleagues who supported and encouraged me as the campaign took shape. Juan Reardon once again took on the role of campaign manager, Kay Wallis was media consultant, and my husband Paul was once again my treasurer. Originally Jim Jenkins handled fundraising for my campaign, although this was short-term, since he decided to run his own campaign for a City Council seat. While Jenkins did not win a council seat, his initial involvement in my campaign, along with his RPA-endorsed Council run, made successful contributions along the campaign trail.

Many people joined us later, but it was the small, mighty team that formed the base of our unstoppable and uplifting mayoral campaign. Sitting around the kitchen table, we analyzed what we were up against and outlined what we needed to win the mayor's seat. There were some serious contradictions in Richmond's political climate that had been boiling up for decades. Now was the moment to address them.

On one side was Chevron, a company increasing its quarterly profits every three months. At the same time Richmond's neighborhoods of low-income communities of color had persistent poverty and high rates of asthma. This incongruity needed to be exposed.

Over the years, numerous groups had cried out for a healthy environment. Chevron felt the pressure, for sure, but rather than investing in effective refinery maintenance to address their environmental impact, they found less expensive ways to silence or minimize the outcries. Chevron funded various non-profits that provided services to the residents in distressed areas of the city. One project they partially funded was the Northern California Breathmobile. This was a regional mobile healthcare unit, operated by an Oakland non-profit, that made numerous trips to North Richmond bringing much needed health services to the community. Ironically one service was to test children for asthma, likely caused by air pollution brought on by the refinery.

The Breathmobile is just one example. Chevron made it a point to periodically throw small amounts of funding at mostly local,

Richmond-based non-profits. These Chevron-funded non-profits were well-intentioned and brought needed services, but they were also doubled-edged swords. The funding was woefully insufficient to address needs in any sustained and meaningful way and these organizations were used to buy a certain debilitating silence. That is, when the refinery exploded or when the oil giant attacked or maligned political progressives, those groups could not speak out against Chevron lest they lose the little funding they were receiving. When Chevron funded these organizations, they were expected to display the Chevron logo on press releases and appear at Chevron-sponsored press events publicizing the donations, thus keeping them aligned in the public eye with their benefactor. On top of that, these non-profits were often solicited into the oil giant's advertising campaigns with the names and faces of non-profit staff members featured in Chevron's newsletters and mailers and plastered on billboards across the city. Through this surreptitious collusion, the refinery sought to take the pressure off themselves and quell outrage in the community. Meanwhile our struggling neighborhoods were left gasping for air, both literally and economically.

We needed to bring these contradictions and disparities before the public before we could begin resolving the deeper issues. Communities cannot be transformed without full disclosure of who is paying what and revealing the hidden costs of those payments.

City officials with ties to Chevron and other big money interests perpetuated the disparities. City officials continued to take corporate money, and made decisions on behalf of their donors, all the while claiming that those interests would spill over and meet the city's and the people's needs. They were unwilling to examine our persistent problems in Richmond apart from the profit-making bottom line of those who funded their political careers. They could not shake free from the shackles of corporate domination and were dragging our community down with them. The old-guard politicians had kept the community in a state of stagnation, tying the city's future to a corporate system that harmed with one hand and placated with the other. We needed to address the people directly and get their voices and opinions on these matters.

So we went to the electorate to see if they wanted to continue having Richmond dominated by Chevron. Was it time for our community to strike out on its own? Were we ready to stand up independently for our own interests? I ran for Mayor in part to pose those questions to the community at large and to propose some answers. This was the time for me to articulate my and RPA's values and mission on the local stage and continue to build our movement for progressive change.

In my campaign kick-off speech, I pointed to the ongoing violent crime, inadequate and non-existent services, and preferential treatment for big industry, presenting bold solutions such as establish a Richmond Youth Corps (RYC) that would create 1,000 part-time, year-round jobs. By providing these jobs, including mentoring, young people would be prepared for more hopeful futures. I proposed funding the program by implementing fair taxation policies. Another position I highlighted was the importance of building a sustainable city—one that stewards, restores, and preserves its environment and is bicycle and pedestrian-friendly, with strong public transportation. I shared my commitment to assure quality of life services for all our residents and to cultivate a vibrant small business economy in place of flawed, quick-fix solutions.

Excited to embark on this next phase of work, I delivered my first speech with great anticipation. Concluding my remarks, I could feel a room full of hopes and dreams, as my team followed up with the dramatic unfurling of a giant banner: "Gayle McLaughlin for Mayor." With that, the campaign was launched. While it was my name on the banner, all those in the room that afternoon knew that we were in this together, working for a better Richmond in solidarity.

Campaign Flames

I ran against incumbent Mayor Irma Anderson and Gary Bell, a former councilmember. Both had deep pockets. Anderson and her industrial supporters spent about $200,000; Bell spent close to $80,000; my campaign coffers had a mere $28,000.

My campaign also supported a ballot measure known as Measure T, a fair taxation initiative that would collect more revenue for the city from large manufacturers, predominately Chevron, underscoring this as a source of funding for the RYC. As was expected, money flowed heavily from Chevron and the Council of Industries into Political Action Committees (PACs). Measure T failed at the ballot box, but it formed the basis of RPA's future fair taxation work.

The Democratic Party was doing their best to stop me as well. Although municipal races in California are non-partisan, the big parties also weigh in with their influence and money. The local Democratic Party, worried about my rising popularity, attempted to organize a press conference with Congresswoman Barbara Lee to denounce me for not supporting the California Democratic Party slate of candidates for state government. I had supported Peter Camejo for Governor in 2006 running on the Green Party ticket, rather than the Democratic candidate. The press did not show up and the press conference was cancelled. But big party political maneuvering was not lost on my local campaign.

Campfires for Peace: Occupying Richmond Parks

Another important event occurred that year apart from the campaign season. It would have an impact on the whole city and amplify our shared values. After the shooting at the funeral of a murder victim in late September, a homegrown, nonviolent response sprang up in response to both that homicide and to the escalating street violence. It was a movement called Tent City and was spearheaded by African-Americans, predominately in the faith-based community, led by Reverend Andre Shumake and Reverend Charles Newsome. The community had had enough violence and started an around-the-clock vigil in Nevin Park, located in one of the city's most troubled neighborhoods. In time, more neighbors joined in and pitched tents. Other parks around the city began to create more Tent Cities in an attempt to draw attention to wanting peace and calling for a truce among feuding factions. Formerly incarcerated individuals—many former drug addicts and "OGs" (old gangsters) who had turned their lives around—became organizers of the effort. Counseling and mentoring of youth took place right there in the parks, helping them deal with their anger and teaching them how to prevent retaliatory behavior.

The community donated food, blankets, and tents. Family members who had lost loved ones to violence joined the gatherings. Day in and day out, there was a welcoming atmosphere for residents who chose to set up a tent or just drop by to chat, listen to music, or enjoy a meal. Children came by the parks after school. People talked long after dark, sitting around trashcan campfires, providing comfort and hope to one another, as well as discussing ideas for stopping the violence. In total, neighbors camped out in four public parks for forty days during a period of relative peace. I gave my wholehearted support, earnestly sharing my vision and platform for building a better Richmond as a candidate who saw this community as integral to bringing about change. I brought supplies and joined in circles of conversation, encouraging them to keep showcasing this kind of peace.

The four Richmond parks included Nevin, Shields Reid, Kennedy, and MLK, each located in a troubled area where there had been repeated acts of violence. Local grocery stores like Safeway donated food and concerned neighbors supplied good old-fashioned home-cooked dishes. A Richmond-style warmth was ever-present.

Many of the mothers who had lost children to violence showed up with photos of their loved ones artistically displayed on card tables and poster boards. These women supported each other, took their healing into their own hands, and shared their stories with the hope that their testimonies would impress others to keep this peace movement going. I remember standing in circles of women, who, with tears flowing, spoke about their loss and grief. These same women sat down with kids in the park, read to them and helped them with their homework. Other people also joined the people in the park and communicated to those gathered their experiences living on the streets of Richmond and what they had learned. Freddie Jackson (no relation to North Richmond activist Fred Jackson) stands out for me as someone who spoke out about the need to reach out to neighborhood street factions to get them to make peace with one another. Tent City was a community mobilizing in its own interest. It was quite a distinction from those corporate-led city officials who claimed to represent them.

Marilyn Langlois, key RPA activist, pitched her tent and spent nights sleeping in these parks in a show of solidarity and support, gaining much community trust. Marilyn's involvement was more than just a gesture, it was her genuine love of the Richmond community. In the 2007 Tent City reunion, Dave Grenell, a staff member from my office, echoed Marilyn's support with his own witness sleeping in the park. Our progressive political movement was there morning and night always lending support, encouragement, and a warm embrace to this independent people's movement for peace.

The dialogue continued after the tents came down, and people continued meeting. The community had a renewed sense of empowerment and self-esteem from this organic and collaborative effort. Beyond the local impact, the phenomenon of this peace movement captured people's interest nationally and internationally as a positive response to violence, leading to widespread news reports, videos, and documentaries preserving this grassroots movement. In addition, an elaborate arts project called "Touchable Stories" displayed commemorative interactive installations reflecting the forty days when the community had taken back their neighborhoods. Even as Tent City wound down in the coming year, we saw its inspiration manifested in marches such as the "Children's March Against Violence" in October 2007, when hundreds of marchers in the cities of Richmond and San Pablo, including Black and Brown students from our local schools, demonstrated for an end to street violence and an end to the violence of immigration raids. In 2008, the "March to Bury Gun Violence" organized by the [Richmond] Iron Triangle Neighborhood Council carried forth that same spirit.

I was moving at the speed of light, speaking at candidate forums and making appearances on radio and television. Driving to interviews and events, I would review my campaign speech aloud in my car, noticing the sideway glances I got from other drivers wondering who I was talking to (this was before blue tooth technology, when seeing people talk to themselves wasn't the norm). I rehearsed because I wanted to make sure I fully presented the details of my platform, as well as convey the passion I felt for my city. Conveying my deep commitment and heartfelt emotions for Richmond was easy—that was ever-present inside of me and rose to the surface when I spoke. But presenting specifics of my comprehensive platform required more practice.

I needed to articulate how we would accomplish effective governance, strong economic development with social equity, prevent more violence and crime, offer better education services, improve the environment, and bring about a better city for families and children. I was also concerned about human rights, including immigrants and homeless, affordable housing, better city planning, and funding the arts and culture, not to mention increasing our global connections. I needed to understand the issues inside and out, and become able to communicate not only proposed policies but how to implement those improvements.

While the incumbent mayor presented the biggest challenge to my campaign, I remember another candidate provoking problems for me. At a panel conducted by the *Contra Costa County Times*, Gary Bell, the third mayoral candidate, who was usually respectful toward me, leaned over the interview table and harshly interrupted me when I was speaking. I was sharing my views about Chevron needing to pay more taxes, and it felt like he was trying to discredit my knowledge on the subject. I was stunned by the interruption and it left me jarred, because I knew what I was championing and I was clearly informed on the topic. I held my ground and learned from that experience to stay focused on my message even as people try to upstage and unsettle me.

In addition to forums and interviews, I traveled to many community events where I would personally hand out my campaign literature. I canvassed door to door in countless Richmond neighborhoods, getting myself known to the people. I knew I needed exposure to defeat the incumbent mayor.

We got the biggest lawn signs we could afford and distributed them in every corner of the city. We never wasted a moment. We couldn't leave the outcome of this race to chance or hope. Plus my opponents were heavily funded by corporations.

In addition to gaining new pockets of support, we kept our current base of support enthused. I gave speeches to our volunteers at the beginning of each canvassing session to get them fired up. I learned how to deliver short, high-energy speeches in those early sessions. Our volunteers were strong-willed and determined and they spread the message that Richmond needed new leadership and a new, fresh perspective on how to turn things around. Our volunteers were also friendly and open to the people they would meet, asking their input on the state of the city. In turn, they would bring back residents' comments so that I could respond personally by email or phone. Responsiveness was key.

After every house party and fundraising event, our campaign group debriefed, often at Juan and Kay's. It was sometimes hard for me to hear the criticism—I felt this campaign in every fiber of my being. But I learned to listen and not take things personally. Ultimately I learned to appreciate constructive critique. RPA campaigns are not about an individual, the focus is on the movement. And every individual, candidate or not, has room for improvement. We needed to learn to let go of our egos.

Fundraising was key, too. One big event we held was at The Baltic, a former restaurant in Point Richmond. Peter Camejo was the special guest and as always, he gave a rousing speech. Peter was running for governor on the Green Party ticket, but that he took the time to speak at a fundraiser for me spoke volumes—he was modeling just what we did at RPA in showing through his actions the willingness to campaign for others.

In late 2006, I was still on the campaign trail moving rapidly toward Election Day. I had put everything I had into being a candidate, and I knew my campaign team had run an extraordinary campaign. Yet we were also aware that the outcome of this mayoral race would be tight. As the votes were tallied, I was tense with apprehension, hoping for the best, while bolstering myself to stand with integrity in case I lost.

As soon as it was certain that I had won the mayor's seat, I found myself breathing an enormous sigh of relief, followed immediately with a profound gratitude to the community who had supported me. The vote count was close—I had won by a mere 279 votes. It had been an incredibly hard-won race, but our grassroots progressive campaign refusing all corporate contributions had prevailed over heavily bankrolled opponents. The Council of Industries, the Chamber of Commerce, major developers, and other big moneyed interests could not buy the highest political seat in Richmond.

Swearing in as mayor

In the aftermath of the election, Paul and I readied ourselves for a major change. We knew that the reality of my work as mayor was about to have an impact on our lives. Winning the race was one thing, but I was now in the leadership position for turning our city in a totally new direction. Although Paul and I were still quite naive about just how much this new role would affect us as individuals and as a couple, we were firmly planted in our love for each other and our shared commitment to the greater good of the community. With this strong bond, we were prepared for the challenges ahead. We had only been married a year, though we had been together for six. Taking on this journey so early in our marriage made it both difficult and wondrous. Hard, because we didn't have the time to devote to each other that we both would have wanted in our first year as a married couple, and wondrous, because we had the opportunity to show each other the kind of commitment that can weather storms.

Throughout the years I was mayor, we often felt a strain on our relationship. We both made sacrifices. My life was taken over by my job as mayor, and most of the household tasks fell to Paul. We adjusted and readjusted constantly, like many couples, but ours included a high-profile job.

On a community level, we were enveloped in something much bigger than ourselves. The RPA had joined forces with an emergent local movement during the campaign. By supporting a community mobilization yearning for peace and providing it with the respect it deserved, we earned a place of esteem for ourselves. When local movements thrive and grow, they often serve as signposts of the times for other movements. Richmond's first Tent City in 2006 was a precursor to the Occupy Movement that would emerge five years later and make similar demands for justice.

While more movements and marches were on the horizon, I'll never forget how in 2006, a burgeoning feeling of pride came to life in our community as they took the lead and created a respite and cooling-off period at a time of escalating violence. I conveyed my admiration and solidarity to all who stepped forward in this mobilization and committed to working with them. In the years to come I was able to put this solidarity into action by providing some funding through my office budget into Tent City reunions in 2007, with people pitching tents once again for shorter time periods. Other actions and dialogues continued into the following year. However, soon after that, the Council majority put an end to these campsites in the parks due to the operational and associated staff costs to maintain those activities. Internal conflicts also plagued the movement, so the Tent City projects wound down on a number of fronts.

But for the time being, as 2006 came to an end, we were completing the year with an electoral victory. I savored our collective success with a sense of awe and humility, alongside a tempered measure of anxiety.

Stoking the Embers for a Better Future

When I was elected mayor, Richmond became the largest city in the United States with a mayor who was registered with the Green Party. What that meant to me was a bit different than what it meant to some people. Mayor and City Council races are almost always non-partisan in California, and that is the case with Richmond. Although my voter registration was as a Green, my political activity revolved around the Richmond Progressive Alliance and our non-partisan organizing efforts. The RPA had pushed the envelope, and we were on the way to putting shared values into action in tangible ways. We knew all eyes were on Richmond, some watching us from the sidelines hoping we would make errors, others cheering us on with a new level enthusiasm, and, of course, others trying to block our way.

Richmond's city government is structured not to give a lot of power to the mayor. We have a City Manager and City Council structure that delegates administrative operations to the City Manager, and a City Council that determines policy. The mayor has a small staff and one vote on the City Council. At the same time, the Mayor's Office often serves the main repository for citizens seeking information, advice, sharing concerns, and frustrations, and of course for expressing ideas and proposals. The Mayor's office has a lot going on. One of my early staff members, Dave Grenell, who had previously worked in both San Francisco and Oakland's City Hall, helped me get my office up and running. Another staff person, Kibibi Culbertson, started as an intern and became administrative assistant. Kibibi's sense of humor carried me through many a hard day—a valuable part of any job description, for sure. Marilyn Langlois, Nicole Valentino, and later Jeff Shoji (who prefers to be called Shoji) would become key political staff people in my office, helping me carry out my tasks as Richmond's new progressive mayor.

The challenges were immense with deeply entrenched problems. I gave my first State of the City Address in January 2007 to give a sense of where the City was at and where we needed to go. I stressed violence prevention, environmental health and justice, and economic development as my top priorities, emphasizing the call to community participation. Good democracy demands our collective actions. I reminded the people that the state of our city depends on us.

The work ahead seemed daunting, but, with the engagement of the community, I believed I could navigate a new direction for Richmond. We were showing a new way of doing politics. Peter Camejo called our political success in Richmond, the "Richmond miracle." I clung to that phrase, that symbolic indication that something extraordinary had taken place, knowing full well (as did Peter) that this was no miracle. It was the relentless hard work of many dedicated Richmond progressives that brought us to the historic moment, where a non-establishment candidate, standing apart from the two-party system and without one corporate dime, had been propelled to the highest elected office in the city.

Of course, the excitement of that collective achievement was tempered by the knowledge that Chevron still held sway among the Council majority. Disengaging this corporate grip on our city government was a necessity. As progressives, we understood that our democracy would never flourish as long as we were being held captive to such undue influence.

Addressing the core needs of our community in real and concrete ways was the mission we had before us. No easy task indeed, but in the spirit of "A better Richmond is possible" we believed we could make things happen. We knew that our complex challenges would not go away overnight, and there were no instantaneous solutions. But I was ready to put in the time and work, along with others, to further our journey to a healthier, safer, and more just city. However, new and more immediate problems would soon surface, and that would slow our work to focus on strategies and policy changes.

Two major upsets happened in the first month of my tenure as mayor. One of these upheavals was a fire at the Chevron refinery (January 15, 2007). Although it was not as big as the 2012 fire that would take place in my second term of office, it was a big concern, triggering a "shelter in place," warning residents to stay inside their homes. The fire took nearly nine hours to put out and resulted in the injury of a Chevron worker. Chevron minimized the seriousness of the fire and presented their refinery as having the safest practices and highest standards available. While their words and reports were a panacea to the Chevron-backed majority on the Council, it only heightened the concerns among many of us who know the billion-dollar profits reaped by this multi-national oil corporation don't come without the heavy expense on workers' health and on the community that lives near this gargantuan, and at times, lethal refinery.

The second upset during my first month in office came by way of the federal agency known as Immigration and Customs Enforcement (ICE) when they descended on Richmond. As part of a nationwide ICE sweep called "Operation Return to Sender," Richmond, along with other Bay Area cities were among the first to experience these raids with 119 residents arrested in Contra Costa

County, some of them in Richmond. Federal agents said they were targeting illegal immigrants with criminal records and those who evaded deportation orders, yet of the 119 arrested, eighteen were criminals and ninety-four were not on ICE's original wanted list, meaning they had no deportation orders.

Richmond is home to a large number of immigrants. One in three of our residents are foreign born. Hundreds of our residents and those in neighboring cities became victims of ICE raids, leaving communities in a state of fear and trauma. Children saw their parents arrested by ICE officials as they arrived at school to pick them up and drive them home. Families were torn apart and even those who were later released were left scarred with the trauma of having witnessed those arrests. ICE officers acknowledged through press reports that its officers identified themselves as "police," which misled residents into thinking they were Richmond police officers investigating local crimes. This created an additional fear that would be transferred to our local police. Our police force was in the early days of transforming its culture to one of a community-involved force so, needless to say, these ICE raids halted a certain level of trust between peace-keeping officers and the immigrant community.

In response a large mobilization sprang up from the grassroots of the immigrant community. There were rallies and community meetings at local churches with one meeting drawing a thousand people. Hundreds came to the next City Council meeting to testify and provide support for a resolution I introduced calling for a moratorium on these raids and resolving that our police department would not act in cooperation with ICE authorities (with the exception of cases involving criminal actions). The resolution approved by the City Council and sent to federal and state representatives also called for a comprehensive immigration reform bill that is fair, just, and humane. Our police chief, Chris Magnus, shared his support for this policy and made it clear that his officers had not been and would not be involved with the ICE raids, assuring the community that they would follow this practice of non-involvement. I made it clear to our community that Richmond was home for all of us—whether we came from the global south, the U.S. south, or any other city or country.

Our immigrant community showcased their ability to organize and speak out on their own behalf. I was proud to stand with them and for them. I also went to Washington, D.C. a few months later, along with representatives of the faith community, to speak at a congressional hearing detailing the trauma these raids had inflicted on our community.

Heat on the Streets

My first year as mayor also demonstrated that the Council, in our ways of responding to the city's violent crime, was even more polarized. Since the RPA had entered the local political arena, we were working to shift the narrative of Richmond from one of a hopelessly dangerous city, relentlessly portrayed as such by the press, to one addressing crime at its roots. As mayor, I used every speech, every presentation, every community event, every city council meeting, and every other avenue I could find to speak about the decades of poverty, neglect, lack of jobs, and the failure of our education system that plagued our community and how we needed to reverse the hopelessness and despair in order to reverse the cycle of violence on our city streets.

Relief for Hot-Spot Neighborhoods

Now that I was mayor, I would lead with new policies for reducing violence. I brought an agenda item to the Council just a few months after being sworn-in, directing the City Manager to fast-track the hiring of a director for an Office of Neighborhood Safety (ONS) to support street-level service and community-building efforts. I also proposed hiring outreach teams made up of individuals who had served time in prison and who had turned their lives around to go out into our neighborhoods in an effort to quell the violence before it started and offer services to our youth. We needed these troubled youth to have mentors with whom they could develop a trusting relationship. Although the Council was more amenable to hiring a director, it took months for them to overcome resistance to actually budget funds to hire outreach workers and peace-builders. The Council originally voted down funding these positions, citing financial concerns, but finally in July they voted after hearing from sixty-four members of the public. Many speakers shared how violence had touched their lives.

One memorable testimony came from RPA supporter Jovanka Beckles, who shared how she and her partner, Nicole Valentino had been invaded in their home by an armed robber. The two women tried to remain calm while he took their belongings. But when the robber came across a photo of their son, Lucio, the robber asked who he was. They answered that he was their son and the robber replied: "It must be nice to have a home and family like this." That spoke volumes to Jovanka and Nicole, who realized this individual was hurting, and if he had grown up with family support, his life might look different and this horrible act of violence would not have been his first course of action.

Getting the funding for the ONS in July was not soon enough. By September we had a spike in gun violence. And the press was all over it. Richmond had made the list as one of the most dangerous cities in the U.S. and that seemed to draw a lurid interest by the press. But reporting on decades of injustices that led to violence takes more than sensationalistic sound bites. Some of my colleagues on the Council spoke only to the need for more police officers, with some of them re-instigating a call for a state of emergency, as they had done two years prior. This of course would have caused city residents to feel more alienation from police rather than embrace the cultural shift toward community policing we were trying to implement. Even the Police Department expressed worries that this would undermine their relationship-building efforts with residents—giving the perception that local police were acting like curfew-enforcing National Guardsmen. Some council members promoted the fear hype and it added anguish. The glare of publicity was not helpful. We needed actual interventions and long-term solutions, and that was the purpose of the ONS, although this office had just been funded and was hastening to get up and running.

Sparks of Irresponsible Reporting

I saw no point in fighting out these different violence reduction strategies in the limelight with my council colleagues. Calm and sound judgment was what was needed, not a city council fight on television and radio airwaves. I put out my own media release on how we needed to address the violence and to state my perspective on our chronic violence. I expressed how after many delays we had just recently approved the ONS, and that the fast-track hiring of a director for this office, which I had proposed in April, had not yet materialized. It was mid-September and by now we should have had "peace teams" organized and hired by the city, but that was not the case. I called upon our residents to assist our police officers and to mobilize with the Tent City Peace Movement that would again set up tents later that month.

I made sure my staff circulated my press release widely. This was not sufficient, apparently, for various reporters. One reporter actually stalked my house. I was portrayed as "missing in action" on Bay Area television. One television reporter misquoted me as saying earlier that year: "Don't contact me for a year." When in fact I had answered his question with honesty when he asked: "What is your plan for stopping the violence in Richmond?" I replied, "I am just getting into office. I have stated throughout the campaign that we need to address the roots of our violence that have been decades in the making. I will be presenting ideas to the Council soon and I will have a lot more to talk about after I've served for at least a year, as some new programs get implemented." It was frustrating to see how my words were twisted and cut short.

I admit to having a healthy distrust of the mainstream news sources, which are controlled primarily through corporate commercials and other advertising. There is also a serious lack of investigative reporting. Sound bites take precedence over bringing forward a deeper understanding. For years, the press had demonized Richmond as a horrible place with crime being the only thing they covered. The spike in homicides in the fall of 2007 affected me deeply as I empathized with the overwhelming impact and suffering it had on families, friends, and neighbors of the victims. I took my responsibility seriously and this was a low point for me in my first year as mayor, as the outcome of decades of systemic injustices played out in Richmond.

Reducing violence remained my major focus throughout my tenure, and I am proud that, under my administration, in a collective effort that included city staff, elected officials and community, we demonstrated how an urban community can transform itself by reducing homicides by 75%. This didn't come easy, and it was a constant fight to make our budget reflect a more balanced approach with multiple strategies to stem the violence, since most of my early colleagues on the Council were beholden to the Police Union, known historically for acquiring special perks as part of their negotiated agreements with the city. In fact the same councilmembers who received campaign contributions from the Police Union also were responsible for providing unsustainable pensions for this union, a situation which continues to have an impact on the city's budget and essential city services today.

But as in every challenge, this experience offered me an opportunity to grow. I learned what I could expect from the press and I needed to confront them head-on. From that point forward, my relationship with news reporters became much stronger. I made it clear that Richmond is not a sound bite about recent shootings for the nightly newscast. There is more to Richmond than that. Our news is an in-depth story of struggle, resiliency, and determination. More recently, we have gotten great coverage about our innovative and bold solutions not only to violence reduction, but also to a host of urban problems. Yet the reasons why we've come this far are not always identified.

And although the media might not be expected to tell the whole story, something only those of us who have lived the experiences can do, a free press certainly has an important role in our society. Unfortunately, too often we see our news reports and broadcasts selling sensationalism over thoughtful reporting and analysis.

Staff Firing

For the most part, I worked with an incredible staff. However, I was faced with a profoundly disturbing situation with regard to one staff person. This most difficult challenge was the hardest one I faced during my entire first mayoral term—it was theft from the Mayor's Office. I found out about this in early 2008, terminated him immediately, set into motion a full audit of his access to the office budget and called for a full investigation from the County

District Attorney. Marilyn Langlois, a Community Advocate in my office and an RPA leader, was indispensable in helping me take the needed steps to address the crisis both inside and outside City Hall.

As a result of the investigation, the person was prosecuted and has since served his sentence, although a light one, allowing him status under house arrest and requiring him only to wear an ankle bracelet. He was required to pay back the money he stole (about $66,000), and has since repaid the entire amount. In addition, his sentencing stated that he can never again work in jobs having to do with financial matters.

What was most difficult for me in this ordeal was the sense of betrayal—the likes of which I had never experienced. I gave this person a job opportunity based on good recommendations; he was compensated with an excellent salary and benefits, and yet he chose to take advantage and engage in illegal activity, somewhat at my expense. This was an egregious breach of my personal trust as well as the trust of the community. Initially, as shock set in, my faith in humanity was shattered. At the same time, I knew this wasn't about me personally—this government worker took advantage of the system and chose to steal. In time I realized that the solidarity and trust I had with the community was never in jeopardy. Adversaries on the Council, along with Chevron and the public safety unions, took every opportunity to politicize this event in an attempt to bring me down. But the people understood the facts and knew my integrity was not in question.

Recently I received an apology letter from the person who stole the money. He added that he knows he will have to live with this horrible misdeed the rest of his life. I accept his apology and wish him well as he carves out a new path for his life. At the same time, I acknowledge that while what he did was awful, this action was not the totality of this person who wreaked such havoc on my life and in the mayor's office. This worker also made positive contributions to the city. Yet I also can't help mentioning that this was a serious crime, classified as "white-collar" crime. This man was treated vastly differently than what would befall an individual who had only known poverty and broke the law. It is the poor, largely persons with Black and Brown complexions, who fill up today's prisons as a result of minor offenses like possession of marijuana and petty theft. People who commit white-collar crime often spend little or no time incarcerated. Our society has a long way to go toward treating people equally who break the law and need to pay restitution.

I was deeply stung by this ordeal and it took a long time to unravel the mess he had left and start anew. And yet I also gained insight and courage as I grappled with it in the aftermath. As an elected official and on a practical level, I made changes in the Mayor's Office. I instituted financial accountability on each and every item I signed for, made sure more than one person was checking expenditures, etc. On a personal level, I learned how to steel myself with fortitude and resolve to keep moving forward toward my goals with a terrific staff, with support from RPA, and with a community in whom I could trust.

Those experiences coming early in my first term as mayor had proved to be really tough, but I had gained more strength and stamina than I imagined possible. Personal and political challenges had not shaken my faith in humanity nor deterred me from furthering my goals on behalf of the community. New challenges would come later, but I had faced my baptism by fire and was still moving forward, still envisioning a better future, and still loving my city.

Stop the Hemorrhaging: A Fair Share for Richmond

My second year as mayor left me feeling braced, bandaged, and yet emboldened after my initiation of trials and tribulations. Now I was ready to dig in and work on the root causes of some of the deeper ills plaguing Richmond. All was not right in my beloved city, from lack of finances to a host of other troubles. This left me with a queasy feeling. I was not alone and that was also how RPA felt even as we continued to struggle to make real differences in Richmond. We were scratching our heads, wondering how to make substantial inroads for our community. We saw how industrialized urban life had festered with untreated sores on our metropolis and we needed emergency care.

It was hard to know where to begin. Creating the Office of Neighborhood Safety (ONS) was a good start, but the needs of our community were vast and widespread, and the difficulties interlinked with one another. Violence, poverty, lack of education and job opportunities, health and environmental issues—all those areas seemed connected and there was a painful stagnation for both our city and many of its residents. RPA knew we couldn't wait on the sidelines for a market cure to heal our ailing local economy. By this time, most people were aware that the invisible hand of the market was bypassing Richmond. No panacea was going to appear and make everything better. We had to come up with our own local solutions to our decades-long sluggish economy.

Diagnostics

Part of RPA's core mission is to lift up lives and enhance the quality of life for everyone in our community. We needed to reverse entrenched social ills with some viable correctives. We were not naïve that in this money-driven system, proposed solutions require financial reserves. Going back to the early days of the RPA, we had been grappling with how to access more resources. Our primary question began by asking who in Richmond wasn't paying their fair share into our city's treasury, and why not. It took just a little digging to unearth the answers. It was big industry, and in Richmond, that was Chevron. The refinery had been given a number of privileges over the years, including a special tax perk instituted in the 1980s.

Chevron, with its billion-dollar profits, most assuredly was not the taxpayer who needed a break. While the fossil fuel giant got this significant financial advantage, our working families and city coffers were left wanting. It was corruption over a number of decades that had given Chevron the tax perk—the company's reach into city government offices with council members doing their bidding had become the status quo. So now we had the origin of the ailment but identifying the symptoms was not enough. RPA knew we needed a tangible strategy to undo the harm.

People instinctively understand fair taxation. It wasn't difficult to rally people around this basic tenet and that's what the RPA did. We had been talking among ourselves about this since our inception in 2003. RPA had just barely come into existence when the city experienced its thirty-five million dollar deficit, and proposals and ideas for improving the city's financial health were part of that discourse. At the 2004 Richmond People's Convention, proposals such as a "gross receipts tax" and the removal of Chevron's Utility Users' Tax (UUT) cap were part of our progressive platform. The UUT is imposed by a city on the consumption of energy and other utilities, including electricity, gas, water, sewer, telephone, sanitation, and cable television. In Richmond, taxpayers pay a 10% tax for such services—every taxpayer, that is, except Chevron. This large corporation pays a flat, capped amount regardless of use. The city did not even receive an account of Chevron's full utility use, so we had no idea if they were paying anywhere close to what they used.

It was mindboggling that the Council did not even have a proper computation for levying taxes on Chevron. The RPA had been outraged over this lack of accountability and it had fueled our work from our beginning. By challenging Chevron on taxation, we knew we were confronting its corporate business model focused on continuously inflating profits at obscene levels.

While we knew that making inroads on this issue was a daunting task, we also knew that when people join together, what seems impossible becomes possible. And, in fact, after a couple years of mobilizing and calling for more taxes from big business, we found our collective pressure starting to have some impact on the other members of the City Council. This was evident in 2006 when four non-RPA councilmembers presented a gross receipts business tax measure at a Council meeting. This is a tax on the total amount of revenue received by a business in exchange for property or services sold, leased, or rented during a given period before deducting costs or expenses. As progressives, we embraced such a policy and were prepared to fight for it. On the night of a Council meeting, members of the business community and the local Chamber of Commerce rallied against this proposal, saying such a tax would cause existing businesses to leave the city and prevent new businesses from coming to Richmond—even though nearby cities like Berkeley had such a tax and were considered business-friendly. With strong resistance showing up, the four council members (Maria Viramontes, Nat Bates, John Marquez, and Richard Griffin) who initiated the item seemed caught off guard. Rather than pursue a vote on it, they backtracked and approved a motion to have a sub-committee of the four councilmembers work on revisions with city staff and stakeholders within the business community. The matter would then return to the Council with revisions for further action.

First Aid: 2006 Measure T

What came back several weeks later was not a revised form of a gross receipts tax, rather a large manufacturers' tax that would predominately impact only one big business, Chevron. Could it be that some of my colleagues were beginning to get some backbone in regard to Chevron? At first this seemed to be the case.

The Council voted to place the initiative on the 2006 ballot with a 6-3 vote. This was actually quite extraordinary given that the majority of the Council were typically unwilling to ruffle the oil giant's feathers. Pressure from below was working—the grassroots community platform influenced enough support to bring forward a democratic vote. The initiative would now go to the voters as Measure T.

Putting this decision up to the people seemed like a great leap forward. Alas it soon became apparent that the same councilmembers who supported the tax initiative were unwilling to take the lead publicly on it in the electoral arena. They had talked the talk but were not walking the walk. It seemed to me that those who were running for re-election would *want* to promote this high-profile measure through their reelection campaigns to make sure it got passed. But that did not happen. The initiators did not become spokespeople. The anti-Measure T forces (which included Chevron and the Council of Industries) responded favorably to their relative silence by not attacking them, choosing instead to focus their smear campaign on me.

The RPA had not planned to take the lead on this, but we knew someone had to be in the forefront, so it was left to my campaign. We organized a press conference and invited other council members to join us, if only to clear up Chevron's disinformation campaign. The titans of industry chose to distort and misrepresent a small increase of the business license tax for non-manufacturing businesses as the main focus of the measure, even though 95% of the new revenue would be coming from Chevron. This small increase—literally a few extra dollars a month—was touted as something that would discourage new businesses citywide. In addition, the opposition intensely focused on attacking the landlord tax adjustment included in the measure. While that would have had a miniscule impact on landlords, Chevron falsely presented it as a tax on renters, exploiting the notion that landlords would pass the tax onto tenants through increased rents. With no rent control in the city, many tenants had no protection, and Chevron manipulated that vulnerability to its advantage.

We countered Chevron's messaging with our own, revealing the truth about the tax. We featured support for Measure T in our campaign literature and funded signs, distributing them around the city thanks to our tireless volunteers. I was the one candidate singled out by Chevron in their deluge of hit-piece mailers where I was repeatedly wedded to Measure T with slogans like "Gayle Should Fail with her Terrible T." In spite of having to ward off this onslaught of attacks funded by hundreds of thousands of corporate dollars, I can honestly say I was proud to have my campaign be the prime mover of this ballot initiative. It wasn't only support for this measure that was driving us. We also set ourselves the task of breaking the illusion that many people had about corporations. Although people had an inherent understanding of the principle of fair taxation, they often assumed corporations were paying their fair portion of the tax base. When educating the voters, people were amazed to hear that Chevron paid only a paltry few thousand dollars as its business license tax to the City of Richmond.

The effort to pass Measure T brought new progressive activists into the RPA, including Jovanka Beckles, who would later became a councilmember. Jovanka came up with a simple and clear slogan for the campaign—"Yes on T, T Taxes Chevron Not You." While Chevron and its PAC put out misinformation to deceive residents and small business owners into believing this tax was aimed at them, we used Jovanka's slogan on our mailers and signs.

Notwithstanding our good efforts, we were faced with a disadvantage. Since we had not been involved in either initiating or developing the ballot measure we had no timeline for rolling it out. In essence, we inherited it by default. Precious campaign time was lost by not having knowledge until July that this was being presented for the November ballot. Getting onto the campaign trail early in the year had been an essential strategy for all our RPA campaigns. We will never have enough money to match the corporate investments, but we use time advantageously, giving ourselves as much as a full year to personally reach out to residents. My mayoral campaign had gotten started months before the measure made its appearance. We were already knocking on doors in every corner of the city introducing my candidacy and vision for leading the city in a new direction. Unfortunately, there wasn't a similar long stretch of time to strategize for this ballot measure, but we did the best we could under the circumstances. While we were handicapped by a compressed timetable, we educated as many people as possible, knowing this would be beneficial whether the measure passed or not. We firmly believe the life-blood of our movement building is a well-informed populace.

Ultimately, the tax measure was defeated, though a respectable 42% of voters had supported it. Chevron's line of attack had been successful but we also witnessed a growing number of people starting to think about wealth inequality in our city. We had planted seeds, which needed to mature and gain further momentum within our population. Democracy isn't a quick fix pill—it is a process that requires full community involvement and support before real signs of growth and healing show.

We were not discouraged. We knew we had laid a sound foundation. This initiative had provided us our first opportunity to mobilize and engage the voters on the ballot measure. It wouldn't be long before we would mobilize further.

Digging Deeper into the Malady

I ran for office to be a public servant, not an agent of corporate interests. In 2007 I was holding the highest elected office in the city, pondering next steps, and knowing I wanted to use my position to bring about justice for the constituents I represented. For too long, the power of money had directed policy decisions in Richmond. City politicians, in service to their corporate donors and an unjust corporate-run system, repeatedly cried "budget crisis" and cut essential human services to balance budgets, while the real crises went ignored. Tax perks and loopholes in the tax structure kept money flowing into the profits of the wealthy, while budgetary cutbacks kept the city from having funds to address the deeper problems. This transfer of wealth is what needed attention and Richmond progressives were bound and determined to tackle it.

Previous to our coming together as an alliance, many of us in the RPA were inspired by Peter Camejo's run for California governor. In speeches and later in his one of his books, *California: Under Corporate Control,* Camejo drove home the point that the actual dilemma of our budget woes stems from the fact that more than half of our California profitable corporations pay no state income taxes—they only pay the $800 corporation fee on a yearly basis.[15] An effective prop he used in televised debates was a chart illustrating that the poor in our state were paying a 57% higher tax rate than the wealthiest 1%. While we've heard a lot about lopsided tax structures nationwide over the course of the 2016 presidential elections, we were building our local movement around such matters over a decade prior.

While Camejo, a third party candidate in a corporate dominated two-party system, did not become California's governor, his progressive voice paved the way for many of us to carry the torch on a local level. Long after the gubernatorial campaign ended, my husband Paul attached a blown-up version of Camejo's tax chart on the back of his pick-up truck in an effort to keep this message in the public eye.

Inequity in our tax system resonated as a key topic for us as progressives who were looking for ways to solve local problems. Our State officials were doing nothing to address this situation. But local government agencies were certainly continuing to provide needed services like fire, police, and street repair to corporate entities. There was a clear imbalance here. While corporations got perks, it is the citizen residents of local communities who are left to pay for taxes corporations are *not* paying.

A prime example illustrates this concept. During the 2012 Chevron explosion and fire (which I'll cover more in depth in a later chapter), refinery representatives called on the Richmond Fire Department for rescue and assistance. Who paid for these services? The average Richmond taxpayer. Likewise, it is ordinary people who shoulder the costs of emergency care for Richmond kids with asthma living downwind from the refinery. People everywhere need to understand that as a community we are subsidizing these corporations with our hard-earned money.

We were also facing the beginnings of the financial crisis that swept the nation in 2007. The housing crisis had hit and the Great Recession was underway. Working-class families suffered the brunt of this plunge, with African-Americans and Latinos being hit hardest, as more and more people lost their homes to foreclosures and the unemployment rate soared. The RPA understood this crisis as a manifestation of growing wealth inequality in an economic system controlled by corporations and Wall Street. We had no trouble understanding that Chevron, in our own backyard, fit into that top income bracket referred to earlier by Camejo. This top 1% continued to pay a smaller percentage of their income in state taxes than the poorest among us. As progressives who had recently won the mayor's seat, we had the onus to do whatever we could through our local efforts to lessen the hardship felt by families throughout Richmond.

This was the economic climate of the times. By this time, RPA had started holding our monthly meetings in office spaces held by other community organizations since we were too large in number now to meet in people's homes. We met for some time in the rented space held by FaithWorks, a faith-based community non-profit, and SEIU 1021, our city public employees union. Later, we met in the rented house held by the Laotian Organizing Project (LOP, a Richmond project of APEN, Asian Pacific Environmental Network). I remember feeling a sense of belonging, sitting around a large table in the LOP office surrounded by the warmth and hospitality of the Asian-Pacific culture and people. We shared food and goodwill, along with ideas as we considered the work ahead. By late 2007, our meetings were focused on the upcoming election, including discussions of new candidates and consideration of a new fair taxation ballot measure.

We wanted to do everything we could to alleviate the economic difficulties facing our community. The city needed more revenue to provide the level of programs and services that would elevate the community and offer pathways out of poverty. We had been talking for years about the need to remove Chevron's local tax perk.

For the RPA, this was simply about what is right and just. Chevron should pay the full 10% of its utility usage, like the rest of us—those funds would yield considerably more city funding. But we had trouble accessing the data from Chevron to make our case. Chevron's refusal to release information was based on what they called "proprietary information." They claimed that the amounts of energy they used in the refining process was confidential and trade secrets would be revealed if they provided the data, compromising their competition on the market. Our response was that they were simply hiding behind a false legal protection. We weren't asking for any chemical formulas used in their refining process where trade secrets might come into play. We just wanted to know how many units of electricity and gas they consumed in their operations in order to calculate taxation, as we gauge *every* taxpayer.

I found it preposterous that a corporation could conceal its energy usage in this era of climate change, but Chevron was able to get away with it. This issue was highly contentious over the course of several years with progressives throughout the community rallying around the banner of full disclosure. There were differing opinions on the Council, however. It came as no surprise to the RPA that most councilmembers were unwilling to push the issue, given the corporation's contributions to their electoral seats. It was very telling how they bowed to Chevron's supposed rights to privacy and later started advocating that members of the Council sign confidentiality agreements with the oil giant if we wanted to get a peek at whatever documents they would release. I was outraged that they would succumb to Chevron's veil of secrecy and would leave the public, who had rallied around this issue for years, in the dark. First and foremost, this was the public's right to know. Secondly, leaving this issue solely in the hands of a City Council still largely in Chevron's pocket, behind closed doors and outside the public realm, had no chance of producing the results we needed. After many tussles on the Council over several years, we hired a consultant to audit Chevron's energy usage and present his findings to the Council in closed session. The Council would only be provided general information on Chevron's methodology for calculating its energy consumption, rather than the full data. It wasn't what we had pushed for, but it did allow us to make some inferences. After hearing the auditor's general analysis, I was confident it pointed to the potential for significant new city revenue.

The passage of this special perk was simply one example of how a City Council can cater to the needs of big industry. All over the country, corporate entities lobby the government that in turn sacrifices the well being of the people. Once in office, elected officials who receive corporate donations feel duty-bound to pay back their corporate donors by passing policies in the interest of that corporation. Given Richmond's history of elected officials taking Chevron money, it is no wonder our city had a special perk in place.

The UUT situation continued to be a mobilizing issue for us in the RPA. However, we were still in the throes of wrangling with Chevron about the data and it seemed we would need more time to effectively present a ballot measure to the public. So we thought it prudent to set the UUT cap removal aside temporarily, and build upon Measure T that was still in the public's memory from 2006 and already had a base of support. We only needed about 8% more votes on top of the earlier measure and we felt certain we could get an updated form of the initiative passed.

Proposed Treatment: A New Measure T

Juan Reardon spearheaded the effort to redo Measure T, this time making it generate more revenue. He revised the past measure maintaining the overall formula for calculating the manufacturers' tax, but required a higher percentage of the value of raw materials used in manufacturing to be paid in taxes. While in 2006, the tax was set at one-eighth percent of the value of the raw materials, the new measure set the tax at one-quarter percent. To prevent a reemergence of disinformation regarding the impact on renters and non-manufacturing businesses, Juan eliminated the landlord adjustment altogether as well as the small increased fee on non-manufacturing businesses. He also included a waiver of the business license fee for all new businesses during their first year of operation in the city, making Richmond friendly to new businesses—with a nod to earlier criticisms.

After making these revisions, Juan presented it to our city attorney, Randy Riddle, who added a valuable edit. Apparently, the previous measure, initiated by other councilmembers, was lax in the enforcement section of the ordinance. There was no provision for withholding a business license or revoking an existing license when violated (that is, Chevron could violate the ordinance and not suffer any consequences). This was corrected in the new measure.

The defeat of Measure T in 2006 could have demoralized us, but with Juan's leadership, we geared up for another go-around. One major difference in how this new measure emerged is that it was a citizen initiated ballot measure. We did not think the City Council would put this new measure on the ballot, given that the previous one had failed and because of its stronger language. So there was only one other way to qualify an initiative for the ballot, and that was to gather *thousands* of signatures.

For six months our volunteer activist movement went door to door and stood in front of grocery stores, post offices, and public transit stations to both get signatures and educate people about the issue. Juan personally collected 2,500 signatures! Other volunteers collected the other 2,500 for a total of 5,000 signatures. Yes, you read that right. Juan garnered half of our signatures. Later he would reflect on how in the future he wouldn't take on such a high volume himself again, since that is truly not sustainable in the long run for one person. Plus, it is important to encourage more people to participate in signature gathering. At the same time, this speaks to Juan's activism and commitment.

Triage and Bringing in the Right Help: New RPA Candidates

By 2008 the RPA had grown to include more people. One of those individuals was Jovanka Beckles, whose principles and eagerness to work for progressive change were apparent from the first Measure T campaign. Jovanka offered a freshness and new energy as we continued to forge the road ahead. We were all too aware that, even in my position as mayor, I had only one vote and no veto power on decisions being made by the Council. While I felt strong in setting a new tone and direction for the city in my mayoral role, we knew we couldn't count on votes from the council as a whole when it came to important progressive policies. We needed more grassroots progressives on the Council. As we prepared for the 2008 electoral season, it was quite natural to approach Jovanka to see if she might consider running for a seat. She was willing to take on the challenge and venture into the electoral arena to assist in building a better Richmond. It was exciting to have Jovanka bring her passion and commitment onto the campaign trail. As an African-American and Latina born in Panama, she had an intimate understanding of unique challenges faced by our communities of color. While we greatly appreciated that she was willing to help expand RPA work, we also knew she would be attacked by our adversaries. By that time it was clear that anyone associated with the RPA would be negatively criticized by Chevron. But Jovanka was solid in her values, pledging to take no corporate money. The RPA fully endorsed her candidacy and she began her campaign side by side with the new Measure T campaign, which we called "A Fair Share for Richmond."

As we moved into the summer of this memorable election year, we were jolted by the unexpected news that Councilmember Tony Thurmond, a young African-American councilmember, would not be running for re-election, planning instead to run for the school board. Tony, though not an RPA member, agreed with us on many issues. RPA did not endorse him in his previous campaign because he did not agree to forego corporate donations, but we considered him an ally. We fully expected him to run for reelection and to win, as he was well respected throughout the community. With Tony not in the race, we knew there was the potential to end up with a Chevron-supported candidate taking his place. By mid-summer we frantically started looking for another candidate.

Jeff Ritterman, Chief Cardiologist at Kaiser Richmond, emerged as the candidate. Jeff had a calm demeanor which no doubt served him well as a doctor. Yet he was also an energetic and conscientious campaigner.

Jeff had already been working with RPA on Measure T, collecting the second most signatures to get the measure on the ballot. He had also worked closely with us promoting oversight by California's Department of Toxic Substances Control (DTSC) for our contaminated south shoreline. Once Jeff decided to run, he entered the race with enthusiasm and he garnered the most votes of all the candidates. It became clear during Jeff's campaign that he was already well known in the community.

Jeff was smeared by the Richmond Police Officers Association (RPOA) with a pitiful and petty campaign against him. Jeff wore his long hair in a ponytail and he promoted "radical" things like yoga and mindfulness through a program called Niroga that combined the two practices. He advocated this as an approach for youth to deal with some of the health and trauma issues they were facing. The RPOA asserted something to the effect that "the only thing Jeff Ritterman would bring to the City Council was yoga." They actually sent that message out in mailers to Richmond voters. I tell this story only to illustrate another attack waged against progressive political activists by the entrenched politics in Richmond. As we move forward today in Richmond, the RPOA has shifted to some extent with less assailing of our progressive movement, although there is much work to be done with holding police unions accountable everywhere. Personally, I think police unions nationwide could use a healthy dose of mindful relaxation techniques.

Other changes made 2008 an unusual election year. We reduced the City Council seats from nine to seven members based on a previous vote of the electorate, which meant there would be only three seats open with four incumbents running. Although Jovanka fell short of winning, losing by less than 500 votes, it was impressive that she came in ahead of Chevron incumbents John Marquez and Harpreet Sandu. They lost their seats by significant margins.

Also marking 2008 as a stellar year, two long-time activists in the broader progressive community, Mike Parker and Margaret Jordan, joined RPA. Both of them came from labor organizing and progressive movement building, and they brought much needed skills and experience to RPA. Mike jumped in as Jeff's campaign coordinator, and he hasn't stopped working to build and expand our movement since. Margaret's passion for social change likewise has helped move us forward by her leadership as campaign organizer, councilmember advisor and as president of her neighborhood council to name just a few of her undertakings. Both Mike and Margaret became tireless activists for our community.

Signs of Healing but Not Out of the Woods: Measure T Passes, Chevron Heads to Court

We won Measure T with 58% of the vote and finally showcased to Chevron and everyone else who had doubted our ability to make this happen, that the people of Richmond were clear about making Chevron pay their dues. With over a hundred years of living with this refinery in our city limits, it was gratifying to see this bottom-up effort gain majority support from the voters. The public understood that this measure would not affect their pocketbooks, but would predominately be Chevron's burden. The many campaign volunteers had educated the community, and successfully immunized them against another deceitful campaign. Volunteers worked for nearly a year gathering signatures and promoting the measure. I was beginning to see a light at the end of the tunnel. Our movement was gaining strength.

Sadly, it wasn't long after the election that Chevron sued the city over our successful ballot measure, putting on hold any implementation of the manufacturers' tax until the courts ruled on the matter. We remained hopeful, but were forced for the time being to sit tight for legal judgment.

As we waited for the outcome the Council had another pressing Chevron taxation issue on our plates. We were still pouring over the audit of Chevron's natural gas and electricity usage. They needed to open up their books and stop playing hide and seek with the data, so we could determine how much they should be paying. Richmond citizens now had a stake in these findings and we waited with bated breath for the test results.

A Bandaid: The UUT Settlement

The old Council was still seated after the November election. The new Council would not be sworn in until January 2009, but it was obvious the incumbents felt the mighty impact of our local movement from the recent election. We had two victories to celebrate: a new RPA councilmember, Jeff Ritterman, had been voted in and the success of Measure T. Chevron was in the hot seat and the Council was feeling the need to adapt to the new reality of people holding our largest corporation accountable. In this climate of progressive strength and momentum, the Council started leaning toward my position of at least getting all the facts in this case, including a willingness to go to court to force a ruling on Chevron's UUT tax payments. I started to feel a little bit of hope. Perhaps the political winds were turning in our direction at last.

This hope was not long-lived. The RPA had gained ground and it was great to have Jeff join me on the Council. I was no longer the only RPA-affiliated officeholder in Richmond. However, it soon became apparent that there were some differences of opinion in terms of strategy at play within the RPA. Jeff chose on his own to work with City staff, the City's UUT consultant, and Chevron on a settlement. This was, of course, something he had every right to do, but given the RPA's leadership role in the issue, it came as a surprise. The next thing I knew the Council was shifting away from its former position, no longer willing to take Chevron to court, instead choosing to negotiate a settlement. Councilmembers needed no convincing to go this route. They had only taken a strong stand with Chevron based on the RPA's great outcome in the election and they feared that they would be politically side lined if they didn't recognize this new political force gaining sway among the electorate. But once they realized that one of the RPA elected officials was promoting a settlement, they jumped at the chance to reverse course and no longer felt compelled to go the distance with Chevron. Whether going to court would have led to a better outcome at that point in time we will never know. It's possible we would have taken steps to settle eventually, if the court case dragged on, but throwing in the towel before we even began to bring this before a judicial body seemed to me a missed opportunity.

Once the Council had abandoned legally challenging Chevron—with my solitary vote to stay the course— I chose to support the settlement, giving all due credit to the community for mobilizing in support of a more equitable city tax structure. It would not be acceptable for me, or for those who looked to me for leadership, to let the Chevron-friendly councilmembers flaunt the settlement money as their political success story, which they surely would have, even though it was our multi-year campaign for fair taxation that brought Chevron to the negotiating table. In the end, the Council, with the inclusion of my vote, approved a $28-million settlement to be paid over three years. While that *temporarily* ended Chevron's worries about having to pay more utility taxes on an annual basis, the RPA made it clear to the public that Chevron would owe us so much more annually if the perk was removed. We pointed out Chevron's willingness to settle quickly as an indication that they had a lot more to lose by letting the courts decide. To this day, Chevron has never provided full documentation to the elected officials or the public on its actual usage of natural gas and electricity.

I was greatly disappointed by how this played out—this was a heartbreak of a compromise for me. I felt blindsided by the push to settle, but when all was said and done, I supported the settlement, hailing it as a partial victory for our grassroots organizing effort in Richmond, based on five years of community pressure led by the RPA.

In spite of this rocky start between Jeff and me, we aligned on most City issues and weathered many a storm during the four years he served on the Council. He contributed greatly to the progress of Richmond over those years, most notably in raising awareness inside and outside of City Hall on health and health disparity issues, as well as a host of other progressive issues.

A Relapse but Strong Recovery on the Horizon: Court Rules Against Measure T but Our Movement Forges Ahead

Meanwhile, Chevron continued its legal battle against Measure T claiming it violated state and federal laws. A year later the Courts ruled in favor of Chevron, with a highly technical ruling about how the tax would be measured—although the judge offered some guidelines for replacement on the ballot with a legal fix. People were again disappointed and we considered resubmitting it to the ballot, but by that time the RPA was already working on a different ballot measure, "End Chevron's Perk," that finally would have lifted the UUT cap. While the UUT settlement would help for a few years, we knew the city needed permanent sources of new revenue.

For RPA, all our efforts to establish new sources of permanent revenue stemmed from our basic principle of fairness. By the time Measure T was struck down by the courts, the Great Recession was in full swing, and our unemployment was soaring higher than ever. It was imperative that we provide job training and program development to help our residents have a fair chance as the society at large spiraled into greater wealth inequality.

So it was onward with our campaign. Chevron, however, presented its own plan. In retaliation to our efforts to close the UUT loophole, Chevron started gathering signatures for a counter measure that would reduce utility taxes for *all* taxpayers. This was their attempt to get voters to approve less taxation for themselves, rather than focus on removing Chevron's special benefit. Chevron's measure, if passed, would have bankrupted the City. If anyone doubted that Chevron played hardball without an ounce of concern for the city's well-being, this was the evidence.

This reactive ballot measure stopped us dead in our tracks since we clearly were not willing to risk the City's financial stability. Chevron, of course, was ready and willing to come to the negotiating table once again to deal with all these tax issues by settlement. They clearly saw advantage to paying settlements, over the course of a finite number of years, rather than a greater amount of annual taxes in perpetuity. Chevron knew we had the people with us, so we were able to negotiate a far larger settlement this time. We reached an agreement for an additional $114 million over fifteen years. In return, the City Council agreed to not go forward with the "End Chevron's Perk" initiative *and* to not initiate any proposed new taxes on Chevron over the course of the fifteen years. This of course would not stop the community (distinct from the Council) from initiating another ballot measure seeking more taxes from Chevron, and although that hasn't happened since 2010, it is an option we have not totally abandoned.

Nonetheless, this $114 million settlement was indeed another victory won by the community and voters in Richmond, whose stance on fair taxation was well known by now. The voter support for Measure T made it clear—people in Richmond expected this massive corporation to pay its fair share.

Slapped with a Secondary Infection: Another Fair Taxation Battle

Just when we thought we could breathe again, another taxation issue. In the middle of the recession, Chevron displayed its brazenness once again when they decided to appeal its property tax assessment. This was no small appeal and there would be a series of appeals that, if won, would have provided a massive refund to Chevron covering the period 2004–2012. Needless to say, this caused an avalanche of indignation and outrage. This was in the depth of the recession, with people losing their homes, their jobs, and their dreams. The RPA, and others grassroots organizations marched, rallied, and attended board meetings to make our opposition known. We even put on theatrical displays with a greedy "Chevron Man" character, demanding more and more profits. The Richmond community was standing up and taking action.

But Chevron continued to bring its appeals before the Contra Costa County Appeals Board. I remember when a decision came forward in early April 2012. I had been invited to speak on a panel at a conference put on by Ralph Nader and the Occupy Movement in Washington, D.C. As I walked to the conference from my hotel, I got a phone call from my husband, who was at the County Appeals Board hearing. Paul told me the board denied the appeal and actually determined that the oil giant owed Richmond *more* taxes! I was so elated I worked this news bit into my speech to great applause by the audience. I also shared that just a few days earlier a Chevron representative had called me (evidently expecting a favorable outcome) saying that I shouldn't worry about this property tax appeal, "since the company would go easy on the city and help us make a 'soft landing' by not requiring all the back payments from the City at one time and waiving the interest." The fossil fuel behemoth obviously didn't have an inside track to the appeals board after all. For our part, we were delighted with the board's decision. There is no question that it was the sustained, multi-year community mobilization that conveyed to the board that anything short of rejecting the appeal would be unacceptable.

Chevron man

This, of course, was not the end. Big corporations don't roll over easily. Chevron sued the County over the appeals board decision, and ultimately reached a settlement in late 2013. The deal settled all open property tax appeals for 2004–2012 with Chevron paying around $50 million in property taxes in 2014 and the City of Richmond receiving around $14 million of that $50 million. Each subsequent year allows for a 2% increase based on the Consumer Price Index. Since property taxes in California are assigned and collected at the county level and only later dispersed to the cities, Richmond did not play a primary role in this settlement, even as our coffers would eventually receive a portion of those payments. The City did play a secondary role supporting the county, which was up against Chevron's high-priced corporate lawyers and was facing its own budgetary problems. On the positive side, the outcome was that Chevron would drop its lawsuit and the appeals board decision (to deny tax refunds to the corporation) would stand. On the negative side, the RPA felt strongly there could have been a much fairer settlement. It turns out, the City and other public agencies, like the school district, got stuck with a less than sufficient assessment of the Richmond refinery. Given estimates that Chevron makes between $2 and $3 billion per year in profits from the Richmond refinery alone, it seemed to the RPA that our city deserved a better deal.[16]

For the RPA, our focus has turned more broadly to State efforts at this point. The only way we can still get more property taxes from the refinery is to work with unions, progressive allies, and cities throughout California to reform Proposition 13, a California state referendum, to require more property tax from commercial and industrial properties. We have also promoted a millionaire income tax at the State level. And we never rule out a citizens'-ballot measure on the city level. Fair taxation, and the challenges we face in achieving it, necessitates we consider many ways to access the revenue needed to serve the community.

Future Prognosis

Today in Richmond, fair taxation has become a well-appreciated course of action. All but the most beholden to or bought off by Chevron understand the basic principle that greater taxation should come from those who continue to make billions in profits year after year in our city. Chevron benefits from its physical location and infrastructure already built and running in Richmond. No new refinery has been built in the U.S. since the 1970s as communities in other places have rightly refused new construction. But this major refinery already exists in our backyard. We have no choice but to find ways to regulate it and seek our fair share of taxes. Our success through mobilization in acquiring more taxes from Chevron helped us bring more services to our residents, but it also brought more consciousness-raising into play. Shifting the discourse to conversations about the public's rights versus surrender to an unequal set of circumstances has been included in all our progressive work. Such exchanges of ideas provide the genes of a new political culture—prompting and activating us toward the creation of a fairer and more participatory democracy. "A Fair Share for Richmond" was all about such a democracy.

We were pleased with the positive steps we had taken on fair taxation—real healing and growth could now happen in our city. While the struggle was long and hard and we didn't achieve all we had desired, the people of Richmond had demonstrated a key truth. In the words of Martin Luther King Jr., "the arc of the moral universe is long, but it bends towards justice." In our case, the overall trajectory led to additional funding for city services and community needs, but more than that, the people of Richmond learned that we can fight and win.

Point Molate, A Love Story

Richmond is seductive. Once it pulls you in, you are hopelessly in love. And this is no passive love; it is the kind of action-oriented love that drives you to do as much as you can to influence life here. As in every romance, there is a quality of deep mystery that summons our hearts, and there is no enticement in Richmond more entrancing than Point Molate. This precious landscape has been described as "the most beautiful part of the bay no one's ever heard of."[17] This treasured natural resource graces the western side of the city on the San Pablo Peninsula, north of the Richmond/San Rafael Bridge that traverses to Marin County and on to San Francisco.

Pt Molate (Winehaven)

Richmond's jewel by the bay, Pt. Molate lies hidden from sight on the freeway, but I can't imagine anyone not being swept up by the splendor of this exquisite masterpiece of nature as they approach the site through its solitary entry point exiting off an interstate freeway. In stark contrast to the setting of a heavily trafficked freeway, a vastly different atmosphere and sensation reaches out and holds you close. A ride by car, bus, or bike into Pt. Molate takes your breath away as a panorama of the San Francisco Bay, San Pablo Bay, and Mount Tamalpais stretch out expansively before your eyes. And the stunning view of a long, gracefully winding bridge connecting Richmond to Marin County enhances the visual experience. Prior to 1956, a ferry service for cars operated on the bay until the completion of the Richmond/San Rafael Bridge.

One step onto the terrain of Pt. Molate you enter a new world. Covering just over 400 acres (290 terrestrial and the rest sub-tidal) with about a mile and a half of unobstructed shoreline, the topography ranges from sea level to steep ridges, rising as high as 500 feet in elevation. On the less sloped land down near the water's edge, historic buildings don a castle-like architecture that conveys a surreal vision, transporting viewers to another place in time.

While the magnetism of Pt. Molate is commanding, it shares the San Pablo Peninsula with a neighbor that wields a power of its own. The Chevron refinery exists right over the ridge line, surrounding Pt. Molate on the north, east, and south sides. Fortunately, the refinery is located on the other side of the sharp wall-like incline of Potrero Ridge, demarcating a unique characterization of the region and allowing this hidden gem to demurely beckon us time and time again.

Smitten by an Alluring Past

From every corner of the site, Pt. Molate murmurs its history. One can feel the presence of the Native American Ohlone and Miwok tribes, with their respectful relationship to nature, living and hunting on the land, and creating burial mounds that have since been destroyed as a result of industrial uses of the land.

Before Richmond's industrial progress and environmental degradation, the land was used by the padres of San Francisco's Mission Dolores in the early 1800s. Later it became one of the Spanish *ranchos* (Mexican land grants mentioned in chapter 1).

In the latter half of the nineteenth century (circa 1865), Pt. Molate's rare location on the bay heralded new pioneers. A Chinese shrimp camp—one among many in the Bay Area—was set up by Chinese immigrants in what is now Pt. Molate Beach Park. By 1904, there were thirty shacks, five wharves, and nearly one hundred inhabitants living in this hidden paradise. The shrimpers would make the daily journey over the hill from Pt. Molate to Pt. Richmond making deliveries of shrimp carried in wicker baskets balanced on ten-foot wide poles. The shrimp was sold to the United Shrimp Company of San Francisco and exported to China. A discrimination campaign against the Chinese fishing industry, which was seen as competition to others in the industry, led to legislation restricting large-scale shrimping on the bay and forced the Chinese shrimpers out of business.

After operating productively for more than forty years, by 1912 the camps were abandoned. While the Chinese shrimpers were among the first commercial entities, the construction of the Belt Line Railway along Richmond's western waterfront made Pt. Molate desirable for commerce. As a result, new operations emerged: an oil-can factory, a brick factory, two rock quarries, a sardine processing plant, and the construction of the Standard Oil (now Chevron) Long Wharf.

With industry marching onward in the early part of the 20th century and Pt. Molate's prime access to water and commerce centers all over the bay, it was only a question of time before more expansive land utilization would appear. And indeed such a new usage came into play soon after the 1906 San Francisco earthquake. Though the devastation created by the major tremor was enormous and San Francisco was left in ruins, the quake brought new economic activity to Richmond. A fire had destroyed the emerging wine industry of San Francisco. As a result, Pt. Molate became the new home for the California Wine Association (CWA). Winehaven District, the name given to the company village, was built on a forty-one acre site along the Pt. Molate shoreline.

The striking red brick Winehaven Building sitting on the shoreline like a castle on the Rhine, adorned with corner turrets, was built as the world's largest winery of its time. The facility produced an amazing twelve million gallons of wine annually. It not only bottled, fermented, and stored millions of gallons of wine each year, it crushed over 10,000 tons of grapes each season and employed as many as 400 workers at the peak of the season. A residence was built for the wine master, along with a hotel to house the workers. Twenty-nine small cottages were constructed for couples and families. You can almost hear the laughter of children as they played in the vicinity of their homes, or dawdled on their way to the small school constructed by the company. Even a post office was erected by the wine company to accommodate the workforce.

Winehaven was productive for twelve years. It was not only a thriving enterprise, it was a tourist attraction bringing in renowned author Jack London, poet Joaquin Miller, and other trendsetters of the era. A pier with an electric tram carried people arriving on excursion boats from San Francisco, Marin, and the South Bay to the hotel.

But in 1919, during Prohibition, CWA tried to sustain itself with the production of sacramental wine, medical wine, and grape juice, only to end up shutting down after a few years, selling off its assets to avoid bankruptcy.

Years later, in 1978, the "Village of Point Molate," was entered into the National Register of Historic Places—a fitting tribute to this thriving early 20th-century period.

Wartime Relationship with the Navy

The site was readapted yet again in 1942. This time it was Uncle Sam who took possession of it, using the Point as a Naval fuel depot. The Navy bought the 413-acre Winehaven site and built infrastructure to receive, store, and disperse petroleum products to thousands of ships, servicing the entire Pacific Fleet during World War II. Winehaven's structures went from storing wine to storing fuel, and the old Winehaven Hotel was converted into barracks and a mess hall. The small Winehaven cottages were renovated for naval personnel, with the commanding officer of the fuel depot occupying the former wine master's house on the bluff.

The Navy installed forty-three underground and thirty-two above-ground storage tanks and constructed a new pier on the shoreline. The area was equipped with rail lines and seventeen miles of pipelines. The facility had a capacity of storing over forty million gallons of jet and marine diesel fuel.

Buildings were utilized or constructed to house a fire department, garage, machine shop, cafeteria, a school, and other necessities for the military and civilian personnel who lived and worked on the site. A sign continues to point to an old air raid shelter in the basement of the Winehaven Building, a reminder of days gone by, before we understood that human survival and nuclear war are totally incompatible. The Navy continued its fuel depot operations during the Korean and Vietnam Wars until it was decommissioned in 1995.

No Love Lost as Whaling Station Closes

Prior to the base closure, there was one more historic use worth noting. One of the two last whaling stations in America remained north of Pt. Molate on the San Pablo Peninsula. It was owned by the Del Monte Fishing Company. The station burned and was dismantled in 1998, but the memory of earlier times can be gleaned from the charred pilings of days when a crew of forty men worked in the maritime tradition of New England whaling men, reducing huge whales to oil, poultry meal, and pet food with record speed. Each year the station hauled in around 175 finbacks, humpbacks, and sperm whales, sometimes unintentionally reportedly killing an orca. They processed the useful parts of these huge mammals. When standing at the site where the butchering occurred, it is left to our imagination to conjure up the smell of blood and brine that must have filled the air, and ponder in our minds-eye the sight of whale carcasses being thrown back into the bay awaiting bottom feeders. Mary Swift-Swan recounts one such fishing trip with her father in these waters.

We could not help but watch the action as whales disappeared up the whaling station gangplank as we fished that day. A high-pitched noise caught my attention. I looked among the whales floating in the shallows where I saw one still feebly moving. I asked my father and the other men on the boat to make them stop. They looked so sad as they shook their heads. If they could not save the whale that held to life so strongly, I asked them to do something to make them at least kill it before pulling it up the ramp and not let it lay there in fear and pain. One got on the radio but got no response. The men aboard said its end was too near for them to make any difference, but surely the whalers would kill it quickly. Pain pierced my heart as I watched it struggle up the gangplank, tears rolling down my face. My dad was clearly disturbed by the site as well. He put an arm around my shoulders as we watched until I turned to him and tried to remember to breathe. We quit fishing early that day.[18]

In 1971, the station closed when the U.S. outlawed commercial whaling. It was the last of its kind. The romance with whaling had pretty much died and Richmond was home to one of its last flings.

City Council Wooed by a Swindler

In 1995, the U.S. Navy declared Pt. Molate surplus property. Once the Richmond City Council was established as the Local Reuse Authority, a forty-five member Blue Ribbon Advisory Committee was set up to prepare a draft Reuse Plan. The completed plan proposed a general mix of uses, including commercial, industrial, and recreational, with considerable parkland and open space. It also proposed, in certain parts of the site, that residential use could be considered, although that has later become controversial, which I'll expand upon later.

In 2003, 85% of the site was sold to Richmond for one dollar—a common transfer for decommissioned bases. The remaining 15% could not be transferred until a determination was made on how best to clean up the remaining acreage, given that petroleum chemicals remained in the soil and groundwater of the former naval fuel depot. After various bureaucratic processes on multiple levels of government, these remaining forty-one acres were transferred to the city in 2010, along with $28.5 million for cleanup.

After the initial sale, an ill-fated idea came forth that dominated Richmond politics for the next few years. A developer proposed a $1.2 billion Las Vegas-style urban casino with two hotels, a conference center, a ferry landing, and a tribal casino with 4,000 slot machines. I vividly recall when the casino idea was put forward in 2004. The city was in the middle of its $35 million financial debacle, and I was a candidate for City Council. The casino idea was touted as a world-class destination resort that would bring jobs and prosperity to Richmond. The developer teamed up with a Native American tribe, the Guidiville Band of Pomo Indians. The Guidiville was a small band of 112 members with roots in Mendocino County who held ownership of forty-four acres of tribal land in Ukiah, California. For the purpose of building this major casino and resort, they claimed to also have a history at the Pt. Molate site. This tribal relationship would later be found to have been a fabrication. This is key, because a tribe's link must be verified before the federal government will allow any land to be taken in trust and used by a tribe to operate a casino. That determination was not even finalized until 2011 by the Bureau of Indian Affairs (BIA), declining the tribe's application, since they had no significant historic connection to the site or in its vicinity.

Jim Levine, principal of Upstream Pt. Molate LLC, the casino developer, is the same Levine associated with a deplorable cleanup plan for the contaminated Zeneca site. As I described in chapter 5, the Zeneca site (once owned by the pharmaceutical company AstraZeneca) is a large swath of land on our south shoreline that contains a brew of toxic chemicals in the soil and groundwater left behind from a century of heavy industrial use. In 2004 Levine defended the cleanup as sufficient and safe for residential development. He was now the point man undertaking this new endeavor in Pt. Molate. Levine had cast his die on an urban casino, partnering with the Las Vegas casino giant Harrah's Operating Company and a Native American tribe without ties to the land.

Casino Embraced

I started speaking out against the casino during my first campaign, and I was hardly alone in my opposition. Once they heard about the casino, most people were opposed to it. However, the developer wasted no time in convincing the City Council and some in the community that this was Richmond's big chance for economic revival. He bandied about with superficial talk with few details. For example, the notion of jobs for our community was held up high, without ever mentioning that these would be low-income, dead-end jobs. The strategy of the development team was to draw in community support by hosting free barbeques and other social activities, where they would toss out tidbits of useless information about the casino but give people goodies as ways to tender their support. From there, the developer would coax people to come to City Council meetings and speak in favor of the casino.

Those of us who opposed this project knew we had to counter the developer's ploys with an organizing strategy of our own. The idea of a casino for our city was something that needed a full public discourse. Upon being elected that November, I was eager to facilitate such a conversation. Unfortunately, I never had that opportunity. The very week after Election Day, the City Council went ahead and voted in favor of it before I was even sworn-in.

Opposition members in the audience were aghast. Clearly this lame-duck session vote was an attempt to cut off further discussion, knowing that my voice on the Council would reflect the anti-casino side. I quickly gathered some anti-casino activists together in my living room where we talked about the initial strategies to fight it—research, community outreach, and education. Carol Telschick-Fall (who I later appointed to the Planning Commission), helped me research various studies about the impacts of casinos and she critically examined the details of Upstream's agreement. Paul and I had initially met Carol when we were canvassing for my campaign earlier in the year. She was out in her front yard pulling weeds and her friendly demeanor and the beautiful flowers in her garden made it is easy for us to begin a dialogue with her. Margaret Hanlon-Gradie, who later worked as a union representative, was another activist in our living room that day, eager to keep the conversation alive.

We shared our passion and determination to save our cherished Pt. Molate, fortifying ourselves with healthy snacks and refreshments that Paul and I had prepared. We had to start somewhere, and as always, we connected with our friends, neighbors, and other local activists. One of the strategies our small group pursued was to connect with other anti-casino efforts around the state. We traveled to places like Rohnert Park, and met with Councilmember Frank Egger of Fairfax, among others, who were pushing back on the proliferation of casinos.

Challenging the Sweetheart Deal

It soon became clear that the debate had just begun. The previous City Council may have thought that their approval of a Land Disposition Agreement (LDA) with Upstream (Levine's company) had sealed the deal, but the long battle to reclaim Pt. Molate was just the beginning. The love that people held for this site would not be dismissed or degraded. One of the first actions after the LDA was approved was a lawsuit filed by environmental groups taking the City to task for not doing an Environmental Impact Report (EIR) on the project.

Bill Lockyer, California's Attorney General, joined the lawsuit, siding with the environmentalists and adding the legal muscle of the State to the case. He specified that the City must prepare an EIR and that the casino project had to be fully analyzed. The EIR would need to identify all potential impacts, including adverse socio-economic impact and local community opposition. And the City Council had every right to prohibit the casino project based on such determinations.

Under the settlement, the City of Richmond agreed it could select any use for the property, including retaining city ownership, and the developer agreed that a decision not to sell or lease the land to them wouldn't constitute a breach of the sale agreement. Indeed, this was a success and helped motivate us to keep our efforts going. The casino project was not assured by any stretch.

City officials downplayed the significance of this settlement. After all, since a majority of the City Council still supported the project, they felt certain the future of Pt. Molate was in their hands. The developer and Council majority continued to portray the casino project as a fait accompli, saying it was just a question of going through the right environmental process. But for those of us who stood in opposition, we were just getting warmed up for this battle ahead.

The Heart of the Matter

I put my argument against the casino in writing the very first year I served on the Council. In 2005, I published an article in the *Contra Costa Times* outlining my opposition to Richmond Mayor Irma Anderson's earlier article in which she supported the casino, saying it would bring jobs and would be a one-stop solution for

Richmond's financial needs. (See full article in Appendix 6.)

I pointed to studies projecting that a few years after the opening of a casino at Pt. Molate, the city of Richmond could expect additional robberies, larcenies, burglaries, auto thefts, rapes, and aggravated assaults every year simply due to the presence of a casino. This information was based on expert findings in the field whose research also pointed to pathological gambler behavior. It typically takes two to four years to complete the gambling cycle: becoming addicted and exhausting one's financial resources.[19] Not only does suffering increase in the community, but mitigation of the crime and health impacts create a price tag for the local government.

Casinos bring more harm than benefit to a city. They make money from those who lose money. Many people gamble away money they can't afford to lose, and often their families lose even more. Those were real-life facts the developer did not mention or address.

I worked closely with community activists and together we kept the issue on the front burner for dialogue. Speaking at community events, meetings and conferences, I kept repeating my position, never wavering from my opposition.

All of my campaigns emphasized the casino as a bad deal for Richmond. Most people didn't have to be convinced that a casino would cause problems in the city. People understood that a casino would pull much-needed income out of the hands of residents. In my talks, I focused on how the false lure of fast money has led many individuals and families to economic devastation. Proponents would argue that it was people's lack of personal responsibility and self-discipline that would be at fault, not the casino. I would counter saying it is irresponsible for a city government to champion false solutions when it should be educating and practicing economic justice to fight poverty and income inequality. City officials should promote and implement genuine fixes, such as taxing corporations, providing educational opportunities, job creation, and higher wages, rather than ushering in a casino mentality to "get rich quick."

Andres Soto continued to play a role in the anti-casino effort as well and helped organize marches, rallies, and letter-writing campaigns to stop the push for expanding casinos in the Bay Area. With megaphones and handmade signs saying "good paying jobs, not Las Vegas style slot machines," we marched up and down local San Pablo Avenue while cars honked in appreciation and apparent confirmation.

Later, I started working with activists Pam Stello, Jeanne Kortz, Joan Garrett, David Helvarg, and other community leaders who founded a new organization called Citizens for a Sustainable Pt. Molate.

Another outrageous maneuver by the pro-casino people was to bring the mayor of Las Vegas to one of our Richmond City Council meetings. They wanted her to tout the successes of casinos in her fair city. I vividly remember the scene as if it was scripted from a Hollywood spoof. The mayor pranced into the City Council meeting clad in flashy clothes and showy jewelry. Her spoken words were just as ostentatious as her dress. All eyes were on her, gazing in disbelief as this caricature of authority sauntered down the center aisle of the Council Chambers, approached the public podium laughing and sucking the air out of the room as she went, singing the praises of casinos. We were not amused.

By 2008, the developer was feeling the heat. In an attempt to get the opposition to back off, he felt the need to promote his project as a "green and environmentally friendly casino." He was clearly trying to co-opt some of the progressive resistance. But RPA's base was having none of that. Community activists spoke to the fact that placing solar panels on a socially irresponsible project does not neutralize the damaging effects of an ill-conceived idea.

The sale of the property by the Navy required the land be put to some economic use, and there were many good ideas to consider that would truly benefit the city monetarily, such as a hotel, a conference center, light industry, restaurants, and recreational rentals like kayaking and camping. We did not believe a casino would be Richmond's ticket to a better economy. This became more apparent as time went on. More often than not, casinos lose their clientele during hard economic times. During the Great Recession that started in 2007, that is indeed what happened in other parts of our nation. In 2009, the *Contra Costa Times* published another guest commentary of mine titled, "Casino Benefit Still Doesn't Add Up for Richmond" (excerpted below):

> Our nation and our state are in the middle of profound economic recession with no end in sight. Are casinos somehow "recession proof?" The answer to that question can be found in countless news articles documenting that tax revenue from gambling proceeds nationwide have dropped for two years in a row now. Even the American Gaming Association (AGA), a proponent of gaming in the U.S., is acknowledging the drop. Their 2009 report states that "With its reduction in consumer spending and freezing credit markets, the recession that began in late 2007 made 2008 a challenging year for the commercial casino industry."
>
> Certainly, all bets are off as we witness Indian casinos suffering in today's economy. Many casino operators nationwide, including in California, are putting off or canceling big expansions and reducing staff. Some casinos have closed and others are filing for bankruptcy. The bottom line is clear. As gamblers spend less, profits shrink or disappear and tribal governments are hit hard.[20]

We need a different kind of development that offers long-term, good paying jobs for our residents; one that creates healthy activities, services, and products that enhance people's lives and is ecologically sustainable. The casino was a losing bet.

Love Blooms Strong Again

We continued to forge ahead with our efforts, but the major obstacle remained the same—the City Council. By 2009, the two lone RPA councilmembers, Jeff Ritterman and I, were the only voices of opposition to the casino.

Since Richmond residents had already expressed their opposition in polls and votes on State initiatives, I was certain they would rebuff this idea at the ballot box in the form of a local ballot measure, if given a chance. In 2010, the public was finally given that chance when the Council acquiesced to public pressure and put an advisory ballot measure out to the voters. Measure U, as it was called, posed a simple question: "Shall the City of Richmond approve a project including a casino at Pt. Molate provided that this advisory measure is considered in a manner consistent with all the City's legal obligations?"

Measure U brought big money into the electoral arena, with Upstream (the casino developer) spending a half million dollars in support of the measure. The pro-casino position emphasized local jobs and much-needed revenue for the city. Our opposition stressed the increased crime and continuing poverty that a casino would bring. We advocated for creating a future for Pt. Molate that would make our grandchildren proud.

The anti-casino vote prevailed with 58% of the vote—a great win for a hard-earned, grassroots effort that brought the debate to a close after seven years of community pressure and mobilization. Along with rejecting the casino, the voters elected two new council members, Jovanka Beckles and Corky Boozé, both opponents of the casino. Councilmember Tom Butt had also latently come out against the casino proposal, mainly because he lost confidence in the developer's financial maneuverings and his failure to provide timely financial reports. Although Butt originally supported the casino, he wasn't blind to the machinations of speculators. So now, for this first time since I had been on the Council, we had a majority who was willing to own up to the flaws inherent in the casino project.

Following the anti-casino votes, the new City Council needed to show their support for the people's vote. And so we did. On April 5, 2011, with hundreds of Richmond residents in attendance, the City Council voted to reject the casino to loud cheers from a triumphant audience. The opposition to the vote came from councilmembers Jim Rogers and Nat Bates. Sound judgment had won the day. I felt a sigh of relief. Five out of seven councilmembers had disallowed the casino option for Pt. Molate, listing a host of findings from serious impacts to the health and well-being of our community, the environment, and our region. The battle for Pt. Molate was long and protracted, but we never gave up.

Once the project was axed, I brought a resolution to establish the Pt. Molate Community Advisory Committee to provide advice to the City Council on all things related to Pt. Molate. The committee has provided oversight for the environmental cleanup, and proposed ideas for use of that precious land.

No casino

Love on the Rocks

The year after we voted down the casino, the City Council completed a final obligation under the agreement with Upstream, which was to review a non-gaming proposal from the same developer. Reviewing and discussing the proposal in closed session we determined it not acceptable. Subsequent to this session, our City attorney wrote a letter informing Mr. Levine of the Council's decision to not accept his alternative, which would have required significant subsidizing by the city.[21] With that, our obligation was completed.

After the City Council finalized its rejection, Upstream and the Guidiville Rancheria filed a lawsuit in federal court claiming the City breached the agreement by discontinuing consideration of the casino project. We knew we were on solid legal footing and were pleased that the judicial system spoke clearly and directly on the case, with U.S. Judge Yvonne Gonzalez Rogers ruling that the City had been well within its rights. She stated that the terms of the agreement gave the City discretion to approve, or disapprove, the casino project and any alternative project. The developer then chose to appeal that ruling and has appealed subsequent rulings for three years with the courts repeatedly coming down on the side of the City and scolding Upstream and the Tribe for baseless appeals. More recently the Ninth Circuit Court upheld a few details of this case. It remains unresolved.

In effect, this development company has tied our hands with their appeals. Our lawyers have advised us to wait until the lawsuit is resolved before soliciting new development proposals. Jim Levine and the Tribe no doubt want to recoup their losses due to their investment of a $15 million "non-refundable" deposit, but that was their cost for taking the City down that road. The City Council majority who supported the project bent over backward, providing multiple deadline extensions to prove their case—clearly they were given fair chances. The two billion dollar casino resort was a poor wager, and the City bears no responsibility to cover the developer's risky bet. It is also worth noting that the City has not been able to move forward for nearly thirteen years now, when we could have been courting a better and more promising project that could be generating revenue for the city.

Even as the city has been constrained in pursuing new proposals until the legal appeals run their course, we need to consider ways to give the public the opportunity to explore and enjoy the natural embrace of the site. Pt Molate needed a new debut.

A Blissful Reunion

Despite delays in development decisions, we were able to reopen the Pt. Molate Beach Park in 2013. The park was originally tended by the U.S. Navy as a recreation site for base personnel and local residents in the early 1970s. In 2004, the park was closed by the city, due to our fiscal deficit and service cutbacks that included maintaining public parks.

Thanks to the steadfast advocacy of community groups, the City, with the help of volunteer groups like Citizens for a Sustainable Pt. Molate (CFSPM), cleaned up and re-opened the park for the public. Funding for the restoration of the beach came from the 2007 Cosco Busan tanker oil spill settlement (this oil leak into San Francisco Bay will be discussed in the next chapter). Today, people enjoy playful times and long walks along the sandy beach, along with picnicking, kayaking, and just taking in the breathtaking beauty of Pt. Molate.

Reclaiming Pt Molate for and with the people of Richmond has been one of the most challenging and rewarding struggles I have ever participated in. As I fought the battle and made my arguments over the course of seven years, my love for this incredible piece of land grew and deepened.

A Deep and Complex Relationship Continues

The story of Pt. Molate is something more than a love of the site in and of itself. It is also the story of what true grassroots action offers a community. The peaks and valleys we experienced in the confrontations over the years are a reflection of how democracy operates. It is seldom a straight-ahead road; often the process is messy. But allowing space for the ebb and flow of majority rule is the quintessential progressive action of our time. When we see a problem, we rise up and respond with many voices and many people taking action to speak their concerns and offer solutions. We educate the public at-large, wrestle with political foes, and take our message to the streets as well as to the halls of government. And of course, we hold elections where every voter has a voice.

Hope is alive at Pt. Molate. For me, it is a magical place where dreams are renewed. Before writing this chapter, Paul and I purposely went there to spend some time, watching children frolic on the beach and families enjoy an afternoon outing. I reminisced how far we have come from the days when the entire site could have been taken over and made into a gambling facility. Those days are mercifully behind us. Today when my husband and I walk along the water's edge, gazing at the waves as they roll in, we are not only spellbound by the magnificence of nature, but we are compelled to imagine new possibilities for the sacred space.

Currently we remain hamstrung by Upstream's legal actions. But for now Pt. Molate has come to life again. The history of the site whispers encouragement to all who are willing to listen and play a role in the creation of a new visionary future—one worthy of its struggles. While much uncertainty remains, my sense is that the next rebirth will be a great one.

Greening Our City

There is a Native American proverb: "We do not inherit the earth from our ancestors, we borrow it from our children." This is a profound adage to guide the management and growth of our cities. It reminds us that many generations will follow in our footsteps, and we have a responsibility to leave them a sustainable world. It is easy to feel overwhelmed by this maxim, especially when viewing parts of Richmond that are overrun by the Chevron Richmond refinery, whose pollution belies that goal. Many battles have already been fought in our city to reverse the damage and many more will be fought, but we have achieved many environmental victories thus far, some of which I share here.

Laying the Groundwork

While most people in our Richmond community were aware of the health and environmental damage caused by Chevron's refinery, a majority of the City Council, along with some sectors of the community, held tight to the idea that they would overlook the environmental impact, because this mega-corporation is central to our local economy.

Yet we can't talk about the economy without thinking about the environment. They are connected. Natural resources are used to build the economy and you cannot bring hardship to the environment without it being felt in the community's pocketbook. The cost of cleanup and restoration of natural systems is incredibly debilitating, and in Richmond, the environmental legacy of 20th-century heavy industries has most assuredly affected our local economy. Some of these businesses packed up and moved elsewhere—often overseas—leaving their toxins behind, while others have remained and continue to pollute. Chevron remains the most powerful of these industries and has caused the most harm, but various other polluting businesses, such as trade and shipping operations at the Richmond Port, and manufacturers along our shoreline, have all created health and environmental hazards.

We take pride in how our environmentally conscious community has courageously advocated for comprehensive cleanups and regulations. We understand that you can't build an economy on a degraded environment. One only has to look at the contamination problems we are still tackling in this century as a result of lack of foresight in the prior century. It was paramount that we present a new environmentally sound economic vision for our city. Not surprisingly, the polluting industries who are legally responsible for cleaning up their toxic messes have resisted.

Those corporations needed help from their cronies in City Hall to make policies on their behalf. The communication was simple, as Councilmember Bates often put it: "heavy industry and Richmond are bound together in a marriage." According to this viewpoint, as a partner in a long-term relationship, Richmond had a responsibility to look out for the well being of the industrial sector, putting aside concerns about health and the environment and not overstepping the rights of these businesses to grow unlimited profits. Previous Council majorities lacked the vision to see an independent economic route. By contrast, progressives sought the kind of business development that would be advantageous to all, and that upheld a triple bottom line—people, planet, and profit—rather than just profit.

To get to such a new business model, we had to set a new tone, one based on a vision for a sustainable city rather than one based on the fear of falling out of favor from those industrial forces. As mayor, I articulated a concept of a new and diversified economy, planting the seeds of a new green economy. But the RPA knew we also had to further our organizing efforts. We needed to counter Chevron's propaganda, which portrayed itself as having the Richmond community at heart. To this day, and now more than ever, Chevron's public relations work is a well-oiled machine. Chevron understands that it must have a connection with the people, even if it is disingenuous, in order to prevent further outrage against its abuses. Even when set back by progressive victories, Chevron finds new ways to shift the narrative. But RPA activism runs deep. We know who we are, what we stand for, and we persist.

Firm Roots Planted

Cap the Crude/Climate Justice

For me personally, fighting for a greener and more environmentally just Richmond was an easy choice. My experience of untouched nature as part of my early childhood years left a positive imprint on me.

As I recounted earlier, I was born in Chicago, and spent the bulk of my adult years in inner city Chicago. Yet despite living in those urban settings, I also had a taste of living close to nature. Just before my sixth birthday, my family moved to Norridge, a little township abutting the northwest corner of Chicago that had not yet been fully developed. It was an ideal place to spend my formative years. The Foster Avenue Chicago bus, right near our home, gave easy access to anywhere in Chicago, while there was still some undeveloped land in my little neighborhood—a small, open-space prairie in close proximity. I have fond memories of playing in our little unscathed plot of land, with its tall coarse grasses, bushy shrubs, and a few felled trees, set alongside a church. It served as a little get-away for my friends and me. Surrounded by uncultivated flora, we entered a world of wonder that provided a space to spark our imaginations. We played games of make-believe, dreaming what our lives would become when we grew up.

In time this little wonderland would be turned into a church parking lot. But playing free in natural environs during those years cultivated in me a love of the environment in its primitive form. Those adventures made me want every child to have a similar opportunity as I did, to both play in nature and learn about our varied landscapes not just from textbooks, but from lived experiences. Those early times in my life implanted in me the seeds to advocate for nature-based activities for our youth.

Preserving Nature's Balance

One of the first Richmond environmental coalitions in which I participated goes back to 2003. I remember the initial meetings at Parchester Neighborhood Community Center with Whitney Dotson, an African-American environmental leader who lives in that subdivision fronting the Bay. It was built post-World War II after temporary housing for shipyard workers had been torn down. This area was originally home to predominately African-American families, but today the neighborhood includes large numbers of Latino families, along with a diverse representation of our community. An eclectic group of people showed up at the Parchester Neighborhood meetings in addition to Whitney: members of the Sierra Club, Citizens for East Shore Park, Richmond Greens (associated with the Green Party), RPA, Urban Creeks Council, the Natural Heritage Institute, and other groups. We engaged in strategic discussions about saving our north shoreline. We talked about naming our coalition and eventually decided on the North Richmond Shoreline Open Space Alliance (NRSOSA). Whitney had been adamant about including "open space" in the name, highlighting the need for keeping it undeveloped into perpetuity. Current and future generations needed to have access to a protected shoreline for exploration and recreation, and for beholding a piece of nature's rich ecology on our northern shore.

NRSOSA was formed to save Breuner Marsh, which is one of the last intact wetlands on the San Francisco Bay. Wetlands are essential to the health of the bay and a natural shoreline. A key to our eventual success, Whitney educated the community non-stop on the importance of this issue. In fact, the entire Dotson family going back to Whitney's father had fought to keep the marsh undeveloped.

Residents of Parchester Village have long believed the marsh would be made into a park for their use, says Dotson. In the late 1940s, his father, a minister, was asked by one of the community's developers to recruit church members to buy homes in the village. Before agreeing to buy into the new development, the church members asked the developer, Fred Parr, to set aside the land for open space. Parr and the area's future residents also approached the Richmond City Council with their request to preserve the land. While a park was not created at the time, Dotson says the community came away with the promise that the city would one day zone the area as open space. Dotson's family moved into the development in 1950, when he was five years old, and he has lived there ever since. "As kids, we thought of all of this as ours," he says.[22]

After years of community struggle pushing back at development proposals, the group achieved victory. Breuner Marsh was finally preserved, with the help of the East Bay Regional Park District (EBRPD), which purchased the marshland from the property owner and is now implementing the Breuner Marsh Restoration and Public Access Project. In 2012 I supported a resolution, approved by the entire City Council, to change the name of the marsh to Dotson Marsh, honoring Whitney and his family.

Whitney currently sits as an EBRPD board member. He is an exemplary elected official, endorsed by the RPA, whose love of nature and dedication to justice comes from his heart.

The fight for Dotson Marsh was part of Richmond's new environmentalism embraced by progressives. In 2007, the *San Francisco Chronicle Magazine* published a cover story about the North Richmond Shoreline in which the author portrayed the unique nature of our new eco-friendly Richmond vision quite vividly: "It is a hardscrabble kind of environmentalism, this push for a greener city amid Richmond's wrecking yards, its chemical ponds and its huge refinery."[23]

The Richmond Shoreline Citizen Response (RSCR) was another example of how Richmond residents rise to ecological challenges. This group came together after the Cosco Busan oil spill on San Francisco Bay in November 2007. The Cosco Busan was a cargo ship that crashed into the San Francisco Oakland Bay Bridge, releasing 53,000 gallons of fuel oil into the surrounding waters. This was one of the largest oil spills in the Bay Area's history, heavily affecting the bay and surrounding natural resources and wildlife. Cities surrounding the bay, including Richmond, felt the impact. I convened a meeting shortly after the disaster to gather community input and ideas on how best to respond to this crisis. RSCR was formed and the group became invested in making sure federal, state, and regional agencies were properly able to clean up from the spill. This accident led to an historic $44.4 million settlement, paid for by the responsible companies—Regal Stone Ltd. and Fleet Management Ltd. A large portion of the money went to various regional restoration projects. Richmond received $669,000. Part of this money was used to re-open Pt. Molate Beach Park; the remainder went to construction of various segments and improvements of our Bay Trail.

Fighting to protect our wetlands and the bay, as well as our hillsides and creeks, earned Richmond the reputation of a community willing to defend our valuable natural assets while also struggling to end Chevron's pollution.

North Shoreline

Reaping What's Been Sown

In the 1980s, Richmond community activists started an organized fight for the health and safety of local residents by forming the West County Toxics Coalition (WCTC). Although WCTC came into being as a local movement, it grew out of a national anti-toxics and Environmental Justice (EJ) movement. It was an outgrowth of the National Toxics Campaign (NTC), founded by the late Johnny O'Connor, who was known nationwide for his work against environmental racism and injustice. Johnny O, as he was called, made a stop in Richmond on a national tour to raise consciousness about the health impact coming from unregulated chemical companies. As a result of the over-abundance of chemical companies in Richmond, NTC decided to send Craig Williams, an organizer from Boston, to help build an organization and train local activists in Richmond. Williams worked with local African-Americans on the frontline of chemical assault, like Dr. Henry Clark, who later became WCTC executive director and a prominent leader of the local EJ movement. Dr. Clark was born and raised in North Richmond on the border of the refinery. He remembers how refinery flaring (the burning of gaseous pollutants through refinery smokestacks) would shake his house. In a February 2005 Global Community Monitoring report, Clark remarked:

> When the flares were blooming, waves of energy would hit the community and rock our house like we were caught in an earthquake. We would wake up in the morning finding leaves dead and burnt by chemicals from the refinery flares overnight.[24]

Ahmadia Thomas, another one of WCTC's early leaders, describes flaring in the same report:

> When you saw the flares—you knew something was wrong.... When they wouldn't tell us what was in their pollution ... [they] called it [a] "trade secret." That was awful. It means you are breathing it every day and you don't know what you are breathing. Trade secret, that was an insult.[25]

Chevron would throw out the term "trade secret" whenever it wanted to hide something from the community, whether to avoid paying taxes or refusing to inform residents about gaseous releases. One of WCTC's early campaigns was the W.H.A.T. campaign—

familiarly known as, "what are the Big Boys at Chevron afraid of?" The initials actually stood for: **W**arning systems, **H**ealthy assessment, **A**ir monitoring and **T**oxic reduction—demands we are still organizing around today. Community pressure led to many health studies conducted in the 1980s that pointed to elevated rates of asthma, cancer, and leukemia in areas around the refinery.

The community didn't need studies, however, to know the sources of these problems. They personally knew the noxious effect of toxins in their daily lives and witnessed the impact they had on their children and neighbors. The studies verified what they already suspected: a disproportionate number of hospitalizations for asthma and lives lost to cancer compared to other, less polluted areas of the region.

WCTC worked with other environmental groups, like Communities for a Better Environment (CBE) and Golden Gate University Environmental Law and Justice Clinic. CBE helped provide scientific information and expertise about industrial plants; the clinic helped the coalition understand its legal rights. By working with each other and other environmental justice allies, a more powerful coalition and local movement emerged. They broke ground by bringing people of color and low-income people into the leadership of the toxics movement. For the first time ever, the community had a voice in compelling the industry to resolve environmental problems. Successful campaigns included forcing the closure of a Chevron incinerator that blew toxic smoke into a nearby schoolyard. Their persistent pressure on the Air Board was the precursor to the eventual approval of new flare monitoring regulations in 2005.

Working in the Fields

When the RPA came onto the scene in 2003, we encountered local groups working on a number of environmental issues in the city. However, the EJ momentum of years gone by was no longer in full swing. Organizers and activists had come up against significant resistance from the City Council of those days. Although achievements made by these early mobilizations helped build a foundation for a healthier Richmond, there were limits to what they could accomplish without support from the City Council.

Our efforts in the RPA offered something fresh. As activists, we had sought and won political power through the electoral process. We offered a new and dynamic political culture, and that's just what the EJ movement needed. My election to the City Council brought forth an activist voice for environmental causes. The RPA and the EJ groups were on the same page. We shared a goal of wanting to create a healthier and safer Richmond. And it wasn't just the refinery we were fighting. In 2006, there was a proposal to move a crematorium to North Richmond, which would have emitted toxins into a neighborhood that had already borne the brunt of other emissions. Working with EJ groups, we stopped the crematorium and placed a moratorium on new crematoriums to preserve air quality.

The majority of our environmental justice work was focused on the enormous harm caused by the fossil fuel industry. RPA and our EJ allies knew we were up against one of the most powerful industries in the world in our fight for accountability from Chevron and to accomplish this goal, we built broad support.

The environmental groups and RPA worked hand in glove. As mayor I made it a point to highlight in my annual state of the city the work of all the environmentally conscious and health-oriented groups in the city. There were groups fighting Chevron's pollution, others working to preserve our shoreline and hillsides, and still others calling for a comprehensive cleanup of toxic sites. Other organizations were working on Bay Trail issues, while other community groups focused on addressing health issues associated with cell tower placements. Overall, there was a shared understanding that we had a lot of work to do. While each group did amazing work on unique and separate environmental issues, there was never any controversy about the fact that we needed to keep the pressure on Chevron. One group, for example, TRAC (Trails for Richmond Action Committee) focused on strategies for completing the Bay Trail, without engaging directly on some of the more controversial Chevron issues. But they became willing to put pressure on Chevron when it related to a Bay Trail issue. When Chevron's permit for use of the Long Wharf to offload crude oil into the refinery came up for renewal at the State Lands Commission (SLC) meeting, Bruce Beyaert (of TRAC) advocated for a bicycle connector path bordering Chevron property and the freeway to assure safe access from one segment of the Bay Trail to another. I also spoke at the SLC meeting making the case to the Commissioners that they had an opportunity to take a strong and fair stand by making this a requirement of Chevron's lease. Alas, the State Lands Commission, with Chevron undoubtedly breathing down their necks, did not have the moxie needed to make this a condition of the permit. But nevertheless, we demonstrated that we were an engaged and active community with a mayor willing to speak up as well as publicize the issue, shining a light Chevron's reluctance to do the right thing.

Oil Giant's Heavy Footprint

In 2007, Chevron proposed a major project, far beyond the general repairs and replacement of minor equipment at the refinery that were now being overseen by the City. Chevron named the project the "Chevron Energy and Hydrogen Renewal Project," but the EJ community more aptly referred to it as the "Refinery Expansion Project." It was a plan to increase the refinery's capacity to allow for processing heavier, dirtier crude oil. Oil companies worldwide were starting to extract a lower-quality crude, given the earth's declining supply of lighter crude. Much of this crude is extracted from Canadian tar sands, a large source of the world's climate pollution. The EJ organizations pointed to the intensified harm and risk that would result from refining this poorer quality crude, especially to the "fenceline community"—those neighborhoods directly bordering the refinery.

We began a massive campaign to raise awareness about this lower quality crude. We educated the community and pressured Chevron to reveal their full intentions about the type of crude oil they were planning to bring into the refinery. As mayor, working closely with CBE, I came to more fully understand the danger this project posed to our already over-polluted and safety-compromised neighborhoods.

When Chevron's Environmental Impact Report (EIR) was released, it proved to be greatly flawed, which prompted us to form a new coalition, the Richmond Environmental Justice Coalition. Partners in the coalition organized a major community campaign that included: CBE, the Asian Pacific Environmental Network, the Laotian Organizing Project, RPA, and other groups. Hundreds of community members showed up at City Council meetings to denounce the project. Hundreds more sent letters and called councilmembers. CBE scientist Greg Karras compiled research, along with experts in the academic community, providing information on the inherently dangerous chemical processing that goes on daily right in our own city and how this project would magnify it. The coalition called for a cap on the type of crude to be refined, disallowing heavier, dirtier crudes to be processed.

Chevron claimed they were not planning on refining such crude oil, but when asked to have their commitment documented in the legally binding environmental report, they refused. That, of course, created a credibility gap for them. We had the facts to back us up. Antonia Juhasz, a leading energy analyst, author, and investigative journalist specializing in oil, discovered in a filing with the United States Security and Exchange Commission (SEC) that there were contradictions in what Chevron was telling us and what they were telling their shareholders. Chevron's SEC Form 10-K for fiscal year 2007 included the following statement: "Design and engineering for a project to increase the flexibility to process lower API-gravity crude oils at the company's Richmond, California refinery continued in 2007." "Lower API gravity" meant heavier crude oil.

In the early part of this campaign, a Blue-Green Alliance emerged, with the "blue collar" Building Trades standing with "green" environmental health and justice groups, calling for a better EIR. But at a certain point the Building Trade international leadership in Washington, D.C. made a deal with Chevron to not oppose the project in return for a guarantee of union jobs throughout the project's construction. I received calls from various local trade unions, apologizing for their withdrawal from our coalition efforts. Some unions took a neutral stance, others came out passionately in support of the project. This turn of events set up barriers between trade unionists and EJ activists, in spite of an organic connection based on health and safety needs in both the workplace and community.

We also faced dueling positions on the City Council—with

jobs and health pitted against each other. This divisiveness is an example of how corporations divide us to meet corporate interests. Our coalition countered by making it known that we want both health and jobs. We called on Chevron to modify the project and adhere to a crude cap, one that prevented heavier crude oil from being refined.

I'll never forget how odd it seemed to me when I first witnessed trades unionists coming to City Council meetings to oppose community members who were rallying for health. I had always thought of unions as having a sense of community. The union movement to me means doing what is right for working class families in communities everywhere. And who was it, if not working-class families in Richmond, that were being harmed by Chevron's pollution? It seemed to me that union workers and Richmond families have a natural bond. Instead, what played out in Richmond is that the trades people would grab seats on one end of the Council Chamber and the neighborhood folks would sit on the other side. Any bonds that may have existed in the past, were no longer present.

The Building Trades never endorsed my campaigns. They chose to negotiate with Chevron to get the jobs regardless of the needs of the community. While fighting for good jobs is certainly part of the role of unions, it seems that basic human values and the common good should not be disregarded along the way. The Building Trades were simply unswayed by hundreds of residents calling for a better and cleaner project from Chevron to protect the health of the community. Chevron had successfully divided our blue-green coalition, at least temporarily.

"Chevron 5" Digs in with Big Oil

The City Council's response illuminated Chevron's deeply embedded influence. Five council members unapologetically supported the EIR and the project. Tom Butt, who stood with RPA and the EJ coalition, dubbed the five members of the Council through his email forum—"the Chevron 5." Councilmember Maria Viramontes led the group, which also included John Marquez, Ludmyrna Lopez, Harpreet Sandhu, and Nat Bates. These five (out of nine), cast their votes in spite of opposition by hundreds of community members.

There had also been talk about a community benefits agreement (CBA) that commonly accompanies these major projects. A CBA model was created in the late 1990s as a way for the communities most impacted by various development projects to play a participatory role in ensuring that developments bring benefit to existing communities. The problem was, the decision-making was coming from the City Council rather than the residents who lived on the periphery of the refinery as the ones to voice their opinions. After all, they are the ones who would be directly affected by the proposed expansion. These beneficiaries needed to have a voice in their CBA. But there were no public sessions for community input.

The Chevron 5 worked out an agreement behind closed doors. On the same evening when the project was brought to the Council for a vote, the remaining members of the Council, including myself, were aghast to see that a legal document determining benefits had already been signed by Chevron, with a majority of votes lined up to approve it. Not only did the Chevron 5 vote in favor of this CBA, but Councilmember Jim Rogers, not to be outdone by the others, jumped on board as well, with six out of nine votes cast in favor. While some of the funding was for worthy causes, such as job training and health care, other allocations were more controversial, including more money for police. In addition, the overall monetary value attributed to the benefits package ($61.6 million) was inflated and misleading. A *Contra Costa Times* editorial explained some specifics:

> But as Councilman Tom Butt and Mayor Gayle McLaughlin have noted, the proposed amounts aren't enough to build and maintain the Bay Trail or to sustain services long-term. Others carry no benefits to the city, and funding for an alternative energy project that Chevron would sell to the city under one scenario is nothing more than a business venture.[26]

This backdoor deal insulted our local movement and further outraged the people. This was clearly a political maneuver by the

Council majority. That same editorial laid bare the shenanigans:

> An advisory board overseeing that fund is to consist of two members appointed by Chevron and three current or former members of the City Council. Those five are to then appoint two members from the community. Quicker than you could say "political opportunity," the council majority appointed three of its members who backed the Chevron deal—Nat Bates, Ludmyrna Lopez and Harpreet Sandhu —to serve on the committee. Bates and Sandhu are up for re-election in November. Critics rightly complained: Officials running for re-election should not be doling out funding to the same sorts of groups from which they will be seeking support.[27]

Chevron felt secure again in its influence, having bonded with its favored councilmembers. With their renewal project approved, the company shamelessly publicized the community benefits package as an example of their big-hearted relationship to the community, with no mention, of course, of the lack of public input and their obfuscation of the actual monetary value.

On the surface Chevron won the day. But their triumph would turn out to be premature. In 2009 a judge stopped the refinery expansion as the result of a lawsuit filed by environmental justice groups. Contra Costa Superior Court Judge Zuniga halted the project because the EIR failed to include a comprehensive evaluation of the effects of the expansion, and whether or not it would enable the oil company to process heavier and more polluting crude oils at the site. This is precisely what we had been saying all along. In the end our local movement prevailed.

By defending the oil giant, the Chevron 5 was politically weakened. The voters removed two of them from the City Council in 2008, two more in 2010, and the remaining one in 2016.

Cultivating Sustainability

With the environmental groups' win in the courts, people were seeing a new trend. Our EJ coalition had won the day and was offering new ideas for a greener, more sustainable economy for Richmond. People were getting it. It was time for new and cleaner industries to help Richmond reach a balanced, sustainable future. Clearly, this type of future was not going to emerge from hitching our wagon to Chevron. The myth of Chevron as the engine of our local economy was starting to unravel. Economically, Richmond had been stagnating for decades, while City Council members tip toed around the oil giant fearing that any misstep would jeopardize their reelection campaigns. RPA challenged those who continued to link their future with the oil giant to instead connect their future to an economic forecast that sustains rather than degrades our environment.

Progressives throughout Richmond knew that we needed to help make Richmond green through renovating parks, preserving our environment, and improving the overall quality of life in our city. That is also what would help shift our city's image to one of a commitment to quality of life for all our residents and attract clean businesses.

By 2009 a new culture was percolating throughout City Hall. Earlier, when I first became mayor, my staff established a Green Team with other City employees and I convened the Environmental Justice Environmental Health (EJEH) Task Force—a working group of community members to advise me on environmental matters. Soon after, an environmental manager came on board who worked on a number of innovative projects, such as the compilation of a greenhouse gas (ghg) inventory that helped us track carbon dioxide emissions data as part of our effort to reduce our citywide carbon footprint. Not surprisingly, it was found that 88% of ghg emissions in our city come from heavy industry, nearly all of that from the refinery.

In spite of the ongoing challenges, we felt new hope. Chevron's loss in the courts over its flawed environmental impact report emboldened us to continue pushing back on this polluting corporation. We were bolstered in our efforts to continue building a cleaner, greener city. As the sustainability work in City Hall started to accelerate, Richmond was seen as a "transition city"—a term coined in Europe to denote a city dedicated to moving away from fossil fuel dependency.

Over the course of my years as mayor, we implemented leading environmental initiatives, such as banning Styrofoam and plastic bags, passing a Green Building Ordinance, promoting and incentivizing solar energy, and approving a General Plan with both a climate change element and a public health element—all of which helped propel Richmond into the forefront as a city leading in a new direction for our times. We gained a reputation as a city on the move, responsibly transitioning to an environmentally healthy future. We created bicycle paths, increased recreational programs, and expanded the Bay Trail along our thirty-two miles of shoreline, all part and parcel to changing the fabric of our city.

Our urban agriculture movement soared, with healthy produce grown in gardens all over the city. Along the Richmond Greenway, a pedestrian and bicycle pathway traverses the city. Fresh vegetables and a full array of fruit trees thrive under the leadership of Urban Tilth, a local non-profit. Other dedicated organizations, such as Groundwork Richmond, emerged to improve, manage, and sustain our physical environment, along with a tree-planting effort called Richmond Trees that was undertaken to beautify neighborhoods, provide shade in our parks, and help take carbon out of the atmosphere. Many Richmond residents wanted in on the action.

Richmond Rivets was another group that came together to find ways to thrive in a world challenged by dwindling oil supplies and climate change. One of their projects, Richmond Grows, was the creation of a seed-lending library, one of the first in the country, that encouraged residents to plant their own gardens and share seeds.

These and other initiatives offered a new vision of vitality for the city. Richmond was poised for prosperity as we welcomed the new green economy. We joined as a signatory of the Urban Environmental Accords, a declaration of more than one hundred municipalities worldwide to build ecologically sustainable, economically dynamic, and socially equitable urban futures, and we became a member of Green Cities California. Attracting green businesses to Richmond, with healthy jobs for our residents, presented a grounded approach to shifting our local economy away from the fossil fuel based economy into a new sustainable one. We became home to many solar and clean-tech companies. More recently we have become a hub for healthy food production businesses. Promoting Richmond as both a green and progressive city helped us get ahead of the curve as new environmentally friendly business trends developed in the region.

When I was still a councilmember I co-founded a grassroots organization with Richmond resident Michele McGeoy. We named the group Solar Richmond, and our mission was to advocate for solar energy. This initiative provided a major boost for the RPA and our city.

Michele was friendly, unpretentious, and approachable. She fit into our RPA style of sitting at the kitchen table and informally working out action plans. Juan initially floated the idea of Solar Richmond and he introduced me to Michele. Michele and I soon met on our own and our work relationship blossomed. I remember Michele's daughter, Helen, getting ready for school as Michele and I sipped herbal tea and brainstormed ideas for our venture. Our work in the RPA is always family-friendly. Family life doesn't stop, even as we transform our city.

It soon become clear that she and I had an opportunity to get this new endeavor off the ground. My role as an elected official was to help reach constituents throughout the city. Michele's role, as an expert in the solar field, was to educate how this form of renewable energy works, including its benefits for both the environment and peoples' pocketbooks. To launch this undertaking, we held a forum in Civic Center to a packed room of interested residents, sharing our vision and building grassroots support for advancing solar in Richmond. In 2006, when I began my mayoral campaign, this effort became part of my platform.

That same year I introduced a resolution commending all the participants in the Solar Richmond initiative. The resolution was unanimously supported by the City Council. It set a goal of reaching 5 megawatts of solar energy, as well as creating one hundred new jobs for Richmond residents. When these goals were surpassed in a few short years, we set new goals of 10 megawatts and 150 jobs.

Under McGeoy's leadership, Solar Richmond (SR) evolved into a non-profit business that trained residents in solar installation through the City's jobs training program, Richmond Build. SR also partnered with the City to create a solar rebate program

Solar Richmond

and to waive fees for solar permits, as well as offering a deferred loan program for low-income homeowners interested in solarizing their homes. Through its work creating a closed loop advancing solar for the planet and creating jobs for local residents, SR grew to become a nationally renowned program that received numerous awards. By 2010 Richmond led the Bay Area in per capita solar installations.

Solar Richmond was the nation's first non-profit to generate green-collar jobs in the solar industry. Today, it has evolved further to become a social enterprise that offers holistic leadership development and transitional employment through referrals. Along with Solar Richmond, groups like Rising Sun, Grid Alternatives, and Solar Living Institute have assisted us in providing green job opportunities and training to our residents.

Thanks to our new green direction, the City of Richmond also began receiving recognition for our sustainability accomplishments, such as our energy-efficient, environmentally sound Civic Center renovation, with its numerous green features, including solar. The City also won accolades for utilizing ecofriendly building practices in the restoration of the historic Richmond Plunge, which has been called "the healthiest [public swimming] pool in America."

To promote efforts beyond our city boundaries, Richmond joined other cities in the East Bay, including Berkeley and Oakland, to share ideas for greening our regional economy, calling ourselves the East Bay Green Corridor Partnership. Nicole Valentino became my staff representative to the Partnership, emphasizing our social justice vision and the importance of green job training for our low-income residents in all aspects of the green economy.

Richmond also became a part of Marin Clean Energy, a Community Choice Aggregation (CCA) program. A CCA is a system that allows jurisdictions to combine the buying power of individual customers in order to secure alternative energy supply contracts, but allowing consumers to opt out if they don't want to participate. I joined then-Councilmember Butt in co-sponsoring this endeavor. Today 85 % of Richmond residents and businesses get their electricity from green, clean, and less expensive energy sources.

Growing our Power

All this "greening" grew out of a city formerly referred to as Refinery Town with smokestacks still looming large on its skyline and neighborhoods still polluted and at risk from fossil fuel production. But we are experiencing a new, emergent power—one that is strong, beautiful, and mighty. It almost makes you forget that millions of tons of greenhouse gas emissions are coming out of the Chevron Richmond Refinery every year.

This is the power of the people. It comes from people who care about the planet and each other and we work together for progressive change. This power comes from people involved in efforts like the Sunflower Alliance, who demand refinery regulations and emission reductions. This power comes from groups like Idle No More, a Native American environmental group, who draw attention to the plight of our city and planet when they lead "healing refinery walks"—solemn marches from refinery to refinery across our region. They advocate and protest the refinery's damage to our land. This power comes from individual efforts that shine brightly—educators like Lana Husser, a former Richmond High School teacher, who led Green Tours in Richmond for young students, aided by Nicole in my office, showing them sustainable ways to shape Richmond's future. And most importantly, this power comes from the observations of these youth, bathed in our better

Richmond. It is for them that we continue to transition toward a thriving, resilient, and abundant low-carbon city. With every step, we get closer to living out that Native American proverb, "We do not inherit the earth from our ancestors, we borrow it from our children."

Walking the Talk: Re-Election

I wasn't sure if I was going to run for re-election as mayor in 2010. In fact, at some point I was sure I would *not* run again. My first four years had left marks, and I was battle-weary. After spending years going up against Chevron and "the Chevron 5," I felt the toll on my body. I felt the need for time away from public office. With worsening knee problems from injuries when I was younger, I wanted to take time for physical therapy.

It seemed the more I stepped away from running again, someone kept pulling me back, supplying bold reasons for why I should run. It wasn't just the local progressive community, people outside of Richmond were urging me to run. Actually, since I was so steeped in local struggles, I needed someone outside my close political circles to help me refocus on the larger movement. One of those people was my friend Frank Garvey. I mentioned him in an earlier chapter—Frank, an artist I've known for decades, has always been attentive to the political landscape, and I value his opinion. We had not been in touch for several years but had recently reconnected. Frank had been following my political work, as I had been watching his accomplishments as an artist. He told me he thought I was the best person to tackle the job for another term. I had always given more attention to our unified efforts as a progressive community rather than particular individual contributions, so Frank was tapping into my working-class values and sense of responsibility for the community. Like Frank, I believe sometimes our historical class struggles carry us into a distinct role for societal change. When Frank encouraged me to keep going for a second term, I also realized how much my being in the position of mayor, and working with RPA's backing, had brought Richmond into the limelight. RPA's political culture was reaching into unforeseen places, including the San Francisco art scene across the Bay Area. That impressed me.

Reflecting on my personal motivation for running for elected office, I realized that I simply wanted to make a difference. And I still had that desire deep within me. As I tapped into that yearning, my reluctance began to melt away.

When I told RPA, they embraced me and helped me see the road ahead with refreshed eyes. I was seeing a self-determined and motivated Richmond able to take further progressive strides with the leadership I would continue to provide. My soul-searching and the support of others reinvigorated me.

What's more, my knees began to feel better, thanks to my husband urging me to stick with physical therapy. I felt bolstered and buoyed, deciding that I still had a lot in me for another mayoral term. I decided to run again.

My main opponent was Nat Bates, who was supported by Chevron and the police and fire unions. The other candidate was John Ziesenhenne, a former councilmember, who was backed by big money through the Chamber of Commerce.

High Profile Kick-off

Despite my initial trepidation, once I was committed to run, I threw myself into the electoral arena with abandon. As in the past, RPA leaders energetically helped me launch this effort. Juan Reardon, Kay Wallis, Marilyn Langlois, and my husband Paul became my re-election campaign team. We wanted to draw on past accomplishments, especially in environmental justice, and particularly in the area of solar energy.

Van Jones, President Obama's former Special Advisor for Green Jobs, came to speak at the kick-off event. Van had spoken at my swearing-in ceremony when I first became mayor. He had also spoken at a press event sponsored by Solar Richmond a year earlier. Van Jones could always be counted on to speak eloquently about environmental and social justice issues. He had a warm speaking style and was embraced by our supporters. We were delighted that a nationally known figure of Van's caliber was focusing in on the successes of our local political work.

This was a good time to bring Van back to Richmond. I had become known as Richmond's "Green mayor," and I had worked to steer Richmond toward clean energy jobs for our residents. Van's vision and mine lined up. His support helped both my reelection and reinforced what we were doing in Richmond.

We have world-class leadership in Richmond, doing visioning things, doing creative things that meet the moment.... Richmond is one of the few cities that is meeting the challenge both in the short run and the long run. Change is hard, but you have in Mayor Gayle McLaughlin an extraordinary leader; you have innovative grassroots projects, and you have hope in Richmond. Keep leading us in the new economy.[28]

Also at the event were Nativo Lopez, an immigration rights activist and the president of the Mexican American Political Association, joined by Richmond Vice Mayor Jeff Ritterman. Richmond's phenomenal Shiloh Singers provided the music. The affair was a monster success, and we were off to a great start feeling strong and confident.

There was a seriousness to this kick-off. The crowd was made up of RPA members and other community members with political interest, all supportive and waiting to hear the speakers. I'll never forget the look of anticipation on peoples' faces—they were eager, excited, and proud to be a part of our local movement. Yet this event was just the beginning of campaign year 2010. It was not lost to those who attended that this wasn't a celebration, but an effort to spark interest in contributing, volunteering, and activating. So while people listened, talked, chatted, and ate, we made sure we had clipboards circulating so we could get names and contact information of everyone there. We would surely bring these new folks into the campaign work ahead.

Walking the Campaign Trail

As I set out to run for re-election, I knew I would be judged on my record. My first term as mayor had been quite a challenge, but our collective movement had made great strides. The state of our city was sound and we were pointed in new, healthy directions. We had made improvements in infrastructure and advanced economic development with new small businesses even

Reelection kickoff

in a harsh economic climate. We had new local hiring goals for subsidized projects, innovative crime prevention and jobs for our youth. We had become a leader in the environmental movement with new policies and grassroots organizing. We were building a more democratic, transparent, and participatory city by re-opening all branches of our libraries, supporting our local schools, and opposing "the Chevron 5's" secret deals.

I held monthly "Meet with the Mayor" sessions, and became known for my accessibility to residents. The community appreciated that I made time to hear their issues. We were building community, social, and economic justice with violence prevention efforts, protecting immigrants, helping renters avoid eviction from foreclosed homes, and renovating our parks in the urban core.

Yet there was still much suffering in our community. We were in the throes of a national recession triggered by corporate bankers and speculators who had left many homeowners facing foreclosures and high unemployment. Systemic violence continued to plague our city due to despair among youth in our most impoverished neighborhoods. I stressed the need to stay the course and continue carving pathways out of poverty at the local level with our job programs, education support, and services to assist working-class families. With state and federal aid to cities decreasing, we couldn't afford to wait for higher levels of government to present answers, because frankly, they weren't forthcoming. We needed bold solutions in the moment at the local level, not more of the thinking that had defined Richmond's past and had resulted in decades of stagnation. Identifying myself as a candidate of hope and change, I spoke of the privilege of having served Richmond thus far and my desire to continue to lead our city in meeting our challenges. I reminded the voters that the road to community, economic, and environmental health and justice is long and hard, but that we were re-directing our priorities and re-inventing our city. I reminded people that I had taken no corporate donations in each of my past campaigns, and was continuing that practice, reconfirming with them that I was beholden to no one but the residents of Richmond.

The Voters' Choice: Take Steps Forward, Not Backward

It was evident that Election 2010 was going to come down to whether the people of Richmond wanted to keep going in the same progressive direction or whether they wanted to head back to the days of corporate domination of City Hall. It was a battle worth fighting.

Jovanka Beckles and Eduardo Martinez, two experienced RPA community leaders, ran for city council. We three were the RPA-endorsed candidates, committed to deepen the work we had started and work in coalition with others.

Of course, Chevron wanted to stop us, as did the Police and Fire Union leadership. I had voted against the recent Police Union contract, which included outrageous, unsustainable benefits that the City could not afford. Some councilmembers held to the tiresome argument that more benefits would help us recruit and retain more police. Our police chief disagreed. He felt the best officers came on board out of a commitment to serve the community.

But the Council majority was not swayed and chose to vote for the inflated benefits package. I voted against.

Both the police and fire unions had a history of corrupt and unethical smear campaigns in local elections. In 2010, they—along with Chevron—outdid themselves to try and stop my re-election. Public safety unions put out large signs all over town, saying "The Mayor doesn't listen to us" picturing anonymous public safety officials with generic uniforms and badges. (Our municipal code doesn't allow uniformed Richmond officials or the use of City insignia in campaign materials.) These signs were countered with homemade signs by the Disability Brigade picturing ordinary people, some in wheelchairs with a counter message, "The Mayor listens to us."

It was a powerful image. In truth I had good relationships with most rank and file police, but these campaign decisions were made by a small group of police association leaders.

Mayor Listens to Us

The police and fire unions formed a political action committee. Other political action committees were also formed, including one fully funded by Chevron to the tune of $1 million. These committees supported Chevron's candidates and paid an investigative research firm, VR Research, to investigate me, which led to the smear campaign. The rudimentary philosophy for this kind of politics is: *Dig deep until you find something.*

Kicked in the Shins

In September I was about to leave the house for a candidates' debate facilitated by the Women's League of Voters, when I got a call from Juan. He said he needed to talk with me right away and that he would be over in a few minutes. His announcement caused my heart to skip a beat. While I had been in Richmond politics long enough to expect political attacks, this one came out of the blue. Our opponents learned about my past experience with depression. Juan added that they also knew about my earlier financial troubles, having filed for bankruptcy several years prior to running for public office. This was a lot to take in. I felt a combination of shock, fear, and dread. But there was no time to stop in my tracks. Juan advised me not to let this throw me off course. He told me people in Richmond would understand and he reminded me that I was running on my record.

I had known I was going to be attacked, but still, this was alarming. I knew things were about to get harder, as the press would be all over this. But I also believed Juan—people would stand by me.

Navigating Hurdles—Past and Present

From an early age, I was self-reliant. While I wasn't raised to climb the traditional ladder of success, I was reared to develop critical thinking. When personal problems arose, I sought help.

At a point in my adult life, I sought therapy to help me explore depression that had built up through some difficult times in my life. As I mentioned in chapter two, there were tensions in my household growing up, followed by some traumatic experiences in my early adult years. I also was involved in a tumultuous and emotionally abusive marriage for five years when I was in my late twenties and early thirties. Not long after my divorce, I lost both my mother and grandmother in the course of two years. As the depression built up in me, I realized it was time for me to deal with it. I wanted to better understand my past and learn how to address some difficult emotions. Therapy was a way for me to further develop and learn how to cope with past pain.

I came to understand many causes of depression. There is certainly a physiological impact on a person that limits one's experience in life, but this impact can be looked at in various ways. While some focus on bio-chemical depression, my personal experience with it, as well as my study of social psychology, lent me to seek a greater understanding of the situational development of depression, both in myself and in others. There are traumas buried in our childhoods that need uncovering and healing. For some, depression is anger held inside that needs healthy expression.

There are also social ills that pervade our society—more reasons to be depressed. I went into therapy to look at the factors that were causing my depression. I mention this because it was a part of my past from which I gained insight. My experience of depression helped increase my compassion for others facing depression and other mental health challenges. I am also motivated to help remove societal factors that keep people poor, hungry, sick, uneducated, and living in harsh conditions, which cultivate despair and disillusionment.

I was fortunate to be able to avail myself of therapy. Psychotherapy provided me a place to explore my feelings, experiences, and early life circumstances. I became a better person for having embraced such a process. It was ironic that years later, powerful political foes waged such a vicious campaign against me, suggesting I was unfit for office for having sought mental health care. In truth, seeking therapy was an affirmative step that made me stronger and more resilient. My healing helped me be able to withstand personal and public trials and tribulations that would befall me in the stressful job as mayor.

Standing Tall

Gayle McLaughlin

What happened in the aftermath was truly transformational. A day or two later, hit-piece mailers were sent to voters and poster boards were set up all over town directing people to a website to learn more about my "lack of fitness" for public office. But that strategy quickly showed cracks. An enormous amount of support came forth in opposition to this low-down politicking. The public was turned off and saw these despicable tactics for what they were. The scheme backfired, and the level of my support grew and grew. People did more than stand by me. They called, emailed, wrote letters of support, and sent campaign donations. Mental health professionals and advocates reached out to me, told me how outrageous and mean-spirited they thought these methods were calling them cynical and bigoted. As usual, my core campaign team also stood by me, helping me smoothly navigate through campaign obstacles.

Marilyn Langlois, in her capacity as campaign volunteer, organized community leaders throughout Richmond to join me in a press conference. Long-time progressive pastor and civil rights leader Reverend Phil Lawson spoke, expressing his disdain for that kind of gutter politics. Millie Cleveland, field representative from the city's general employee union, supported me referring to this as political mudslinging. A couple of my councilmember colleagues, Tom Butt and Jeff Ritterman, even stood by my side as I read my statement to the people:

Many of you are now aware of a campaign by the Richmond Police Officers Association (RPOA) disclosing personal information about my medical and financial history prior to entering public office. While I respect and work well with the Richmond Police Department, certain members of the RPOA have a long history of doing the dirty campaigning in the last weeks of the election. In 2008, you will recall that they were responsible for the racist hit piece against the Latino community.

Some years in my earlier life were extremely challenging. I was the victim of multiple crimes and experienced a host of personal losses, including debilitating illnesses and deaths within my family. My health and personal finances

157

suffered as a result.

But that is all in the past. I overcame those challenges. I believe my past challenges have strengthened me and made me a wiser and more compassionate woman, leader, and public servant.

It is not the adversity that one faces, but how one emerges from that adversity and overcomes one's challenges that defines a person.

Those who oppose our program for positive change in Richmond have decided to attack me personally, in an attempt to distract voters from the important issues and decisions we face.

This kind of campaigning—attacking with personal information—has damaged our political process across the nation, and has contributed to the cynicism and powerlessness with which too many people regard government. Good people are discouraged from becoming active in public life.

But I know, with great certainty, that Richmond voters will support candidates on the basis of their values, ideas, and vision. I know that you will look at my record in office over the last six years and judge me on the merits of my consistent hard work and achievements. I stand on my record as Mayor of Richmond.

For anyone in Richmond who has ever struggled with adversity, I stand with you and for you.

A Better Richmond is possible, and we can build it together.

While it was unnerving to stand in front of the media that day with microphones thrust in my face and reporters questioning me about very personal experiences to be covered on the evening news, the power of the community carried me through that press conference. People showed their solidarity with me. My heart swelled with pride, seeing how our community had been offended by this personal attack and stood by me, their mayor.

Still Standing

As we neared Election Day, the smear campaign boomeranged. I was supported as a popular mayor who had steered the city in a new, healthy direction. Trying to tarnish my reputation didn't work. The public boldly criticized that shameful campaign.

The people of Richmond had more basic human decency than to let these attacks affect my re-election. At the same time it bears saying loud and clear that reaching out for support—whether for mental health or other kinds of assistance—needs to be encouraged and regarded as a sign of strength.

The people of Richmond, like working people everywhere, understand hardship. Depression is all too common in this world. Many people in Richmond have struggled themselves or had a friend or family member who has struggled with serious difficulties at one time or another. Financial difficulties are also common among Richmond families. We all have our personal histories—sets of circumstances that can weigh us down in later years. What is more important is that we deal with hardship. It isn't the depth of our challenges, but the height of our climb that determines our mettle.

It's those individuals who don't seek help for mental health problems that should raise concerns. Often those who don't tackle their own personal problems create new problems that can cast aspersions on others.

Crossing the Finish Line

While my reelection campaign was receiving the heaviest blows, City Council candidate Jovanka Beckles had also been on the receiving end of hostility from the police and fire unions due to her association with the RPA and me. The first attacks against Jovanka took place in 2008 when the RPOA issued the infamous racist flyer—blaming Latinos for the drugs and violence in Richmond—in an attempt to defeat her and Jeff Ritterman, both of whom were supportive of our immigrant community. The police union issued a four-page mailer that attributed the city's crime to drugs: "Drugs come to Richmond from across the Mexican border." The RPOA president linked Beckles and Ritterman to immigration rights policies I had spearheaded as mayor, claiming we wanted "to identify a special class of people who are exempt from the rule of law." (Not unlike the kind of defamation we witnessed on a national level in the 2016 presidential election.) Our community mobilized against such outrageous statements and widely denounced the flyers.

While Jovanka did not succeed two years earlier, this time she was victorious in spite of the slander. Jovanka and I had weathered difficult storms. Eduardo narrowly missed a win, but he remained committed to continuing the work as a community leader. This was his first run for city council and he gained experience that would later lead to success.

We also won the Pt. Molate casino advisory ballot measure. RPA had shown well in 2010—we now had three RPA officeholders on the City Council—Jovanka, Jeff, and me as mayor, all without corporate money.

The RPA showed that change from the bottom up could happen, even in the face of dirty politicking. All three of the Chevron-funded candidates that electoral season—Maria Viramontes, Ludmyrna Lopez, and Nat Bates—lost, in spite of Chevron pumping a cool million dollars into their campaigns: icing on our RPA cake.

Not a Sprint, but a Marathon

The 2010 campaign provided some lasting lessons for me. The personal hostilities were a reminder of the way our system operates every day. And yet it is not a reflection of what works for people when they vote. Faced with such distasteful politicking, most people were repelled, and many spoke out against it. The level of support I received was astounding.

All of us have personal challenges in our lives whether physical or mental health, relationship, educational, or financial issues. At different times of our lives old problems get resolved and a new resilience takes hold. Having support from good therapists, friends, and family in my life gave way to the collective support of the Richmond community that had seen me in action over the prior four years and judged me on my record. They were convinced that I was the person to continue leading Richmond into a better future.

Richmond's police and fire unions were left with an argument no one was buying. In an article in the *Richmond Globe* right before the election, Reverend Alvin C. Bernstine, pastor of Bethlehem Missionary Baptist Church in Richmond poignantly addressed this hypocrisy:

> To make the statement [as police and fire have made] that "I believe it is important for the citizens to know everything they need to know about the people who serve them" is disingenuous. The same could be said, and probably needs to be said, about firemen and police. Many of Richmond's citizens would feel a lot safer knowing the psychological histories and profiles of men and women with guns—more so than a mayor with a pen.[29]

With the success of the 2010 campaign behind us, we were excited to move into more work ahead. The new year started out with a great achievement in rejecting the casino. Before long, however, the year would quickly morph into a period of major disruptions that would last throughout my second term. Though I would face daunting challenges, my administration was on solid ground because I had learned something valuable over the course of the campaign: we are long-distance runners on this progressive journey and when the road gets rough, we fortify each other with support and solidarity, equipping ourselves for the long run.

Disruptive Waters—A Pirate on Board

As I entered my second term, I felt strong and hopeful. I had reaffirmed my commitment to the people of Richmond and shown I could withstand character attacks. I had been expecting the road ahead would be smoother, but it took a mere three months before I was forced to deal with a developing storm that no one could have predicted. A new councilmember's out-of-control behavior would force a fierce battle for civil decorum in our Council chambers. This would play out ferociously over my second term in office.

As the new City Council was seated, a new member, RPA-endorsed Jovanka Beckles took the seat next to me. Seated to her right was another new councilmember, Casper. Casper is not his real name and Richmond locals know him well by reputation, but I have changed his name to recount this story. I do that because I don't want to publicly shame him, nor make a spectacle of a person who has mental health issues and, in all seriousness, needs help. In addition to his wild and unruly behavior, this person's piracy included accepting loot from the corporate oil giant, that had no qualms about paying big dollars to rock the boat and create big waves. I tell this tale because most political groups at some point encounter disruptive individuals who can wreak havoc on the business at hand—whether in small, close-knit activist groups, city councils, or, writ large in national politics. One of these major disrupters came upon the Richmond City Council. He would become the bane of my existence for the next four years.

Calm Before the Storm

Casper had been a perennial candidate in Richmond. He finally won a Council seat after seeking office ten times. He was known in the community as a gadfly; a colorful character who spoke at every council meeting and had something to say on many Council agenda items. My acquaintanceship with him went back several years.

I remember one of the early RPA meetings when we invited Casper to join us. We were still trying to get a larger slate beyond Andres Soto and me. At that point I knew little about him, except that he would likely run again. We asked him if we could interview him for a possible RPA endorsement. At the meeting we questioned if he would agree to not take corporate donations, particularly from Chevron. He responded matter of factly: "Depends on how much they offer!" Casper's answer was both classic and comical to those of us sitting around Juan and Kay's living room. Looking back, his response revealed his politics: he could change as the wind blew depending on what it offered him.

While he was clearly not a good RPA fit, over the course of my early years in elected office, the RPA and Casper had a friendly relationship. We had built some community ties with him through Tent City in 2006 for which he had been a strong proponent. He liked the fact that I, along with RPA community leaders, supported this spontaneous movement for peace on our streets that had sprung up in our city parks. It was an intersection in which we found grassroots compatibility.

As the 2010 election neared, Casper also joined RPA in opposition to the Pt. Molate casino. He had not previously been on board with us, but we welcomed his support.

As expected, Casper ran for a seat again. For our part, the RPA as an organization wasn't going to endorse him, given our no corporate money rule. However, RPA takes the position that *individuals* within the organization can endorse whomever they want, since the alliance has separate rules for organizational endorsements. Many of us decided to support Casper based on the two positions we shared in common. He also had the confirmation of long-time Councilmember Tom Butt. Editorials in the local paper speculated that it might finally be "Casper's time." And so it happened. Casper was elected with the support of many who wanted to believe the best about him.

We found out soon enough his "best" had been overrated. It wasn't long before he would reveal a troubling shadow side. To be fair, in April 2010, Casper did live up to his campaign promise and joined me and others on the Council in voting down the casino. But that was the only progressive-friendly step he took while in office. It wasn't long after that vote that he proved to be led by pure, unadulterated self-interest.

Within nine months sitting on the Council, Casper ceased voting with the Council's majority. He parted company following a fight with another councilmember over a Richmond start-up having to do with a transportation system. At that point, Casper chose Councilmember Nat Bates (a long-time Chevron-supported councilmember) as his new buddy and they teamed up on every vote henceforth They cast their votes in union with what Chevron wanted, all in contrast to what we supported—parks, the environment, health initiatives, preserving historic sites, and the like.

Councilmember Casper's four years of service on the council proved challenging for everyone—me, other council members, and the public. As mayor I had the responsibility to chair our meetings, but it became increasingly daunting. Casper's "service" would more accurately be coined as "performance." He *acted* on the Richmond City Council. It seemed his goal was to draw attention to himself. He did so with flagrant, hostile behavior, throwing insults at council members and progressive leaders in the community. His behavior became a huge public embarrassment, and his antics deterred many members of the community from coming to Council meetings to share their views.

Trying to Anchor the Ship

There is no question that Casper's behavior set back the democratic process at work in Richmond. He would often speak for thirty to forty-five minutes at a stretch and whenever I, as chair, urged him to wrap it up, he would snap back at me with an insult, calling me a dictator, and claiming I was being rude. He would often address his remarks to the people watching from home, since our meetings are shown on a local government station. Looking into the camera, Casper would say something like: "To my people watching at home, see what this lady is doing. She doesn't care about you." I learned to hold in my outrage, even as my character, integrity, and commitment to the community were being attacked.

My instinct was to defend myself, but I quickly learned that anything I said in response to Casper's rants would only feed his fire. He was like a time bomb ready to explode. Once he started his tirade, he would seem to gleefully get more and more worked up. It was as though he thrived on this personal performance. He was an act onto himself. Some of his comments were comic in their peculiarity, while others were tragic and shocking, filled with acrimony and rancor. My initial approach had been to use kindness and respect in all my dealings with Casper, since this is my general demeanor. When things started going astray I would respectfully refer him to our *City Council Rules and Procedures*—a document the Council had approved in 2006 as a guidebook for meeting comportment. RPA leaders tried reaching out to him as well, using whatever they could muster to reach a level of respectful engagement with him. Nothing worked.

By this time, Chevron was giving Casper safe harbor regardless of his actions. The oil giant no doubt delighted that our meetings devolved into disorder, with Casper pointing the finger at me as the source of the problem. And Casper had no problem cozying up to Chevron. For example, Chevron had made a commitment of $200,000 for our job-training program. A check for $100,000 was handed directly to Casper, who claimed he coaxed Chevron into providing it, when he was clearly attempting to secure Chevron support for the next election.

At one Council meeting, as I was trying to control the meeting that he and his supporters were disrupting, Casper asserted in a scathing way that, "I'd better watch out." He said there were street-tough people out there in the community who were capable of doing harm—implying that such harm could come to me. I asked him if that was a threat. He didn't reply.

But Casper went overboard when he and his supporters ruthlessly started attacking an RPA colleague, Councilmember Jovanka Beckles, and other members of the LGBTQ community at Council meetings. Even Chevron could see how that would create a backlash. So Chevron held a Pride Celebration at the refinery, where Casper was forced to read a letter saying he has close friends and family members who are gay. In the progressive community, we have come to refer to that as Casper's "I am not a bigot" letter. Enduring the strikes against her as a lesbian, councilmember Beckles stood strong and courageously responded, not only for herself, but for the LGBTQ community, using the hateful remarks as a teachable moment. On one occasion, she presented a study session for the Council to examine the struggles and accomplishments of the LGBTQ community.

Divide and conquer seemed second nature to Casper, and nothing could stem his penchant for turmoil. As an African-American man, he would try to divide the Black and Brown communities with such comments: "Councilmember Beckles isn't really African-American," playing on the fact that she was also a Latina, having been born in Panama. Jovanka would respond with pride in both her African and Latina roots, highlighting the importance of our diverse community coming together as "One Richmond." This is not to say that there weren't times when she had had enough and called out Casper or one of his supporters for their abominable behavior. But she found, as I did, that this was not effective. Maintaining our composure in the face of hostility became our conduct of choice.

I needed to navigate the fine line between allowing free speech and disallowing Casper's hate speech, so I found myself in the role of referee calling things as I saw and heard them. As chairperson I had to rely on my own judgment and I did the best I could, keeping my personal feelings at bay as I made on-the-spot determinations whether or not he had crossed the line of decency. But what really helped was the amazing stand taken by the greater community who mobilized against the hate speech, homophobic harassment, and disruption at City Council meetings.

As Casper's antics escalated over the years, only his few supporters and some of our very committed progressive activists could bear to come to Council meetings. Although Casper was by far the instigator, he also had a couple of co-conspiratorial councilmembers who either aided and abetted him or refused to play a role in stopping it. Though previously on opposite sides of issues, Casper's new ally, Bates propped him up. They now shared a new commonality in wanting to turn back our progressive direction and those of us leading it, with Chevron backing them both. Casper also had the implicit support of Councilmember Jim Rogers, who refused to vote to end debate when Casper went off into one of his many soliloquies. As well, Rogers refused to vote in favor of changing our meeting rules to limit the amount of time each councilmember could speak on agenda items. We tried to enact that change on several occasions, with Rogers always opposing, unwilling to alienate whatever level of support he thought Casper might have. The fact that Casper was taking up the bulk of the time in every meeting was not a factor for Rogers. In actuality there was a majority vote *against* changing the time allotment rules—Bates, Rogers, a recently appointed councilmember, Jael Myrick (who had gained his seat by the good graces of Rogers), and, of course Casper. Only Beckles, Butt, and myself voted to try to rectify the situation.[30]

Needless to say, without majority support for limiting Casper's rants, I was left with few options for controlling our meetings. I was continuously frustrated not only by this unrestrained councilmember, but with his cohorts as well.

While we struggled to get through the issues on the table, Casper performed with abandon. He stirred up his three or four supporters in the audience so they would start calling out insults at me and other council members. The situation got so chaotic I would have to instruct the officer on duty to escort these disruptive audience members out of the Council Chambers. There were even times when I had to clear out the entire Chambers.

Looking for Ports in the Storm

We considered recalling Casper. But recall campaigns take enormous amounts of time and effort in non-electoral years, and for the RPA that would mean lots of volunteer hours and fundraising. It just wasn't practical. We needed to focus on the upcoming regular campaign season. The community's response to Casper was horror, disgust, and outrage. For me, it went further. It was an enormous test of my patience and tolerance. But as mayor I had to do my best to handle this situation with the dignity that our community deserved. We would have to wait until his term was over. RPA's position became focused on preparing good, progressive candidates for upcoming elections to both defeat Casper and add more progressive voices to the City Council. At the same time, RPA representatives would attend every Council meeting speaking at Open Forum, denouncing those responsible for the discord, and providing a narrative of the situation through our newsletter, social media, and other publications.

The conflict reached such an apex that we brought in one of our police officers to read a statement before each Council meeting, explaining that disrupting Council meetings could result in citations. This offered only temporary help. Some citations were given and things calmed down for the remainder of a meeting, but it would all start up again at the next meeting. I insisted our officers act with restraint, knowing there was the possibility of making a bad situation worse. Above all, I wanted our community-involved policing approach to be upheld. In keeping with this, their approach was to calm down the rowdiness and not add more fuel to the emotional fire. While this did not solve the problem long term, it gave us some breathing room so meetings could continue.

There was a time when a few of Casper's supporters brought a megaphone to a Council meeting and started marching up and down the middle aisle of the Chambers, shouting noxious and fighting comments such as "this is war." Having the officers clear the Chambers was the only way to restore any semblance of order. As someone who stands firm for our constitutional right to protest, let me be clear, this was not a protest, it was a theatrical ploy meant only to interfere with our meeting. Casper had no apparent goals, demands, or issues on the table. He meant only to bring mayhem to the meetings. It became apparent to most of us in the RPA that the purpose of such displays was a cynical attempt to make me look bad for not having control over the meeting, knowing that if I looked bad, the RPA looked bad as well. He wanted to diminish our strength as an organization, and creating disorder was one way to do that with Chevron's continued support. It was obvious that the corporation behind the councilman believed they had much to gain if our progressive movement could be stopped. Yet regardless of motives behind the attacks, quelling the disturbances rested on my shoulders, and this continued to be challenging.

Had this simply been a case of unruly audience members, it

would have been bad enough, but, this motley crew had a champion sitting right there up on the dais, not only sanctioning their raucous behavior, but hurling out his own unbridled venom. Finding a way to curtail a councilmember's disorderliness was a whole different challenge. As progressives, we were aghast at Casper's behavior, as he signaled with hand motions from his Council seat to his small assemblage of supporters, encouraging them to keep up the rancor.

Disruptive audience member

I sought advice on legal maneuvers for how I might deal with Casper. I went to the City Manager, our City Attorney, and the Police Chief. They all sternly advised me not to exile Casper. The attorney cautioned me that it could put the City at legal risk if an elected official was banned from a meeting. Short of Casper threatening or assaulting anyone, I could not have him escorted out of the meeting, even as his words stirred up so much hate and disturbance.

Time and again in between meetings, people would sincerely approach me and say: "I don't know how you do it." To be honest, the only way I was able to manage the situation was to spend most of my time at meetings on alert with a readiness to intervene whenever Casper would go off on a tirade. He would simply disregard my calling him out of order, and I had to find other ways to keep some civility and try to make progress in our meetings. At one point we held a Council retreat with an outside facilitator. This also proved fruitless. At the end of the meeting the facilitator asked that each of us commit to being respectful at Council meetings. While the majority of the councilmembers agreed, it was disheartening to witness Casper and Nat Bates refuse to even make an initial commitment. Eventually, I started calling recesses whenever Casper's behavior needed calming down. That worked surprising well, if only for short periods of time. There were meetings when I had to call ten to twelve recesses throughout a four to five-hour meeting. Tiresome, indeed, but at least we could conduct city business.

Not Jumping Ship

When patience and tolerance wore thin, I used my delegated power to protect the democratic space. It is vital that we promote civil discourse in the political arena and that elected officials address each other with respect, even as we disagree. Ground rules of engagement are important for political bodies, but such rules can only be helpful if they are followed or, should they not prove useful, that a majority of the body care enough about the democratic process to strengthen the rules. Unfortunately, that did not happen during the Casper years.

Nevertheless, we had the community behind us and we knew there was power in our numbers. We continued to organize in spite of the chaos. Although the Council's business slowed down, it never stopped. There is no question we could have accomplished a lot more had our meetings been more decorous. Still, we made important progress. In 2012 we passed the 2030 General Plan—a major project of the City of Richmond, which had vigorous input from the public and laid the groundwork and guidelines for sustainability, equity, and health in our city planning. Only Casper and Nat declined to support it. Their allegiance to big business provided their opposition votes. So while much of my attention as mayor was, of necessity, focused first and foremost on keeping order in our Council Chambers, the passion for progress that I shared with all my RPA colleagues led us to bear fruit under these horrible conditions. We never stopped countering the crazy antics of the few with the dedicated passion of the many.

When either Jovanka or I presented a controversial item at a Council meeting, we made sure we had enough public speakers to counter the reaction we knew would surely come. Those who were unwilling to speak at Council meetings, given the repulsive climate, were encouraged to write emails and make phone calls to councilmembers urging their votes. RPA helped create public pressure campaigns geared toward influencing the swing votes on the Council.

Our organized efforts were well thought out ideas and initiatives on how to improve our city, and that gave us an edge time and again. Those councilmembers who leaned more toward the center politically were often compelled to support our policies because to not do so would link them with the irrational "acting" members of the Council. In this way, we took positive steps forward, in spite of Nat and Casper, who became known as the "party of no."

A Spotlight Through the Fog

While we felt adrift at times in the sea of conflict that Casper brought to the City Council, the record of this atrocity would later be documented and shown for all the world to see. Richmond resident and member of Richmond's Arts and Culture Commission, BK Williams, produced a documentary film titled *Against Hate* in which she tells the story of how Casper ransacked the City Council meetings with his hate speech. She examines the vicious campaign that ensued, particularly against Councilmember Beckles. BK's film focuses on the barrage of hostility and homophobia that unfolded from Casper and his clique.[31]

In 2014 Casper and a handful of supporters brought their hate crusade to a crescendo. Their fulmination against Richmond's LGBTQ community, replete with religious anti-gay zealotry, was an example of how a small but unruly group led by unrestrained and unprincipled leadership can put rampant chaos into motion.

Casper and his group's defense of free speech led to a larger discussion for many of us. Free speech is indeed a hallmark of our democracy, and needs ardent protection. At the same time it needed to be clear that the halls of Richmond's city government are intended for all our residents. There is a difference between free speech and acts of disruption of meetings that prevent huge swathes of people from participating. These principles are embodied in the following passage from the Supreme Court in Chaplinsky v. New Hampshire:

> There are certain well-defined and narrowly limited classes of speech, the prevention and punishment of which have never been thought to raise any Constitutional problem. These include the lewd and obscene, the profane, the libelous, and the insulting or "fighting" words—those which, by their very utterance, inflict injury or tend to incite an immediate breach of the peace. It has been well observed that such utterances are no essential part of any exposition of ideas, and are of such slight social value as a step to truth that any benefit that may be derived from them is clearly outweighed by the social interest in order and morality.[32]

Righting the Ship

It is both troubling and worth remembering Casper's four years in public office. This was a time when an elected official and a few supporters were able to halt the democratic process with behavior that served only to disrupt. Richmond voters, the overall arbiters of our local democratic process, made this point clear by not re-electing Casper in 2014. By this time, even Chevron was willing to let Casper sink. Incredible as it sounds, Casper even ran again in 2016. Fortunately, the voters remembered his toxic mix in our city politics and they rejected his twelfth run for a Council seat.

Looking back over those unsettling years, I showcase this person's behavior to point out an example of mental illness getting acted out in the political arena. It was both irksome and tragic for me personally, for our city's functioning, and for the community at-large who witnessed this travesty. This person clearly has mental health issues, if not a personality disorder, and his actions damaged our city's democratic process.

There are emotionally disturbed individuals in many sectors of society, including elected positions on all levels of government.

We saw this on the national scene in 2016 to the horror of many of us.

What we witnessed in Richmond is what happens when someone doesn't acknowledge or seek help for dealing with emotions or problems that have been festering for years. When I witnessed Casper's emotions turning to hostile spewing and experienced the trauma and disturbance spill over onto other people's lives, I couldn't help but ponder how essential it is that the stigma of mental illness be lifted and how we, as a society, must provide services for all people who struggle like this. And while I have compassion for all those who wrestle with emotional pain, we in Richmond saw how one person's unresolved issues could harm our social fabric and governmental process. Serving in elected office requires a level of personal decorum, integrity, and dignified behavior. We don't expect completely restrained conduct because we know that elected officials, like anyone, can display passionate feelings on the political stage. But when those fiery responses veer into unruly demeaning outbursts, they need to be addressed and firmly dealt with for the greater good of the community.

This was also a display of a corporation's unethical behavior that degraded the public sphere. The fact that a major corporation would prey upon a person with mental health issues to further its own aims illustrates how a corporate culture can operate in our political arena. Left without regulations, corporations can use their power and money to stop the sea change of progress that so many of us are working hard to advance.

The political culture we are shaping in RPA is about building relationships. Casper's self-promotion, manipulated by corporate interests, ran counter to those goals. It was, however, in many ways similar to patterns of behavior we witnessed in the 2016 presidential election—Donald Trump, too, seemed detached from those he disparaged. True leaders engage with the people they serve. No leader is infallible, but to be oblivious to people's struggles, or worse yet, to denigrate them, is a barrier to an inclusive, democratic society.

It was raw endurance and deep commitment to the people of Richmond that carried me through those four years when Councilmember Casper sat on the dais. But we endured the attack on our democratic process together.

Disruptive Industry: Chevron Explodes

Chevron Fire

In December 2016 I set about writing this chapter to share our Richmond story on the horrific Chevron refinery fire of 2012. But before I settled into the experience of telling our story, another Bay Area fire took over the news waves, shocking our region and nation. I refer to the tragic fire that occurred at the Ghost Ship Warehouse, an artists' work and performance space in nearby Oakland, that left thirty-six people dead—trapped in a building described as a tinderbox that went up in flames. It had been a fire waiting to happen in a structure jam-packed with combustible items, flammable materials, serious safety hazards, and building-code violations. While triggering enormous sadness for the families and friends of those lost lives, this fire also caused me to remember similar feelings of shock and distress that I felt during the Chevron fire some years earlier. This is every mayor's nightmare.

Duck and Cover

Our Richmond tragedy happened on August 6, 2012—the same day when we remember the devastating U.S. bombing of Hiroshima during World War II. Paul and I had just finished dinner when we heard the sirens. A countywide warning system had gone off signaling a serious public health or safety hazard in the area. We were accustomed to hearing test alarms on Wednesday mornings, but this was a Monday evening, so we knew to take heed of the blaring sound-off. We immediately suspected a problem at the Chevron refinery—that's a Richmond resident's automatic response, even though the system is in place for any hazardous materials incident. Stepping outside, we saw a dark plume in the sky off in the distance in the direction of the refinery. Simultaneously I got a phone call. It was Marilyn and others at the RPA office witnessing the ominous cloud of smoke moving across the city. I started making calls, as per protocol, and the Police Chief confirmed that the Richmond police and firefighters were at the refinery working directly with Chevron's in-house fire department. I left a message with Chevron's General Manager. One of their representatives called to say they were working to get it contained. Meanwhile television and radio stations broadcast a "shelter in place." We were warned to stay indoors to protect against breathing in toxic fumes. People were told to secure doors and windows with duct-tape, wet towels and blankets, and to turn off air conditioners. Richmond residents were in a state of fear and confusion. Parents rushed to whisk their children from our city parks and their early evening activities. BART, the Bay Area Rapid Transit system, as well as our regional bus system, stopped coming into Richmond. Many people were unable to return home from work or to leave Richmond to their homes in neighboring cities. In some places the loud, public warning system failed, in other locales the phone alert system did not work correctly, making matters even worse. Most people got their information from television and radio.

People talked later about how traumatizing it was watching this poisonous blanket of smoke move overhead with its accompanying chemical smell. The media reported all night, with footage of the flames and images of the dark moving cloud, seen as far away as San Francisco, twenty miles across the bay. It was terrifying.

That panic continued through the night. Phone calls and emails kept on coming through. I could hear fear in people's voices, concerned about the health and safety of their children, elderly relatives, and neighbors. While I wasn't a first responder or a medical professional, I could only tell people what I was hearing from our public safety providers to stay indoors, make sure your homes were tightly sealed, and call 911 if they had serious medical concerns. I felt both helpless and worried sick for all Richmond residents who are so dear to me.

Public Fallout

By the next morning the shelter in place was lifted. The fire had been contained, although controlled burns would continue for days. Luckily there were no reports of fatalities. Preliminary probes indicated that nineteen refinery workers had been engulfed by flammable vapor on the evening of the fire, and eighteen of them barely crawled to safety facing what workers later called a "wall of fire." Another worker, a Chevron firefighter, only survived due to protective gear he wore as flames encircled the cab of his engine. But it wasn't just workers who experienced the disaster. On the night of the fire and over the coming days, 15,000 people sought treatment for respiratory ailments at local hospitals and clinics. Emergency rooms were packed with people experiencing symptoms such as breathing difficulty, stinging eyes and nasal passages, heavy coughing, and skin reactions. People with compromised immune systems, the aged, children with respiratory ailments, and others were particularly struck. The health impact on our community was vast and pervasive.

Chevron knew it had a major public relations problem at hand. Its image wasn't doing so well anyway, but this explosion and fire thrust them into a whole new level of public relations work. The next day they held a town hall meeting in the auditorium of our civic center. Chevron representatives apologized and tried to assuage people's fears, asserting that safety is their highest priority. The public was incredulous. So was I.

I flashed back to 2007 when, in my first month as mayor, there was another fire at the refinery—lesser in size and scope, but one that also triggered a "shelter in place." After that fire, Chevron raved about their safety procedures. They assured everyone that they operate the safest refinery in existence, claiming it was just a small glitch and the public had not been put in danger. Here we were again five years later with nineteen workers barely escaping with their lives and Chevron telling us once again how they are tops in safety. I reminded Chevron at that very town hall meeting that they had told us this back in 2007 and that our community would not be deceived again.

Hundreds of people gathered at that meeting, expressing their outrage, fury, and fears. A whole range of raw emotions filled the room. People clearly recognized that their safety had been compromised. One memorable action that night came from Urban Tilth, the city's premier urban agriculture group. Members of the group brought produce they had pulled from their gardens that could not be harvested and eaten due to contamination concerns. In street theater fashion, they tossed the produce at the feet of the panel of Chevron representatives and public agency officials.

Chevron's post-fire town hall meeting turned into a public relations fiasco. Our community stood up to Chevron and showed they were not buying the corporation's attempt to smooth ruffled feathers. Richmond residents demanded better answers.

Source of the Blast

The community spontaneously rose up in protest in the aftermath of the fire and RPA sprang into action, working hand in hand with environmental justice and labor groups, publicizing actions and meetings to mobilize as a united front. The power of the people was needed.

Early reports indicated there had been a leak in a pipe carrying hot, flammable gas oil in the refinery crude unit. When Chevron employees discovered the leak, rather than shutting operations, their managers instructed them to keep the unit running and remove the insulation from the leaking pipe. This led to the pipe's rupture and the formation of the huge vapor cloud. Within moments a fireball ignited and poisonous black smoke rapidly spread over our city neighborhoods.

But community and union workers were up in arms and wanted answers. As mayor, I was also determined to lead in that inquiry. The City held meeting after meeting with panels of representatives from both Chevron and the regulatory agencies.

Thanks to an investigation by the U.S. Chemical Safety Board (CSB), an independent federal agency with board members appointed by the U.S. President, we learned that the pipe was seriously corroded, worn down to less than the thickness of a dime, due to the presence of sulfur compounds at high temperatures in the crude unit.

Other agencies—federal, state and regional—also investigated. In time more problems would be revealed. I introduced resolutions at City Council meetings demanding better safety procedures and technology in the rebuilding of the crude unit of the refinery. RPA and our allies organized, mobilized, and made statements at the many public meetings that various agencies held. The RPA electronic newsletter continued to inform the public with calls for action in the post-fire period, our vision of community empowerment always leading the way. We weren't about to let up and leave it in the hands of Chevron and the regulators.

Chevron, Guilty as Charged

As time went on, investigations began to further unfold as criminal charges were filed, violations cited, and fines levied. The Chemical Safety Board did the most extensive investigation. Over a period of two and a half years, it published three comprehensive reports that included a host of recommendations for Chevron, the regulatory agencies, and the City of Richmond and Contra Costa County.[33] CSB meetings were predictably well attended. To explain the situation to the public, the Board created an instructive animation video vividly depicting the incident.[34] When the video was shown at various community meetings, the public watched with horror to see how quickly the fire engulfed the workers who narrowly escaped the raging fire.

The CSB reported that Chevron's managers had heard from their own engineers, by way of at least six reports, that pipes were corroding and needed inspection and replacement. The tragic reality was that managers ignored those warnings, including the corroded pipe that had failed back in 2007, continuously deferring action. It was only by sheer luck that none of the workers were killed, and it's clear that had weather conditions been different, the plume could have remained closer to the ground, rather than thrust high into the air, creating an even more catastrophic impact for our community.

The California Occupational Safety and Health Agency (Cal OSHA) issued twenty-five citations with penalties totaling nearly $1 million for willful and serious violations. That fine was the highest the agency could institute, but it seemed trivial compared to the harm afflicted on our community. Another agency, the U.S. Environmental Protection Agency (EPA), found sixty-two regulatory failures, stating that these violations indicated "an overarching failure to implement an effective management system."[35]

In August 2013 the oil giant had to pay $2 million in fines and was given three years probation after pleading "no contest" to criminal charges filed by then California Attorney General Kamala Harris and Contra Costa County District Attorney Mark Peterson. During the probationary period, Chevron was required to inspect every piece of pipe identified as susceptible to sulfidation corrosion to ensure sufficient thickness. The criminal violations included failure to correct deficiencies in equipment, negligent emission, and failure to prevent employees' exposure to hazardous conditions. Both this $2 million and Cal OSHA's $1 million were woefully inadequate considering the trauma and harm this fire presented to workers and the community, and, of course, it was just a drop in the bucket for this billionaire corporation. However, it was good to see that regulatory agencies and the courts validated what RPA had been saying for years—that Chevron is a direct threat to our community and acts blindly and willfully in pursuing its profits to the detriment of life, health, and safety for workers and the Richmond community in which it resides.

Holding Industry's Feet to the Fire

One glaring omission in these settlements was that there was no compensation to the City of Richmond for the harm and economic damage endured by the city and community. We lost millions of dollars in property taxes. And who knows how many new business prospects, home buyers, and developments were deterred from settling in Richmond following this travesty? Many residents felt downhearted, as the fire was once again giving our city a blemish. At the same time there was no time to grieve, we needed to keep moving forward. All this was happening in the midst of a new progressive direction with an emergence of a new image, further opportunities, and a positive outlook for our city. We would not sacrifice this, but we knew we had a lot of work ahead of us to regain momentum.

In reality, the fire had slowed our progressive movement. It was time for us to act on our own behalf. The City Council had many discussions about potentially filing a lawsuit. In my eyes, it was clearly the right thing to do, and Jovanka strongly agreed. But we would have some tussles with other councilmembers.

Some members of the Council wanted a negotiated settlement with Chevron rather than taking them to court, so we agreed to have our staff talk with Chevron representatives first and see what agreements we could get without going to court. Predictably, the company was unwilling to bargain for much. Still, there were councilmembers who pressed for the City to be more compromising. Over and over again it became clear that there was a lack of political will even as Chevron had been so horrifically negligent.

For me, it was time to use the court system to address Chevron's crimes. The City of Richmond had never before initiated a lawsuit against its largest corporation and major polluter. I questioned how long the City could sit on the sidelines while our community was put at risk. Richmond couldn't just slip into quietude with the hope that regulators would make everything safe for us, ignoring the damages this fire had caused. This would be negligent on *my* part. As mayor, I wasn't about to let up on our progressive efforts. That meant standing up for ourselves in the face of a profit-hungry corporate culture that disregards everyone and everything in its path. So I kept the pressure on my council colleagues, knowing we needed at least four votes out of seven to set things in motion.

As always, it was the community that made the difference. RPA members and our allies came to Council meetings repeatedly laying it on the line that they expected their elected officials to do what was in their interest and not deter justice for Richmond. It was time to go to court.

Much to my delight, eventually, the City Council voted unanimously to file. Looking back, that Council vote was a momentous occasion. While some on the Council were not initially for it, they realized that this was one of those historic votes when it really mattered to be on the side of justice. While the lawsuit is still in the court system, this was already a political victory for progressives. When your opposition swings to your side, knowing it as the side of the people, you have politically advanced. Bringing this lawsuit forward was historic in that the people of my city, for the first time ever, are having their government stand for them in a battle with the big polluter in their own backyard. The lawsuit calls for the utmost safety for Richmond residents and seeks financial compensation for economic damage, including the costs of emergency response, firefighting, environmental cleanup, alleviating harm to public health, and loss of value in city property. A year after the explosion, on August 6, 2013, at a press conference held in City Hall, I announced to the public that the City of Richmond had just filed a lawsuit:

> We need accountability from Chevron to ensure safety for our community so this never happens again. And we need to safeguard the public's right to health and to enjoyment of our city without the threat of injury—due to yet another failure by Chevron to ensure the safe operation of their facility.

> So we filed this lawsuit today to bring forward this issue through the transparency of the public courtroom. We think our community should not have to live in fear of another fire and explosion. Fourteen incidents have occurred since 1989. So this is about, first and foremost, a change in Chevron's corporate culture to place safety as a top priority.

This was a major accomplishment from a city which just a

mere decade ago was run by Chevron. One of RPA's consistent goals has been to hold Chevron accountable, and we have never veered from that mission. We know we are not alone. Confronting the oil industry takes the power of numbers, and our call for environmental justice in Richmond is echoed by people across our nation and around the world.

In fact, just two days prior to the press conference, 3,000 people marched to the refinery to mark the first anniversary of the Chevron explosion. There were unions, environmental organizations and community activists all taking to our streets calling for no more toxic hazards, no refining of dirty crude, no Keystone Pipeline and yes to clean energy. Mostly this was a Bay Area march,

First anniversary of Chevron fire

but people came from across the nation, and some international guests joined in the demonstration. Over 200 people nonviolently risked arrest that day. The action was orderly and planned ahead of time with our police department, who also respected the peoples' right to peacefully protest. Even our police chief attended the rally. He was clad in plain clothes, but came to the event and shook hands with the protesters.

But when the crowds leave, it is the people of Richmond who remain here, as is the case in any urban center that lives with toxic dangers. It is up to us to continue to be vigilant in the struggle for a safe and healthy city. There have been subsequent fires at the refinery and major flaring incidents since that August fire, and while those have not been as severe, they are a reminder that we can't rest secure and leave safety measures up to Chevron's vigilance.

In addition to Chevron, new fossil fuel dangers have emerged in our fair city. We have taken up the fight against highly explosive Bakken Crude that for a time was being transported by rail to Kinder Morgan, an off-loading terminal in the city, without an Air District permit.[36] We have also called for federal regulations on the overall movement of crude by rail (often called "bomb trains") and championed new rules for coal and petcoke transport and storage as well.

The fossil-fuel industry is still largely unregulated. We have a long way to go, but every victory sets us closer to our goal. Every win for safer and healthier communities sets a precedent and example that communities are not willing to be pawns in the big business race for quick profits, given the dangers they pose.

As I write this chapter, I can't help noting the remarkable environmental campaign waged by the American Indian tribe at Standing Rock in North Dakota. Valiant and courageous protestors, known as "water protectors," staked out their ground for weeks and months in cold weather, suffering abuse and hostility at the hands of police who protected the fossil fuel industry against the health and safety of the people. Their political will and perseverance temporarily stopped the pipeline from going through their land and polluting their water resources. The pipeline company, aided by local and state law enforcement, ruthlessly pushed to keep construction moving so that they could send their crude oil to Gulf Coast refineries. What happened at Standing Rock was well known to the Richmond community. We are familiar with an industry's insatiable hunger for profit that is a disaster for land, people, and our planet.

Richmond continues to play a strong role on the environmental battlefront in our city and in solidarity with others. As we continue to grow our local movement, RPA links with progressives everywhere to stand up against the fossil fuel industry's irresponsible and unsafe practices. Our struggles unite us, and through each other's victories, we become stronger. Each step is important even as we know that ultimately the way to protect our communities from these dangerous fossil fuels is to shift toward renewable energy. Corporations will not lead the way to this better world; their indifference to our lives and the planet must be challenged for our own sake and that of generations to come.

A united, energized community will usher in a green economy and a shared porsperity.

The Art of Governing and a Symphony of Successes

Richmond's political theater was filled with enough drama, disruption, and dysfunction to almost derail the RPA from advancing our progressive agenda. But I held onto my dreams for that better Richmond I had campaigned on. And indeed, we accomplished much in my council and mayoral years. Despite the downturn of the economy during the Great Recession and the deep-rooted challenges facing many of our residents, we carried the day in many tough areas. This chapter recounts some of those successes in areas as disparate as supporting and spreading the arts throughout our city, promoting community empowerment, immigrant rights, health and wellness, education, and addressing crime—all with dwindling resources.

Each production had its own theatrical struggles, tussles, and skirmishes before we saw progress or victory. And yet each play brought us closer to fulfilling our foundational RPA goals: restoring democracy and efficiency, community safety, financial health, environmental safety, basic justice and the joy of living in our city. Every act and scene enhanced the set for the progressive design of today's Richmond.

Painting Broad Strokes to Keep the Arts Alive

I was fortunate to learn and be inspired by dance during my youth through subsidized lessons at a local Chicago park. That experience stayed with me as an adult, imbuing in me a love of art in all its forms, including an appreciation of art's power to heal, uplift, and expand my outlook. I knew that if our city was going to seriously play a role in bringing enrichment to the lives of our residents, I needed to make space for the arts.

One of my first appointments as a councilmember was serving as liaison to our city's Arts and Culture Commission. At that time funds for the arts were about to be eliminated from the City budget. A commissioner and a city staff person asked for my help to keep funding available, and I worked with them to come up with a plan. From my Council seat, I spoke with sincerity and passion about supporting the arts. Together with advocates throughout the city, we successfully compelled the Council to preserve the funding. Standing strong for the arts came easy for me and was a key RPA priority. We were clear that artistic and creative pursuits were essential to Richmond's transformation.

We began the arts insurgence by continuing a number of festivals as one way to demonstrate support for cultural diversity and celebrations. These festivities included Juneteenth, Cinco de Mayo, the Homefront Festival, the North Richmond Shoreline Festival, Martin Luther King Jr. Day of Service, Sisters in Solidarity, a Native American Powwow, a literacy fair, Spirit and Soul Festival, and various youth and music events. These festivals, parades, and special days have been a vital part of Richmond's community life. Many people in our community hold dear the importance of creating and producing cultural expressions to celebrate our ethnic heritages as part of what it means to live in the United States and as a part of our democracy.

By 2011, we seemed to be on a trajectory for artistic advancement. The City helped fund three major arts institutions: the East Bay Center for the Performing Arts, the Richmond Art Center, and Nurturing Independence through Artistic Development (NIAD). We also helped the East Bay Center renovate its historic downtown building, so that young dancers, musicians, and actors—mostly from low-income families, could be subsidized by the Center and have a state-of-the-art performing space.

Our Arts and Culture Commission and the Public Arts Advisory Committee both established and spearheaded the Public Art Program. This program reviews public art proposals that are funded through a one-and-a-half percent allocation on all eligible capital improvement projects on public property. This small provision has led to a robustness of the arts throughout Civic Center and some of Richmond's neighborhoods.

Each cultural celebration offers its own enrichment. For example, the annual Richmond Powwow, launched and organized by Richmond Native American organizer Courtney Cummings, brought a new level of awareness to the broader community. Today the Richmond community-at-large is more mindful and has a fuller appreciation of the history and traditions of our nation's first people, who lived here thousands of years before our city came into being.

Guerilla Art

In early 2011, Richmond's Arts and Culture Manager, a local art teacher, and some of our Arts Commissioners informed me that our Department of Code Enforcement had ordered the destruction of a mural on the bare wall of a building facing the Richmond Greenway. This mural was designed and painted by students at Gompers High School, located across from a community garden that was also created by these young people. They had received permission from the building owner to paint the mural and did so under the guidance of their art teacher. They had tried to get permission from the city, only to discover there was no established procedure in place.

The mural was created in the style of graffiti art as an expression of the students' pride in their school and community. After the mural was completed, it was declared a code violation of the City's graffiti ordinance and the young artists were told they had to paint over it. They obeyed. As mayor, I stood with these young artist activists. City Hall needed to become educated on graffiti art as a valid form of art. The young people explained the difference between "tagging"—acts of vandalism that warrant abatement—and the use of graffiti art embedded in the visual design of a mural.

This wasn't the first time Code Enforcement had erroneously ordered the destruction of a mural on private property, it had happened twice before. It was time to educate the adults in the city, and Richmond youth were eager to take the lead. To support their agenda, I placed a study session on the City Council agenda and invited the Gompers students to speak before the Council. The Gompers artists came to the Council with their painted signs and spoke about how devastating it was for them to have their artwork destroyed, especially after they had made every attempt to do the right thing in the right way.

With the support of allies from a local youth center, the RYSE Center, along with the ACLU, who supported their First Amendment rights to free expression, the young people made their case. At first some councilmembers were reluctant to resolve the issue, supporting the City's right to control graffiti as part of our beautification plan. It took just one more meeting a month later, with more intense organizing, to bring all the councilmembers on board to grant them permission to repaint the mural without censorship. The city even supplied the paint.

When the new mural was finished, we held a magnificent unveiling, inviting the press and members of the public to view this public art gracing our Greenway. What we saw on that day, and still behold to this day, is a bright and colorful wall with graffiti art lettering woven among jungle animals, flowers, and frogs. The students gave themselves a name, "the Gompers Guerillas." They had not only created a mural, they had spearheaded a campaign challenging City Hall.

Guerilla art mural

The lesson was twofold. This group of young people learned they could organize on their own behalf and win, and City Hall had listened to both young people and artists. City Hall embraced creative pursuits on behalf of artistic expression as a benefit for the city.

Richmond's cultural terrain continues to develop. One can't rush such a changing landscape, but it is important for cities to embrace the arts and make space for art and artists who add depth and beauty to our lives and our cityscape.

Folk Art: A People Bouquet

In addition to promoting the arts as part of our municipal experience, I wanted to expand and develop cultural empowerment more generally on the political and social landscape for our city. I had learned of the term "community cultural development" promoted by two Richmond residents and experts in the field, Don Adams and Arlene Goldbard. They define the concept of culture as "the sum total of signs, beliefs, artifacts, social arrangements and customs created by human beings."[37] Adams and Goldbard go on to describe community cultural development as "the work of artist-organizers ('community artists') who collaborate with others to express identity, concerns, and aspirations through the arts and communications media, while building cultural capacity and contributing to social change."[38] For me, this was the next step in using the arts and community advocacy to build bridges among separate groups in Richmond.

I envisioned collaborations and dialogues on how to resolve issues of mutual concern among residents and organizations throughout the city that would both elevate individuals and help spur a new collective identity for Richmond. Toward that end, I proposed to the City Council that we hire Don Adams to facilitate such conversations. Though the Council didn't approve my request, I was not discouraged. After all, we had already been promoting an atmosphere of engagement through the RPA in the socio-political sphere. It just reinforced the need to continue changing the political culture within our city to develop dynamic and vigorous community culture. The raw material for this change was alive and well in the hearts, minds, and aspirations of our people.

The rich diversity of race, history, and cultural background that make up our city formed a sound foundation for building a united and emboldened community identity that valued and lifted up each and every resident. The Council rejected my community engagement proposal (to hire Adams) but I knew that cultural empowerment would still be a platform to promote the dialogue and engagement needed to bring social change.

This work of building unity and empowerment had deep roots in Richmond and stands on the shoulders of many community activists. One of these advocates was Fred Jackson, a long-time community leader who lived in North Richmond. Fred was a deeply loved African American community advocate, political activist, poet, writer, and singer/songwriter. Fred could turn a phrase and create vivid metaphors that aptly described community. He coined the term "people bouquet" which he described as "the idea that our earth is a garden of humanity, populated with human flowers of many colors and shapes. Although we have many variations in appearance, language, culture, and beliefs, we are all part of one human family."[39]

Richmond is a lush example of this garden of humanity, with all our accomplishments and possibilities. Together with RPA's grassroots efforts, I worked as an activist mayor to find ways to break down barriers of race and cultural differences so that we could grow and nurture our common experience as a united community. We needed to build bridges between our Black and Brown communities. While these residents were neighbors and had a shared experience of discrimination, injustice, and oppression, other tensions kept them from working together on their mutual problems. As Richmond's population shifted from a predominately African-American one to a majority Latino demographic, tensions rose between the groups. This was understandable, since neither group had access to sufficient opportunities for sustainable jobs or financial advancement. Many among each community knew that these divisions were unproductive and sought to come together.

My office helped to stimulate one unifying effort through an annual "Sisters in Solidarity" event, a celebration of International Women's Day, begun in 2008. An offshoot of that inspirational event was the beginning of another women-led effort, "Building Bridges." These conversations transformed into an ongoing program organized by women of color to learn about each other and promote a supportive environment. The first of these dialogues was sponsored by Black Alliance for Just Immigration (BAJI),

The Latina Center, Black Women Organized for Political Action (BWOPA), the City of Richmond Human Rights Human Relations Commission, and Neighborhood House of North Richmond. RPA participated, represented by Councilmember Jovanka Beckles and Nicole Valentino, in her capacity as Community Advocate in my office. Today, many of these women join together as leaders in a number of important struggles in Richmond.

Harmonizing with our Newcomers

Richmond's diversity is enhanced with significant groups of immigrants. The mere sound of the word immigration conjures up discord in our local and national arenas. The controversy over how to best deal with the influx of people to our region is far from settled, but Richmond offers some steps in addressing this pressing issue. While it may seem precipitous to mention this in a chapter focused on successes, it bears mentioning that many people who live and work in Richmond have been spared greater pain and anguish by the measures we have taken to protect immigrants. Even as our actions may seem incremental, they offer solutions for other cities to emulate.

As mentioned in my first chapter on Richmond's demographics, of Richmond's hundred thousand plus residents, one-third are foreign born, two-fifths are Latino/as, one-quarter are African-Americans, less than one-fifth are White, and under a sixth are Asian-American. We are also home to small populations of Native Americans and Pacific Islanders. Immigrants and refugees have long been on Richmond activists' agendas, including the RPA, which has listed justice for our diverse populations among its highest priorities.

I remember one day in particular, going back to the early years of RPA. It was May 1, 2006. We designated it as the "Day of the Immigrant." Thousands of people congregated in Civic Center Plaza and out onto the city streets to demonstrate our united efforts toward unity and support for immigrants. Advocates, elected officials, faith and community leaders, and others came out in force. Our rally for immigrant rights felt like a human chain of solidarity threaded by the diverse layers of our community. Fred Jackson was there, among community leaders of all races. As a councilmember, I spoke alongside Fred and others raising awareness of our broken federal immigration policy. I felt connected to the struggle of so many who had undergone hardship as they fled poverty and war. I knew their aspirations were like those of so many others in our city and country, wanting to pursue a decent life by working hard and wanting to raise their families in safety and security. I wanted to do everything I could to assure a pathway to achieving those goals.

After the march, many of us took BART to San Francisco, where we participated in the 100,000-person immigration rights march. Latino leaders organized that bigger march as part of "The Great American Boycott"— a one-day action led by immigrants who attend schools and work in businesses. It had an international reach, with even Mexico and some Central American countries participating.

Richmond had already implemented a number of protections for immigrants (see chapter "Baptism By Fire"). We had in place a non-cooperation with Immigration and Customs Enforcement (ICE) policy meaning our police department would not cooperate with ICE authorities, except in criminal cases. Then, with RPA leadership, we successfully launched a campaign to stop driver's license checkpoints. These checkpoints were found to be discriminatory, as the vast majority of cars being towed belonged to individuals with Latino surnames. We also assured that day laborers have the right to solicit work in front of Home Depot, seeking to get hired for construction, moving, and landscaping work. We believe these workers have a right to solicit work. In addition to these changes, we implemented a municipal ID, regardless of immigration status, to assure services for all our residents.

In 2009 Richmond joined two other cities across our United States by proclaiming our city as a Human Rights City. We adopted the United Nations Resolution to Human Rights as an initiative that started in our Human Rights Human Relations Commission (HRHRC). The Commission has been honoring December 10, Human Rights Day, in various ways since the resolution was adopted. The first Human Rights Day action was a day of support and unity with and for day laborers, delivering breakfast, coffee, and bilingual literature providing legal assistance and health care

Municipal IDs (immigration)

information to those congregating at Home Depot and another location in the vicinity.

We have also reaffirmed our stance as a sanctuary city. We have asserted our refusal to scapegoat immigrants for the problems many politicians heap upon them. We welcome refugees and people coming to settle in our city. Immigration is a complicated issue that needs to be resolved on many fronts. So while they fiddle in Washington over who is to blame, who should pay, and whether to keep people in or out of our nation, in Richmond we unite as a community and sing our song together. Every voice is welcome to the choir.

The Culinary Arts: Sugar Overload

The simmering obesity crisis among the poor, and especially young people, caught the attention of the City Council in 2010. Dr. Jeff Ritterman, the Kaiser doctor and RPA councilmember, connected the dots of poverty, childhood obesity, and diabetes, as those issues are connected to increased consumption of sugar, particularly sugary drinks. Jeff cited a report prepared by the Contra Costa Health Services showing that more than half of Richmond's children were overweight or obese, and medical experts asserted that sugary beverages were a huge part of the problem. Today this concern has broad appeal across our nation, resulting in many creative solutions, from taxing sugary drinks to citywide public health programs advocating less sugar consumption. But Richmond was the first city to take this issue on legislatively.

We started our campaign with two local actions. The City Council placed an ordinance on the 2012 November ballot mandating a one-cent citywide tax per ounce on the sale of sugary beverages. This came to be known as the "soda tax." Recognizing we needed to use those taxes effectively, we placed a companion initiative on the ballot that would advise the Council to spend those tax dollars on sports and recreational programs—in effect to address not just stemming the consumption of sugar, but also to combat obesity through exercise and better health habits.

Our focus had been to address obesity and health. We had not intended to take on Big Soda, even though we knew they directly market to youth with their millions of advertising dollars. We simply wanted to dish up healthier prescriptions and begin addressing the obesity problem. Big Soda responded with a recipe overloaded with sour politics. Pepsi, Coca-Cola, and other beverage suppliers descended on Richmond, spending $2.5 million to oppose the measure. They outspent our campaign by a ratio of thirty-five to one. Big Soda made claims that the tax was discriminatory, that it was a blatant attempt to hit low-income people, largely people of color in Richmond. We responded by citing dire public health statistics for Richmond youth, as well as our expectation of revenue of $2–4 million a year that could be used for the youth activities and health education.

This campaign would become fraught with more tartness than just Big Soda's money. The soda tax became a wedge issue and spoiled more than just the added cost of sugary drinks. Big money from pro-corporate sources (including $1.2 million from Chevron) was used to attack our progressive, corporate-free City Council candidates, Eduardo Martinez and Marilyn Langlois, who both passionately supported the soda tax bill. Alas, we did not bring down Big Soda. While we vigorously responded to all their lies and raised this issue on the electoral stage to our constituents, we lost the soda tax initiative. Our two RPA candidates were casualties as well.

So what was the success? We educated our community about the public health problem of obesity facing significant populations in Richmond, and we highlighted the health problems of too much sugar, particularly in beverages. RPA also gained more name recognition, and our community benefitted from hearing the views of two principled, corporate-free candidates. We gave Big Soda a run for their money and made an impression on other cities across our land. Four Bay Area cities—Berkeley, San Francisco, Oakland, and Albany—have since passed soda tax initiatives, as have Philadelphia and Boulder, Colorado, among others. Mexico even followed suit on the issue. Some cities are instituting other ways to curb consumption of sugary beverages without taxation, so we recognize there is not just one way to address this public health crisis. But the fight started here in Richmond, California—we prepared the taste tests.

While perhaps lacking the perfect sweetness of success on this public health crisis, we did not stop addressing it simply because that one attempt did not go our way. Democracy can be messy. Each venture we take on can take a long time to bear fruit. In the aftermath of the soda tax, the City Council adopted Health in All Policies (HiAP). This is a strategy and ordinance that sets a framework of collaboration within city departments, community groups, and other agencies to continue working toward health equity. We are implementing an innovative program, thanks to a multi-million dollar grant, called "Healthy Richmond" that looks at broader aspects of health beyond the physical, including health education and violence prevention. Working with non-profits, foundations, and organizations, we have made health a centerpiece of our city's practice.

Rhyme, Reason, and Education

Cities with majority populations living in poverty face other challenges beyond health and welfare. Their schools also suffer. Failed federal policies, like No Child Left Behind, left the most needy schools with scant resources. Many Richmond schools were also bereft of books and other essential tools most of us took for granted in our early public education systems. Richmond's educational cupboards were threadbare.

On top of that, our school district, which encompasses five cities including Richmond, was still reeling from the effects of a California State debt produced by district financial mismanagement nearly two decades earlier. Schools were one of RPA's prime focus since our inception, so we organized and educated many people, and we allied with other groups in those early years. We took to the streets and joined the "2004 March4Education to Sacramento" demanding forgiveness of the debt. A few hundred students, parents, teachers, and community members walked ninety miles from Richmond to the steps of the State capitol in Sacramento during spring break, sleeping in churches and community centers along the way. Taking this battle to the steps of the Capitol was just one testament to the political will of our community. Our first triumph was achieving a reduction of the debt, including improved district finances.

In time, the debt would be totally eliminated, but not before the school district would propose closing three Richmond neighborhood schools. I wrote an editorial in the *Contra Costa Times* with a call to unify and organize to save our schools. With the school community mobilized and unified, the City Council ultimately agreed to provide three million dollars to keep our neighborhood schools open. It was another victory fueled by working together and amassing large numbers of parents, teachers, and students to make it happen—democracy in action, for sure.

RPA then partnered with the city and our school district to make sports fields available at low rental rates all across town. We formed a group called Safe Fields Coalition that organized sports teams to advocate with one voice and hence have more power representing more students. In addition to sports, a scholarship program has been established for every Richmond high school graduate as part of a community benefits agreement with Chevron.

My personal focus on education has extended beyond the monetary support. Having briefly been a teacher myself, I knew the value of engaging with young people in my role as mayor, both to encourage them in their learning as well as to listen to what they say. I visited many schools, where I heard our young people read aloud and share their poems and essays with me. I was often brought to tears with the depth of emotion they expressed as well as the earnest teachers who guide these developing minds. I was constantly reminded too, of the value of art as a vehicle for human enrichment. I was moved by the creativity and thoughtfulness these young students put into their communications on topics such as ending street violence, saving the planet, and, of course, friendships and family. Staying close to the youngsters who are the beneficiaries of school funding and educational advocacy reminded me time and again why I fervently fight in their corner.

Other school challenges in Richmond include the rise of charter schools. RPA certainly understands a parent's choice to send their kids to charter schools, especially when they have seen failure in the public education system up close and personally. Yet we remain concerned that charter schools, largely funded by public education money, drain resources from those students who attend public schools. And charter schools are not equal opportunity education providers—they do not accept every child, unlike public schools whose mission is to assure education for all. The fight to stem the tide of charter schools is part of RPA's School Action Team. We continue to stand for education as a right, not a privilege.

And speaking of not providing for all, Richmond's low-income families face other challenges. With RPA's resourcefulness we promoted after-school services for children and rallied around the preservation of the district's Adult School. Richmond has a large number of people who need English language classes—programs often on the chopping block for funds. Realizing that many of our poorer students' parents need to learn English in order to increase their employability, we pressed to keep the Adult School running. We've also promoted a community school model, fostering partnerships between the school and community efforts, to share resources in order to further academic, health, and mentoring services for both students and the surrounding neighborhood.

Beyond the language skills adults need, City Hall sponsors a free program called LEAP, Literacy For Each Adult. This is a one-on-one or small group tutoring that helps adults earn a GED and other certificates. The program has boosted people's self-confidence as an added bonus. As mayor, I took particular joy when I was invited to participate in LEAP graduation ceremonies. Some of those grateful adults would later become more active participants in their neighborhoods, communities, and their children's education.

It gives me hope and inspiration to see students, teachers, and volunteer support staff advance so many efforts that cultivate a love of learning in our community. We have a lot to do to assure quality education for Richmond residents from early childhood onward. Every child deserves a quality education to peak their curiosity and tap into the wealth of their intellect and creativity. Their rhyme, reason, and keen study will lead them to become the poets, scientists, doctors, teachers, and critical thinkers required for our changing world.

Tuning Up the Minimum Wage

We do our best to educate our young people, yet, in a community such as Richmond, many are still not able go to college, given its extravagant cost. Additionally, like many young people, Richmond youth often work part-time while in high school, often contributing to their household income. After high school, many of these young adults want to enter the workforce full-time. Yet most establishments will not provide enough wages to help these new hires live as fully independent, self-sufficient adults. In Richmond, as throughout the nation, most workplaces that hire young workers—as well as immigrants and other workers—offer hourly wages that are nothing close to a subsistence level. In fact the federal minimum wage languishes at an inflation-adjusted amount lower than it was in the 1970s, a shameful level for such a wealthy nation as the United States.

Long before the Fight for Fifteen Campaign we passed an ordinance to raise the minimum wage in Richmond to $13/hour with a phased-in approach. In January 2017 we increased the wage to $12.30, and in 2018 it will be raised to $13/hour. Every year hence, the wage will increase as per the rate of inflation.

By comparison, California's minimum wage is currently $10.59 and won't increase to $13 until 2020. Once again, our local movement-building efforts were put to work. This accomplishment included many community partners. RPA's Juan Reardon brought the idea and draft ordinances to the forefront, and the final policy was brought to fruition by one of my staffers, Shoji, who worked with youth and community organizations, small business owners, and UC Berkeley researchers to achieve this major win. Shoji is taking the lead again in organizing a new effort to increase Richmond's minimum wage to $15 dollars in 2019. Upping the notes on this scale won't be complete until everyone can earn a living wage.

Striking a Chord for Peace

In Richmond's urban core, you'll meet a majority of people who can name a brother, father, uncle, or cousin who is or was in prison. Generations of poverty, racism, neighborhood neglect, the crack cocaine epidemic, and the practice of incarcerating so many of our Black and Brown brothers has laid the foundation for Richmond's school to prison pipeline.

Wanting to understand what we needed to do to stop this cycle of violent crime in our community, I, at the invitation of some faith-based community members, visited a nearby prison, San Quentin Penitentiary, just across the Richmond/San Raphael Bridge, and met with some incarcerated men.

The first time I ventured into this world was while I was a councilmember in 2005. I visited a group of men who were part of what was known as the "Richmond Project." This group of Richmond men organized themselves into a self-help group, aided by non-profit organizations and volunteers from the outside. San Quentin is one of the few prisons that facilitates positive programs for their inmates, and the Richmond Project rates highly. I was impressed with the way these men were transforming their lives. They explore social and psychological factors underlying their behavior and past actions, they further their education, and they engage in artistic endeavors. All of this was evidence that these men could find ways to better their lives even behind prison walls.

After that first visit and throughout my years as mayor, I regularly visited the men, often a number of times a year. I assisted in projects facilitating communication from the men to the outside community, especially our Richmond youth. Their messages, sent through videos or essay contests, were of peace and guidance. They implored our Richmond youth to utilize opportunities available to them to better their lives and not become engaged in the downward spiral of violence that could lead them to prison.

These men shared with me their heart-wrenching stories, their deep regrets, and their motivation and desire to make a contribution to our community. I could see first-hand the progress many of them made inside those prison walls. Many of the men were repeat offenders, and they explained to me the recurring problems they would have upon release that contributed to their return to prison. They could not find the same level of support in Richmond that they had received inside prison. I knew we needed to find a way to reduce the 70% recidivism rate and help formerly incarcerated individuals experience healthy re-entry into our community.

Our first attempts were the formation of two groups: Safe Return Project and CEASEFIRE. The Safe Return Project was largely made up of formerly incarcerated individuals. Its goal has been to help those returning from prison to get jobs, housing, and other needs. This program initially started as a program under the Office of Neighborhood Safety (ONS). The second group, CEASE-FIRE: Lifelines to Healing, was staffed by faith-based groups and dedicated community activists who used a two-layered approach to help the most vulnerable in our community. They began implementing Friday night walks with residents walking different neighborhoods of the city, having a presence on our streets and making sure young people of the neighborhood know that there was support for them. The other layer included "call-ins" where members of the faith community would telephone known offenders (often individuals affiliated with street factions) and offer them the option of accepting special services to get them off the police department's list of potential re-offenders. This went a long way in building trust for the ex-offender, being able to relate to someone who wanted to help him turn his life around but hadn't found the support. CEASEFIRE and Safe Return have helped many individuals stabilize their lives and have guided these men into services, providing them layers of community support.

While most of our re-entry service efforts centered on young men, women need these services as well. For women, the group

Reach Fellowship International, a religious organization, took up the mission to help women inmates returning from prison. They offer health services to assist women struggling with HIV/AIDS, and other ailments that have often prevented these women from being able to re-start their lives. Reach Fellowship International has held educational forums, workshops, and conferences for the community in which they identify some of these women's unique needs and distresses of women while in prison (for example, pregnancy). Working with the County, they created a women's transitional home, Naomi's House, where women are united with their children after they've served their time. Thanks to wonderful community leaders such as Bishop Edwina Perez-Santiago and Belinda Thomas, many women have come to experience light, hope, community, and sustenance for their futures.

On a legislative level, Richmond enacted some bold policies. We became one of the first cities in the nation to come up with a Ban the Box policy on City of Richmond employment applications to give equal chances of employment to those re-entering the job market after being incarcerated. We would later require all City contractors to adhere to this policy.

Our support for the formerly incarcerated was then put to the test in 2012 when Assembly Bill (AB) 109, came into play. This state-based law enforcement policy transferred responsibility for supervising certain felony offenders and prison parolees from state prisons and parole agents to county jails and probation officers. Each county in California was given funding to help restructure forthcoming prisoner releases in their regions. Two distinctly different ideas for how to deal with this process surfaced. The Contra Costa County sheriff wanted to build a new jail; RPA and other Richmond activists had a different vision. As mayor, I joined with our police chief and groups like the Contra Costa County Interfaith Supporting Organization (CCCISO), Safe Return Project, Office of Neighborhood Safety, and other community groups with another agenda. We countered the Sheriff's approach with ideas like: "Invest in people not in prisons." We came out in huge numbers at meeting after meeting, speaking up as a united community beseeching the use of AB 109 funding for re-entry and violence prevention programs to keep people from ending up in prison.

The sheriff relented on AB 109 and gave up his prison-building agenda, at least temporarily, demonstrating another success of people power. This shift toward investing in services rather than prisons resulted in building our Reentry Success Center in downtown Richmond. This is a welcoming, one-stop center that connects formerly incarcerated people and their families with services and resources to help them meet their short term and long term goals, whether family reunification, employment, health, housing, or other needs.

The sheriff kept coming back with more prison expansion proposals—first in 2013, again in 2015, and now in 2017. Two attempts have been roundly defeated with hundreds of people showing up at Council meetings, protests, and rallies. A current mobilization is underway to stop an expansion of the West County Detention Center, likely to make room for immigration roundups proposed by the current President's anti-immigration stance. But public sentiment in our city is that mass incarceration is not an answer to public safety.

Singing New Songs

We push back on bad ideas like expansion of jails, and we put that same energy into promoting and supporting good projects, like the construction of the West County Family Justice Center. This center provides a safe haven and pathway to healing for victims of rape, domestic violence, and sex trafficking, using the integration of a full service approach.

The need for such a center became clear in 2009 when a sixteen-year-old female was gang-raped on the night of a homecoming dance at one of our Richmond high schools. Adding to the horror was a group of onlookers who watched and did nothing. When this tragedy hit the national news, I was faced with not only needing to respond to this shocking crime, but also to figure out how to deal with our community which was in the spotlight in an unfair and harsh way, with cruel typecasting of our Richmond youth. The act was appalling, for sure, but this heinous deed represented a small number of young men—certainly, an aberration.

Hundreds of school youth accompanied by their teachers and supportive adults responded by choosing to present a different picture of their school and our city. Their first action was to hold a press conference and vigil. These concerned individuals brought attention to the serious issue of rape as it occurs not just in Richmond, but across our nation and world. The young people wrote and read poetry and recited heart-wrenching statements. They told the press that *they* were the youth of Richmond that the press should be highlighting. The press should emphasize what these young people had to say about their hopes, dreams, academic achievements, and aspirations. They demonstrated that Richmond youth care, citing statistics about the prevalence of crimes against women in our society, and expressing deep concern about the problem of rape and onlookers who stand aside and do nothing.

I was stunned watching the press latch onto this new story of Richmond where the youth led and acted responsibly with strength and courage. Those young people had been able to turn a tragic national story into a treatise on hope for their future, and they showed the public a profound lesson they had grasped. Richmond had shown its true colors for all to see as we continued our march forward to a better Richmond with heads held high, even as the tragedy left tracks in our hearts.

The Craft of Healing

We made significant inroads as we dealt with crime and violence over the years, but many Richmond residents still grieved from the losses of the tragic killings of their loved ones. I found myself deeply touched when I engaged with those families. I did not just attend those funerals, I worked with community organizations like Mothers Against Senseless Killing (MASK) and A Mother's Cry, where I heard the stories of mothers who had lost their children to violence. Family members shared their pain and gave each other support, eventually forming a collective to help others deal with the sadness. These women came together with open minds and hearts to seek ways to move beyond their grief. Families turned their pain into power. That became MASK's motto. My office partnered with MASK and other community groups to foster support groups for family members of victims.

I will never forget the heart-wrenching, sobbing mothers who held tight to the memories of their children. Their faces showed a deep sadness. I remember how they physically held their surviving children a bit closer, as they shed tears of grief for the sons and daughters they had lost but had once also held close.

I remember the first time I locked eyes with one of these mothers at a memorial service. The pained look in her eyes was a moment of truth for me. I felt helpless, knowing words of comfort would never be enough to ease her pain. My eyes welled up, too, but I held back the tears, believing I had to convey a strength and commitment to reverse the violence that had been at the root of her loss. Each of those grieving mothers also wanted to prevent other families from similar suffering, yet I felt the pang of needing to lead this struggle from my place as Mayor. I committed myself to redoubling efforts to violence prevention as one way to begin to comfort these mothers.

I attended many funerals and memorials, each one as heartbreaking as the next. Each phone call from the police announcing a homicide made my heart skip a beat—another lost life added to our yearly homicide count. My promise as mayor was that we remembered the victims not as statistics but as real human beings with grieving families and friends. One way I commemorated this vow to Richmond was by officiating at a special memorial every year. I held a simple and meaningful end-of-year gathering in which I would read the name and age of every victim who had been killed by homicide, as community members stood in a circle of healing and hope.

In time, due to a variety of violence prevention strategies, I can report a poignant success. The vicious cycle of violence slowed. Each year's list of victims grew shorter and shorter. By my last year as mayor, our homicide rate had decreased by 75%, with the list of victims down to eleven from a high of forty-seven. Richmond has been a beacon of hope to urban communities struggling with street violence. Yet we are also a place that holds the sacred memory of every precious life that we have lost.

Part of this success comes from our community-involved police force. Our officers deserve enormous praise for having shifted our city toward a new culture. This was started under the able leadership of Police Chief Chris Magnus. Our policing in Richmond is not totally rosy—there have been two fatal police-involved shootings over the span of a little over a decade, not as many as some urban centers across our nation, but still of grave concern.

One of those troubling deaths has become a project supported by RPA. Richard "Pedie" Perez, a 24-year-old, unarmed man was shot by a Richmond police officer in September 2014. The fact that this incident was the only police-involved shooting death since 2007 brings no comfort to the Perez family who seek justice for their son. But at the urging of the family and other activists, the City Council authorized a Civilian Police Review Commission to conduct a new investigation and strengthened their powers as a commission. In a groundbreaking ordinance, we now have a provision that all police activity that results in either a killing or serious bodily injury will be automatically investigated. We believe our community deserves a police force that is accountable and upholds the trust of the people it serves. We are working to create a culture of justice that permeates throughout the city.

An Expanding Mosaic of Social Change

Over the years, we have witnessed many progressive changes and successes in Richmond thanks to joint actions by many alliances. RPA has stretched itself again and again, forming coalitions with others to reach our goals. We've accepted that democracy does not come in a neat package, frustrating though that may be.

By 2013, Richmond's progressive changes were making headlines everywhere. Against all odds, we were becoming an empowered community finding our way to better health, crime reduction, quality education, and enhancing the arts. We have painted our future with boldness and sensitivity. With both fine and broad strokes in every local struggle and as part of national movements, we have created a montage of accomplishments.

The art of governing begins with democracy—government by our people and rule of the majority. Democracy is messy, takes a lot of time, and needs scads of people working together. Richmond's symphony of successes didn't happen overnight and we still need to improve some of our orchestration, but we have more pieces to play, and we are staying in tune with the songs our people want to hear and sing.

Housing, A Space Odyssey

The Great Recession may have officially spanned from late-2007 to mid-2009, but for Richmond the crisis loomed large for quite some time for the majority of our low-income population. Our city continued to live with an aging infrastructure amid rising costs to operate and maintain city functions. We wanted to break through the barriers and provide for the needs of our communities on a local level, but were feeling the enormous weight of the broader economic crisis. In 2010, we passed a resolution that called for a massive national public works program similar to the Works Progress Administration (WPA) of the 1930s. While my less progressive council colleagues kept wailing their time-worn phrase, "we are not the federal government, we must stop wasting our time discussing matters over which we have no control," the resolution was part of an important dialogue. While a new WPA-like program has yet to emerge, the discourse educated the public and kept the pressure on higher branches of government for real solutions.

The truth is that help from the federal and state government, even when promised, was not adequate. We had a few sources of aid: President Obama's Stimulus Package helped us create some new city programs, but that didn't last for long, and federal agencies like HUD (Housing and Urban Development) significantly cut its funding for public housing. In 2012, Governor Brown ended California's Redevelopment Program, which had brought funding for revitalizing large swaths of Richmond neighborhoods that had been identified for redevelopment. I did not agree with my fellow councilmembers that we should let the state and federal government off the hook and simply discuss matters under our municipal control. The Great Recession was a time to discuss our deeply flawed system and the inequities that it had produced. I strongly felt that it was this kind of provincialism and self-imposed limitations that the Council needed to overcome. As an elected official, it was incumbent upon me to promote discussion about these civic concerns, ensuring that our local constituencies are participants in building a better political set of circumstances in this country. As such, our conversations necessarily need to overlap from city to state to federal politics.

Richmond had insufficient revenue to serve our communities. Housing issues in particular needed to be addressed given the crisis at hand. Rent control had been an RPA priority from our inception in 2003 so we were poised for that battle. But in those early days even we did not foresee the foreclosure crisis that would emerge and have such a devastating impact on homeowners in Richmond. We also needed to address homelessness, which was increasing. All of it needed to be considered under the umbrella of a just economy for our entire community.

Star Burst: The Occupy Movement

In 2011, Occupy Wall Street drew attention to the inequities and wealth disparity unleashed by a largely unregulated financial industry. Protests, marches, tent cities, rallies, and other calls-to-action erupted throughout the nation as well as the Bay Area. They became known as the Occupy Movement, which was the political campaign that surrounded my second term as mayor. RPA embraced this spontaneous movement from its inception as a parallel effort to ours. I believed that Occupy was a moment whose time had come, one that we progressives had been working for. Our local movement in Richmond knew all about this inequality, given the billionaire oil giant in our city, it's history of corrupting local politics, and the economic strife left in the wake of those years. We were ready to become part of this greater movement.

During Occupy's rise, the City Council passed a resolution supporting the Movement with the expectation that our police department would respect and support the rights of protestors while refraining from the kind of tactics and police actions that had been used in neighboring cities—from spraying teargas into Occupy protestors' faces to shooting a protestor (a war veteran, no less). Police Chief Chris Magnus' support of our resolution boosted the vote for our more reluctant councilmembers. To show our city's solidarity with the greater movement, some RPA members created an Occupy Richmond group that held various activities in the city.

Occupy Richmond arose not in conflict with City Hall, but side by side with the RPA model of governance already in motion, mobilizing the community around our own needs and interests. RPA organized marches and speak-outs where people gathered and spoke about their concerns. One gathering took place on November 11, 2011 in Civic Center Plaza. It was a public forum organized for people to voice their concerns about the state of our economy and our nation. The purpose was to build community empowerment for further struggles in our city and beyond. That was surely where I wanted to be and I joined the Occupiers in solidarity and celebration of this budding movement.

Shining Lights: Celebrating and Remembering

The Occupy Richmond event wasn't the only affair I was invited to that day. I had received an invitation to speak at a Chevron-sponsored Veterans' Day gala at the Red Oak Victory, a restored World War II ship built during Richmond's shipbuilding era that has a special place in Richmond's history. I have enjoyed many tours and talks on board this amazing vessel.

I chose to speak at the Occupy event. With that simple decision, an avalanche of rightwing attacks came hurling at me. I received more vicious hate mail on that decision than on any other issue during my time as mayor. The right-wing media launched a full-force attack on me. Before I knew it, television, radio and print media, both local and nationwide, were all over this story about Richmond's disrespectful mayor who chose to attend an Occupy event championing Main Street over Wall Street and skipping the chance to honor a Veterans' Day event sponsored by a billionaire oil giant. Fox News covered the story, which I imagine is what triggered the flood of emails and letters, filled with obscenities, vile name-calling, and impassioned calls for my expatriation.

But joining the Richmond speak-out that day was more consistent with my values and the principles upon which our country has been built. When asked by the press why I chose the Occupiers over the Chevron-sponsored event, I explained that I choose to honor our veterans, not only on Veterans' Day, but daily, by supporting an end to military warfare and to prevent further fighting and dying in needless wars. I also brought out the fact that the speak-out was honoring Scott Olsen, the Iraq War vet who had been shot by Oakland police as he participated in an Occupy Oakland protest. Participants at the speak-out included Iraq Vets Against the War and Veterans for Peace. When I was an activist in Chicago, I had occasions to work with Vietnam Vets Against the War, so I was aware of the plight facing so many of them. It seemed hypocritical to me that our nation was not providing these men and women sufficient medical care to help them and their families overcome health issues and other hardships that are the direct result of having served in combat. Yet when the national budget gets carved out year after year, the lion's share of our country's spending goes to U.S. wars of aggression, causing immeasurable pain and suffering all over the world. Those much-needed funds enrich the pockets of the weapons industry and leave little for those who fought in those battles.

Meanwhile I also received numerous letters sounding a different tone, some from veterans themselves, telling me they respected my choice to attend the Occupy event. I'll never forget one letter from a Korean War vet who wrote to tell me that he respected my decision and has watched with horror over the decades as our country has gotten mired in war after war, illegally and immorally, with so many lives sacrificed. The America he thought he knew had become diminished in his eyes.

I was uplifted reading those letters, as well as by comments and concerns of others at the speak-out. At the same time I shared my thoughts about how Richmond has been leading the way toward a more equitable and sustainable transformation for several years, with the emergence of the RPA. The Occupy Movement offered a positive convergence with RPA's efforts already in play, as we participated in Occupy marches, rallies, and forums in Oakland and San Francisco as well as in Richmond.

On several occasions our police department escorted Occupy marchers through the streets of Richmond, stopping traffic to assure the safety of all participants, showcasing a different kind of police response from what people saw in the nightly news aired in other cities. And when Occupy Education, a subset of the Occupy Movement, marched through Richmond on their way to Sacramento to protest the rising cost of higher education, a local church—St. Mark's Catholic Church—gave them a place to sleep, and local volunteers made sure there was healthy food for them to eat. I felt a sense of gratification that the road to democracy was running through Richmond, as we opened our hearts to "occupiers" who, like us, were mobilizing to confront systemic injustices.

Eclipsing Wall Street: Eminent Domain for Homeowners

My parents bought a home and struggled with mortgage payments, believing that their hard work to maintain home ownership had the value of putting down roots for our family. While my parents were able (though often just barely) to make ends meet and continue to pay the mortgage, today many families in Richmond can't do the same.

By 2013, many in Richmond were still reeling from the foreclosure crisis. Though it was a gargantuan task, I saw my job as mayor to look for ways to help struggling homeowners. Here are some figures that tell the story about what this crisis looked like on the ground in Richmond. It will probably sound familiar, because many other cities across our land were hard-hit. Richmond home prices had plummeted 58% since the 2007 peak. Many neighborhoods had been (and still are) devastated by foreclosures. Citywide, the community of Richmond lost over $264 million in wealth in 2012 alone, and nearly half of the mortgages in the city were underwater. Our city government lost millions in property tax revenues. We thus had to cut funds for roads and other needed repairs, plus reduce many municipal employees through attrition. We had to spend scarce funds to deal with abandoned buildings, crime, and drugs, among other problems that were by-products of the foreclosure epidemic. Walking the blocks of North Richmond and the Iron Triangle, one could see the metamorphosis. Many homes sat vacant, with boarded up windows, copper wiring torn out by thieves, and yards that had become dumping sites.

Many of our Richmond homeowners, especially people of color, had been targets of predators in the financial industry. Bankers and brokers peddled high-cost rip-off loans to people who assumed that bankers wouldn't lend money if it was a bad risk. These bankers lent money knowing full well that these were bad loans and then turned around and sold the loans back to Wall Street. When teaser rates commonly associated with subprime mortgages jumped to higher rates, homeowners unable to afford their monthly home loan payments defaulted and faced foreclosure.

One homeowner, a Latina, became a spokesperson for these problems. She and her husband, a mechanic for a nearby school district, have two kids. They thought they were having a chance at the American Dream when they bought a modest home in 2005 for $420,000. By 2013 the home's value had dropped to $125,000 while they were making interest-only payments on the loan. With payments increasing due to the variable interest rate, and the family living paycheck to paycheck, they feared they would just have to walk away from their home, along with their dreams.

Another homeowner was a 57-year-old jazz musician living in the largely African-American Park Plaza neighborhood. He owed more than $400,000 on his mortgage, but his house was only worth about $130,000. Due to the unfair terms of his loan, in twenty-two years a single lump-sum payment of $194,000 would be due. How would he and his wife ever afford that balloon payment, especially when they are expecting to retire on fixed social security incomes?

For other families, financial disaster was more abrupt and immediate. One could only imagine the troubles that people were facing when all that remained of their possessions were boxes and furniture strewn across the yard—remnants of packing that wouldn't fit in the car as the family took off to stay with Grandma.

Things were bad. Our neighborhoods felt the impact in a host of different ways: people lost their homes, their stability, and their social support systems. One homeowner put it simply: "The banks won't help us. We have to help ourselves."

So we took matters into our own hands and acted where our federal government had not. We launched a Local Principal Reduction program. It was officially known as CARES (Community

Eminent domain

Action to Restore Equity and Stability), also known as the Eminent Domain Program. The purpose was to save homes and stimulate our local economy by putting money back in the hands of local residents. This plan was the brainchild of Robert Hockett, a Cornell law professor who specializes in the securitized mortgage market. But it was our bold embrace of the program in Richmond that gave it national attention. This venture required multiple partners: the City, special funders, and most important of all, the community. In Richmond, our main community support came from the Alliance of Californians for Community Empowerment, known as ACCE. Together, along with other groups, we led this mobilizing effort with vigor, including marches, protests at banks, Civic Center demonstrations, and public theater.

RPA had worked closely with ACCE, going back to the days when the organization was known as the Association of Community Organizations for Reform Now (ACORN). More recently, we joined efforts fining the big banks for not maintaining vacant properties and worked on various strategies for affordable housing. In 2013, we got national and international attention for the

Eminent Domain Program. We held marches, assemblies, and press conferences at the site of big banks throughout our city and region. As Richmond's mayor, I became a spokesperson for the program, and worked with ACCE publicizing both this program and Richmond's progressive direction as a city. The events were covered broadly by major media such as the *New York Times, Los Angeles Times, Nation Magazine, USA Today, Mother Jones,* Democracy Now!, MSNBC and other national and local news outlets. I even had inquiries from Europe and Latin America.

In essence, the Eminent Domain Program was a foreclosure prevention program which would stabilize our neighborhoods by keeping people in their homes with affordable mortgage payments and end the blight and crime associated with vacant properties. The City, with a funding partner that was prepared to cover all costs, stood poised to step in to buy certain mortgages—the loans, not the homes themselves—and thus help homeowners refinance or modify their mortgages to be in line with current home values and interest rates. Hundreds of families stood to see their mortgages lowered by an average of $130,000 and their monthly payments lowered by hundreds of dollars. We knew if we could make it happen, we could then expand and help thousands more homeowners.

Our point was simple. Legally, a city has the right to use eminent domain for a public purpose. Stabilizing neighborhoods to prevent blight and crime, as well as helping a city's homeowners stay in their homes and keeping the city's property taxes coming in, met this goal. The banks had repeatedly broken the law. In my opinion, a whole lot of those bankers should be sitting in jail for their white-collar crimes. When those bankers sold the predatory loans, there were next to no consumer protections in place to stop them. With or without the protections in place, their actions were ethically and morally corrupt and innocent people suffered. That was a gross injustice.

What we were seeking to do in Richmond was to step in and right a wrong, as well as prevent further devastation to both people and city government. A number of other cities also took steps to research and advance this program. Community groups and unions worked with their elected officials on this effort. Richmond even attempted to get a group of cities together to form a Joint Powers Authority to take further steps.

Here is what we said to Wall Street: there are a whole lot of troubled loans headed toward foreclosure. If you're willing to fix them, do so. If you are unwilling or unable to fix those troubled loans, sell the loans to us, the City, and we'll fix them. But if you aren't willing to let us buy the loans at fair market value so we can prevent further foreclosures, then we will use the power of eminent domain to advance this public purpose. So you, Wall Street, will then have to sell them to us. We'll still pay you fair market value and we'll do what is right by our homeowners by reducing the principal on these toxic loans you sold our community.

Wall Street would have nothing of this revolutionary project. Their lobbyists spent a whole lot of time in Richmond telling lies about the program, saying city officials were trying to acquire their actual homes rather than their underwater mortgages for modification. Their lobbyists also went to Washington D.C. and put pressure on Congress to kill this innovative program.

Still, we moved full speed ahead in Richmond. I was fascinated by the idea of utilizing the power of eminent domain to help homeowners rather than to displace residents for highways, shopping malls, and other commercial structures, as eminent domain had traditionally been used. Here was a wonderfully positive use of governmental power to help our working-class population in a city that had been devastated by foreclosures.

By late 2014 the program was killed by those D.C. lobbyists and politicians who do Wall Street's bidding. Congress passed a new law that refused government insurance for any new or modified mortgage that came about through an eminent domain transaction. That presented an insurmountable barrier for our program. I think what was equally at stake was Wall Street realizing that its dominance over the financial system had been challenged by a local community and its mayor.

We subsequently shifted our efforts and have made some gains getting delinquent loans sold to non-profits (rather than speculators) with the same mission of preventing foreclosures. We need to do more to both expose the financial industry's hegemony and help unwitting victims. But the courage and fortitude we showed in taking on Wall Street from the grassroots has built up the political muscle of a community willing to level the housing and economic playing fields.

A Stable Landing Pad: Richmond's Rental Market

Nearly half of Richmond residents are renters. While RPA had rent control on its priority list from our beginning, the history of this activism started even earlier. In spring 2002 an organization called Richmond Vision 2000 held a housing summit at Sojourner Truth Presbyterian Church in Richmond. The following year a number of groups formed the Just Cause Coalition: Richmond Vision, Urban Habitat, Faith Works, Richmond Greens, the newly formed RPA, Laotian Organizing Project (LOP), ACORN, Contra Costa Central Labor Council, and Reverend Phil Lawson, a local activist pastor.

In 2003 this coalition held a town hall to hear from residents and tenants. The people articulated the need for rent control and just cause eviction. The issue had also been strongly affirmed as part of the platform out of the People's Convention in 2004 (mentioned in chapter "Waging a People's Convention"). RPA and Richmond Greens was represented by Marilyn Langlois, and Torm Nomprasseut spoke for the LOP, often bringing Laotian tenants to speak at public meetings.

By 2004 the Just Cause Coalition started meeting regularly with pro bono legal assistance and drafted an ordinance, "Just Cause and Fair Rent," with components for fair rent, just cause for eviction, and a rent board. As a first-time Council candidate, I attended meetings reviewing language, comparing what other cities had done, etc.

I championed the ordinance throughout my campaign. By the time I had a seat, I was the only voice in favor. We had fierce opposition by the California Apartment Association (CAA). The coalition brought the issue to the City Council, knowing I was the only reliable pro rent control voice. It never came to a vote. Instead, then-Mayor Irma Anderson appointed a special task force with representatives from both sides to try to come up with an ordinance that everyone could live with.

That task force was convened in the summer of 2005 and met

through the end of the next year. Various coalition partners sat at the table, including RPA, along with the CAA, the Realtor's Association, and the Richmond Chamber of Commerce. That long effort took the steam out of organizing for rent control. From the outset the landlords, realtors, and business community vowed to have rent control taken off the table. They refused to ban "no-cause evictions" as well, clinging to the notion that there are some cases when a landlord has to be able to evict without stating a reason. They kept coming back with proposals to simply inform tenants and landlords of their rights and responsibilities, which we agreed was important but not sufficient in itself, and they declared that no ordinance was necessary to do that.

In 2006, it became clear that this task force was going nowhere and would have no ordinance to recommend to the City Council. The landlord and realtor interest groups were willing to do whatever it took to delay and obstruct any kind of rent control or just cause ordinance from being adopted. The task force was disbanded when Mayor Anderson left office.

After the 2008 economic crisis set in, evictions and rising rents were less pressing because rents stagnated as real estate values precipitously dropped. In 2010, Councilmember Jeff Ritterman and I introduced a Just Cause for Eviction ordinance for the Council to adopt that covered only tenants living in bank-owned foreclosed properties. At that point the Council composition had shifted a bit in the direction of the RPA, and we were able to get it approved.

By early 2015 we were facing an out-of-control rental market. We knew it would take a coalition effort. So we formed a group now known as Fair and Affordable Richmond (F.A.R.). F.A.R. brought together nineteen groups: ACCE, AFSCME Local 3299, APEN (Asian Pacific Environmental Network), Building Blocks for Kids Richmond Collaborative, California Nurses Association (CNA), CCISCO (the interfaith organization), Centro Latino Cuzcatlán, Causa Justa, CUIDO (Communities United in Support of Olmstead), Eviction Defense Center, EBHO (East Bay Housing Organization), Iron Triangle Neighborhood Council, RPA, Saffron Strand, SEIU Local 1021, Tenants Together, Urban Habitat, Urban Tilth, and West County Concilio Latino.

After months of discussion, much publicity in the news, and significant outreach by all coalition partners, the Council approved the new law. On August 5, 2015, in a hard-won battle, Richmond successfully adopted a Rent Control and Just Cause for Eviction Ordinance, the first such new law passed in California in over thirty years. The Council had made it clear that housing stability, something every human being deserves, is worth preserving in Richmond in the face of skyrocketing rents and unjust evictions in the Bay Area, with its obscene housing costs. I was among four councilmembers who supported this ordinance with Councilmembers Beckles, Martinez, and Myrick adopting the law. It was a great victory for our coalition, especially given the long history of failed attempts. We made major news throughout the nation, giving hope to other cities, especially in California, where rental markets have run amok.

But nothing is ever easy where big money interests are involved. The CAA carried out a successful, albeit deceptive, campaign to repeal the ordinance. They spent nearly $100,000 on a referendum effort with highly paid signature gatherers making misleading and distorted statements, along with outright lies, to unsuspecting voters. Lynda Carson reported: "Many Richmond voters were tricked into signing the petition by devious signature gatherers who were being paid anywhere from $12.50 to $20.00 per signature, according to numerous reports. The signature gatherers lied to people by telling them that the petition made rent control stronger or kept rents from increasing, according to testimony from renters and media reports."[40]

We were not deterred. We knew we could still put rent control on the ballot for the voters to decide. With no time to waste, we rewrote the ordinance as a ballot measure. Landlords would be able to increase rents each year by no more than the annual percentage increase in the Consumer Price Index, with petitions for additional increases to cover unexpected legitimate costs brought for review before a rent board. As per California law, single-family homes, multi-unit buildings built after 1995 and condominiums would be exempt from rent control. But our ordinance would protect 20,000 to 30,000 people in nearly 10,000 rental units from unfair rents and unjust evictions.

After the ordinance was rewritten as a ballot measure, we could have had the City Council put it on the ballot. But Councilmember Jael Myrick, who had supported the ordinance in 2015, altered his position and was unwilling to vote for a Council-initiated ballot measure. Without Jael's fourth vote, the only other option was to collect thousands of signatures to get the ordinance on the ballot, which would require lots of work on our part even before we could campaign for the measure. We tried to get Jael to change his mind, but he closed the door saying "good luck with the signature gathering."

Rent control

It was time to hit the pavement.

After a year of hard work gathering signatures and knocking on doors, making phone calls, reaching out through social media and holding many town hall and house meetings, in 2016 we won the ballot initiative, Measure L. It was a campaign to be remembered. We had lots of opposition from the CAA, the Realtors Association, and Mayor Tom Butt, who continues to remain a strong opponent. Our *Richmond Sun* newspaper, launched by the RPA and mailed to voters in the city, featured many articles highlighting the issue. We corrected all the misinformation being thrown out to confuse and scare people.

The rent control issue also served as a wedge issue that helped us gain two new RPA-supported City Councilmembers, Melvin Willis and Ben Choi, both strong supporters. Unlike the previous wedge issue, the soda tax loss of a few years ago, not only did we win rent control and two new councilmembers, RPA would now have a super majority on the 2017 Council.

Just a couple months after the election, the CAA retaliated with a lawsuit against the City attempting to overturn Measure L. The City and the community vigorously defended our democratically approved and constitutional law. Early on, the courts weighed in favor of our side by refusing to stop the rent program while reviewing the merits of the case. On May 8, the CAA dismissed its challenge.

Rent control is just one part of the housing crisis. We still need to build more affordable housing. Many of our residents have been displaced, leaving neighborhoods unstable and forcing families to move their kids from school to school, interrupting their education and social ties. We listened to the voices of our people in distress over rental rates and those facing displacement.

Under the Night Sky: Homelessness

Richmond has one of the largest homeless populations in our county. My participation in the Homelessness is Not a Crime Coalition dates back to my earliest activist work in Richmond. This was a coalition effort to overturn a city law referred to by many activists as the Anti-Homeless Ordinance that disallowed sleeping in public places. There was a massive community pressure campaign in 2003 to reverse this policy. Led by Richmond Greens, residents sent thousands of postcards and regularly came to speak to the City Council calling for a change to this inhumane law. The effort was ineffective at the time, but it laid the groundwork.

It took a federal appeals court ruling in 2006 on a case in southern California, Jones vs. City of Los Angeles that forced the Richmond City Council to reverse course.[41] The U.S. Circuit Court of Appeals ruled that arresting homeless people for sleeping, sitting, or lying on sidewalks and other public property when other shelter is not available was cruel and unusual punishment, essentially nullifying an ordinance that Los Angeles police had been using to clear the streets of people who are homeless.

Today, given a constant shortage of shelter beds, Richmond police do not cite homeless individuals for sleeping in public places, forcing them to keep moving from one place to another. We understand that sleeping is a human need and to cite someone and force them to move is just cruel.

Throughout my public service, I have continued to shine a light on homelessness and the need for lasting solutions. The RPA supports an organization called Saffron Strand that helps people who are homeless enter the workforce. I'll never forget when Yvonne Nair, Executive Director of Saffron Strand came into my office to talk about her idea to create a membership organization for the homeless to help them help themselves. She was both inspiring and amazing in her commitment and zeal for this work. She has helped many people find employment and get their feet back on the ground, and she educates city officials and Richmond residents on the topic. Each year Yvonne also brings a national conference of homeless service providers to our city auditorium.

One unique event held by Saffron Strand took place in 2012 when a number of Richmond and other Bay Area residents gathered for an overnight vigil in Civic Center Plaza. Their purpose was to draw attention to the plight of homelessness as a social justice and human rights issue. Tyler Osburn recounted the story:[42]

Guest speakers gave inspirational speeches, and before it got too dark everyone shared a light meal and conversations of hope. When the cold wind and nightfall overtook them, thirteen people sat in a circle, lit a candle, and shared roofless stories over an open mike.

The event was organized by Saffron Strand, a Point Richmond non-profit focused on helping the homeless find meaningful employment and achieve economic independence. Its founder and CEO, Yvonne Nair, said there are nearly 20,000 people living without a home in Contra Costa County, and that 1,200 of them reside in Richmond. "We hope this event brings awareness," Nair said, "and to help people volunteer—to do whatever it takes to help the other person back on their feet."

Nair said homelessness doesn't end with just a roof. To get the homeless back on track they need a space to learn how to work and gain social skills. Nair said Saffron Strand has about 150 homeless members and that they've put around sixty people back to work.

Mayor Gayle McLaughlin addressed the small crowd bundled in jackets and blankets to champion the work done by the non-profit. She said there was no value in turning away from the plight of homelessness because every struggle that goes ignored diminishes the community.

McLaughlin said an imbalance of wealth distribution has not helped people off the street. Taking inspiration from British novelist John Berger, she said today's poverty was imposed by the rich. "It's not like there isn't enough [money] to go around in this world," the mayor said. "We know that big corporations like Chevron make billions in profits, and yet we have one of the highest homeless rates in the Bay Area right here in Richmond. That's really an obscene fact that we have such disparity in our community."

The Final Frontier: A Just Economy

Our city, like cities everywhere, suffers from fiscal year to fiscal year under the impact of shrinking budgets due to loss of state and federal funds, among other reasons. We don't delude ourselves into thinking that we can do it all on a local level. We need lots of changes that need to be implemented through state and federal efforts, such as a millionaire's tax, an oil severance tax, and fixing loopholes in assessing corporate property taxes. At the same time, cities like Richmond cannot wait for higher levels of government to enact such policies. As a body of local progressive activists, RPA felt an obligation to do as much as possible on the local level. In addition to the significant leadership we have provided advancing the new green economy and forcing Chevron to pay their fair share, we have sought other reforms, including those mentioned in this chapter for homeowners, renters, and those struggling without a stable home. We need to create ways for more services and opportunities for our residents, especially those in the most neglected areas of our city.

Equity refers to fairness in economics and equal life chances. We should all be outraged that we are so far away from this basic principle in our country. This is part of what the Occupy Movement was about. Rest assured, while that movement has faded from the foreground of public view, various sub-groups and many other activist groups continue the work. We should not end our pursuit for equity until it is firmly embedded in the fabric of our culture and systemic structure.

Moving communities toward equity is a key priority for any progressive elected official. We have found many ways to do this in Richmond, and we are working on many more. Increasing corporate taxation, raising wages, setting in motion new requirements for local hiring and small business promotion are all part of that equation. All these efforts have helped bring additional money into our city coffers and local economy.

The RPA has been the primary force offering a grassroots model of social change that has put Richmond on the map. We have helped shift popular consciousness away from relying on an external locus of control, that is, failed market approaches to economic development (with little trickling into our city) to an internal locus, taking the reins as an engaged community. Of course the RPA does not do this alone. We work in coalition with other groups, and other elected officials have made significant contributions. New municipal management, led by City Manager Bill Lindsay, and a hard-working, dedicated frontline staff have played a strong role as well and have skillfully implemented the good policies adopted by the Council over these years.

Reaching our final destination of a just economy doesn't just happen. But with a foundation of democracy, empowering large numbers of people, and outlining new policies, we can stop wandering in outer space and waiting for solutions to drop out of the sky. We only need creative strategies and a fully engaged and dedicated citizenry. Progressives know, too, that our most profound efforts radiate from a place deep inside. A place we call heart.

Travelogue: Labor, Land, and Revolution

I have long had the desire to gain a better understanding of the world and not be limited by my own journeys, experiences, or personal endeavors. I have tried to gain a well-rounded education that includes learning about other cultures, lifestyles, geographies, and the formations of cities, nations, and empires. My parents were also influential in shaping that interest within me. They were not much interested in my sisters and me moving up the social ladder. Rather, they wanted us to discover each of our unique qualities that might lead us to better understand the wider world in which we live. For me, that became a search for what ties the human family together, as well as gaining a grasp of what divides people.

My antiwar activism was one way I tried to help remove barriers between peoples and nations. To this day, the essence of my political work emanates from a belief in peace that will never be won through wars. We will have peace when we embrace, value, and preserve our common threads and our commitment to community.

I bring those values to my work as a local government official. While my efforts center on tackling local problems, I also realize Richmond residents are citizens of the world and our civic responsibilities extend beyond the borders of our city. We feel the impact of events unfolding across our nation and in other countries. We have the capacity, and, I believe, the onus, to think and act beyond our provincial issues and not merely watch international events develop as if they don't affect us. When we voice our concerns about injustices that happen here in Richmond, we need to connect the dots in other places so that we can share both concerns, as well as solutions to similar problems.

One example is climate change. In California we have had droughts, sea level risings, flooding, tragic fires, and other

earth-shattering events. In Richmond, these environmental ca-
tastrophes have been on our activist agenda for years. We know
how keenly important it is to seek global connections and collaborate in international affairs to assure the survival of our planet.
Climate change is happening in Richmond, across our nation,
and in the world. The way we address those problems here can
serve other cities and countries, and likewise, their solutions can
be applied here.

Though we did not have a rich tradition of introducing international affairs into our city government, I and some other councilmembers would occasionally bring resolutions in support of
struggles happening in other regions. We were often met with resistance by other councilmembers with the excuse that local matters were of greater import. I couldn't disagree more. A provincial
Richmond that does not express concerns beyond its borders is
missing the bigger picture. All cities live in the context of a greater
world whose problems can come home to roost (take immigration
and refugees fleeing war for two), not to mention offer support
and aid where appropriate. Local government can make a difference on statewide, national, and international matters, especially
when cities join together in action.

Our progressive movement in Richmond mobilized around a
number of resolutions. We had taken stances against the Patriot
Act during the George W. Bush era, spoke out against various wars,
the occupation of Iraq, and called for non-intervention in Iran.

I believe we need to help build a sense of internationalism,
as well as support a more sustainable and just world. When we
take positive steps in our home cities, whether voicing support
through resolutions, traveling to other nations in joint ventures,
sending or receiving money, or protecting people fleeing war and
other strife, we become better citizens both locally and globally.

During my eight years as mayor I took three trips abroad with
those values in mind. I visited Spain, Ecuador, and Cuba. Those
voyages broadened my horizons and gave me an opportunity to
convey what we had done in Richmond through our progressive
politics. This travel afforded me the opportunity to learn from
other nations as well as establish relationships for further collaboration and support.

Workers Unite

In the summer of 2010, Praxis Peace Institute was embarking on a trip to Mondragon, Spain to study that community's fifty plus years developing worker-owned cooperatives. I had only been familiar with small consumer-type cooperatives, and was eager to learn more about the kind of cooperatives owned and managed by the workers themselves. To gain knowledge of this, a group of us from Richmond decided to join Praxis Peace on the delegation— including my husband, Paul, and colleague Marilyn Langlois. In preparation for this trip, my office contacted the Evergreen Cooperative Initiative (ECI) of Cleveland, Ohio. ECI had brought several stakeholders together and launched a series of cooperative green businesses along the lines of Mondragon's model. Since we were also interested in green businesses, connecting with them made good sense. We also got in touch with the United Steelworkers, who had signed an agreement with Mondragon to create good-paying, sustainable jobs in an equally supportable economy. In the middle of the U.S. recession, even unions were stepping out of their traditional roles, and this intrigued us.

We joined with others from all over the country to learn from Mondragon's example. We visited their co-ops and talked with the worker owners to better understand what this productive engagement was all about.

These people shared with us their history and the development of the cooperatives. The people of this once impoverished city had lived under the repressive regime of the Franco administration. At that time a Catholic priest by the name of José María Arizmendiarrieta, known as Father Arizmendi, had a deep commitment to these struggling Basque people. He started the cooperative movement in Mondragon. I was heartened to learn how a community could rise up under a dictatorship and take such a radical departure from traditional economic structure. Their example gave me hope for Richmond's transformation while our own federal government, though not a dictatorship, still left so many of our people in economic despair.

As early as 1956, Mondragon had implemented a strategy for job creation, worker empowerment, and local wealth building.

Since that time they have employed over 100,000 people—nearly the entire population of Richmond (!), and they have created a network of over one hundred cooperatives. They are collectively known as the Mondragon Cooperative Corporation, with sales topping fifteen billion Euros.

Our delegation saw firsthand how the worker-owners structured and organized themselves and aligned their work with their life style. They spoke of their shared values as more important than the rule of money and that both are weighed in the design of the cooperative structure. Co-op members determine maximum salaries. Lay-offs are virtually non-existent. Instead, members vote to take collective pay cuts, work fewer hours, or take unpaid leave during hard economic times. The co-op model is preserved and grows for the benefit of the entire workforce: people are not expendable.

The Mondragon model is a bottom-up approach. Management and administration provide advice and technical assistance, but the cooperatives are autonomous and the worker-owners are the decision makers. These workers certainly maintain the importance of earning a decent income, but they report that each worker's sense of dignity and community is more important.

Empowered and encouraged by these workers and their organizational structure, I wanted to take this knowledge and newfound relationship back to Richmond. Our guide for the trip, Mikel Lezamiz, Director of Co-Operative Dissemination, and I signed an agreement committing to sharing advice, ideas, and assistance to foster worker cooperatives in Richmond. I signed the letter on behalf of the people of Richmond, and Lezamiz signed on behalf of Mondragon Cooperative Corporation. Richmond and Mondragon were now joined by shared values and goals.

Our delegation returned to Richmond with new hopes and dreams. We had some innovative strategies for Richmond workers based on what we had seen abroad. We had a commitment to promote and create worker-owned cooperatives in Richmond for jobs, local wealth, and workplace democracy in line with the principles of economic, social, and environmental justice. Upon our return, we held community forums to educate and share the prospects of what worker co-ops might offer our community. Richmond residents were receptive to these new ideas and the community meetings were packed with standing room only crowds.

From there we built and deepened relationships with cooperative organizations, non-profits, and other networks throughout our region and state. We also sought advice from other co-ops already existent in local Bay Area cities, and we set up field trips for interested Richmond residents.

We took another bold step by hiring a cooperative consultant to the Mayor's office, Terry Baird, a co-founder of the worker-owned Arizmendi Bakery in Oakland. The bakery has grown into the Arizmendi Association of Cooperatives, and now includes six independent bakeries in the Bay Area. Remembering Father Arizmendi of Mondragon, it made sense to have a co-founder of Arizmendi Bakeries consult the Mayor's Office. In time we developed the Richmond Revolving Loan Fund as a non-profit organization to provide small grants from private donors as seed money to start up more co-ops in our city.

My trip to Mondragon inspired me both personally and professionally. I was uplifted by how much we in Richmond shared similar work and life principles with the people of Mondragon, as well as values of social justice, democracy, and equity. We brought their spirit home to Richmond.

We were all impressed by how those workers were able to balance the importance of working for income with personal dignity while also fostering a sense of community. Those concepts are not easy for many in our nation to hold in tension. Personal value is often equated with how much money one makes and that keeps us from looking at the workplace in new ways. Father Arizmendi explained it well when he said, "It is worthwhile to live and work for something besides earning money and accumulating things for oneself. Community with others, peace, justice, understanding, sensitivity, [sic] fraternity are things to be sought and found, and, to attain them effectively in a world of struggle, it is necessary to think of another way to align the people who work and struggle."[43]

Trudging through Oil Fields

From worker justice to the environment, I would soon find another international reach for Richmond—this time in South America. We had gained quite a reputation in our fight for environmental health and justice in our victory against the Chevron Corporation and all the harm they had wrought in Richmond. News of our success had spread internationally, just as the conglomerate's spread also oozes across the globe. Chevron's business model allows them to cause damage to communities in many cities and countries.

Having brought some good ideas and news of enhanced life for workers from Mondragon to Richmond, now I would take more steps to expand relationships across the miles, this time with people who were being harmed by the same fossil fuel giant that operates in our city.

I contemplated a number of questions: What should Richmond's relationship be with other communities who have also been damaged by the oil industry? As I have sought to explain to my own people what Chevron has done here, is it my responsibility also to point out what that industry has done in other places? And if I believe that climate change is something that is happening to our entire interdependent planet, is it not incumbent upon me to connect the dots, speak out, and take action?

The answer to these questions is, of course, a resounding yes. I need to link up with other communities, help us find collective solutions, and bring justice for all peoples, not just Richmond. Our community has lived for over one hundred years with pollution and other ill effects due to Chevron's poor environmental practices. People in other parts of the globe have similar experiences.

Our local work did not go unnoticed. Our lawsuit against Chevron reached across the miles to others throughout our world. Richmond had become "ground zero" for holding the oil industry accountable. A full-page ad placed locally in our own *West County Times* by the government of Ecuadorian President Raphael Correa said it well: "In the fight against Chevron, the people of Ecuador and the people of Richmond can deploy the most devastating weapon ever invented...the Truth!"

Gayle McLaughlin

Ecuadorian newspaper ad

I had been aware of the Ecuadorian struggle for many years and had connected with groups like Amazon Watch, who host delegations to be with indigenous communities and small farmers from the Ecuadorian rainforest to the U.S. In 2003, before I was even on the City Council, I helped organize an event in Richmond to welcome one of these delegations to our city and share experiences. So in 2013, when I was invited by the government of Ecuador to come see the contaminated areas of the rainforest, I heartily accepted. I would spend five eye-opening days in Ecuador, joined also by a number of other intensely interested observers: Doria Robinson, Richmond resident and director of Richmond's Urban Tilth (an award-winning community garden and urban agriculture non-profit), and John Geluardi, reporter for the *East Bay Express*, a local weekly newspaper. On this trek to help document the Ecuadorian story we saw close-up the contamination of a vital rainforest, among other carnage.

The devastation left by the oil company (at that time it was Texaco, which would later merge with Chevron) was truly an indefensible and an inexcusable environmental disaster. The indigenous community and farmers who lived in the rainforest were equally affected. Eighteen billion gallons of wastewater, called "produced water," were dumped into rivers and streams, and more than 900 open-air, unlined toxic waste pits were constructed that

Three mayors with oil on hands

leach toxins into the soil and groundwater. When I reached down and touched the unlined oil pits, my hand came up covered with thick, molasses-like crude. I was joined by the mayors from two polluted areas of the rainforest—Lago Agrio and Shushufindi—who also reached into the pits. It was awful.

Throughout the trip, I talked with people who had lost family members due to high rates of cancer, birth defects, and other health ailments as a result of the contamination. For years, these people drank the water, washed their clothes and dishes, and fished in contaminated streams and rivers. Their lives were gravely disrupted when they were forced to move from areas where they made their homes and farmed the land. Of course Chevron should be held responsible for cleaning up the mess. And of course, Chevron has not done right by these people or this land mass. The people of Ecuador sued Chevron and won a multi-billion-dollar settlement that Chevron continues to avoid paying. Chevron, like many other international corporations of their size and reach, has put up obstacles at every step to avoid paying, including countersuing the indigenous community and farmers, accusing them of racketeering.[44] (Yes, you read that correctly, "racketeering"—poor villagers in an undeveloped rainforest were accused of mafia-style organizing.) This is painfully familiar to us in Richmond—our lawsuit against Chevron is not coming quickly or easily.

Despite the harsh conditions and the terrible damage done to these people and their land, our delegation was inspired. We connected in solidarity with similar issues and felt a sense of purpose, despite our vast differences in culture and geography, not to mention the great distance. We formed a community of shared hardship and commitment to speaking truth to corporate power.

When I returned home from Ecuador I received a letter from Chevron indicating their desire to meet with me and "let me know the truth about what they had done in Ecuador to clean up the contamination." I think they hoped they could sway me from what I had seen and experienced in that far away land. I was even criticized in the press for not immediately meeting with Chevron. But I had other things to do, like speaking to the people of Richmond about what I had seen and felt, and how important it is to know that we are not alone in our fight against the irresponsible and criminal activities of this oil giant. I did eventually meet with Chevron representatives. After listening to their disturbing testimonies about how the area had been cleaned up, I simply thanked them for sharing their perspective. Honestly, I trust my senses of smell, touch, and sight that showed me quite vividly the billions of gallons of oil and oil-contaminated wastewater cavalierly tossed into open pits and spilled along the rainforest roads.

Sister City and Brotherhood

In December 2013, I led a delegation to Richmond's sister city of Regla, Cuba. This was the first official delegation in fourteen years. Having traveled on my own to Cuba in 1986 with the Vinceremos Brigade, I was aware the country had changed dramatically since that time. Still, the people, their ingenuity, hospitality, and determination to build on their revolutionary history shined bright as ever.

A theme ran through our visit—"The Cold War is over. When is the U.S. going to return our Cuban Five brothers to us?" The Cuban Five was a group of men who had been wrongly imprisoned in the U.S. and sentenced to long prison sentences. One of them had two life sentences. These men were charged and convicted by U.S. courts for espionage. In fact, they had been doing anti-terrorist work, gathering information about certain Cuban exiles in

Miami who had already attacked Cuban citizens in Cuba and were planning to attack again. These five patriots were protecting their own people.

It was truly Orwellian—the real terrorists were allowed to continue to do harm, while the men trying to prevent terrorism were convicted. While Mayor, I had worked with the International Committee to Free the Cuban Five to bring attention to this case. I was also part of a worldwide movement standing up for their release.

My coming to Cuba in my role as a U.S. mayor meant a great deal to the Cuban people I met on that trip. It was significant to them that I was making a contribution to help free their brothers. The warmth I experienced in the country as a result of my solidarity work on behalf of René, Gerardo, Fernando, Antonio, and Ramon was moving.

Our group met with René González, one of the five who had recently been released, having served his shorter sentence, as well as family members of the remaining Cuban Five. Their deep love and respect for their loved ones was apparent, as was their grief for not being able to be with them.

Love of family and country profoundly come together in Cuba. You could see it in the admiration the community displayed for these men. The Cuban Five were considered brothers and heroes. Bulletin boards and banners spoke to Cuba's love for these compatriots who had put themselves on the line for the greater good of their nation. When we met with one of Cuba's parliamentary representatives, she told us that freeing the Cuban Five was one of Cuba's top three priorities. The other priorities were to end the embargo and travel restrictions, and for the U.S. to withdraw from Guantanamo Bay and return that land to Cuba. A year later President Obama would finally agree to free the Cuban Five.

Cuba has a place in the hearts of many of us who have visited the island and learned first-hand the enormous progress this small country has made in a relatively short period of time. Cuba has built its own revolution and is carving out its place in the world. They have reasons to be proud of their country and their accomplishments, including literacy, free education, free health care for all, and a new budding economy. As a matter of fact, two economists we met told us how the Cuban government, after much discussion with the people at all levels, is starting to diversify its economy by promoting the conversion of certain state-owned enterprises into worker cooperatives. To this end, they have consulted with experts from all over the world, including Mondragon, Spain.

The pride that Cubans show for their country is one of a people courageously working together to build a better society in the face of hostile forces. Our Cuban brothers and sisters live less than one hundred miles from the U.S. It was uplifting to experience the Cuban people and their system of social change.

Our Richmond/Regla Friendship Committee continued to build bridges with our neighbor to the south through elevating the arts and hosting guests. One visit included a performance of La Colmenita (Little Beehive), a Cuban childrens' theatrical group. More recently, our Friendship Committee hosted a visit from Kenia Serrano, president of Instituto Cubano de Amistad con los Pueblos (The Cuban Institute for Friendship with the Peoples), or ICAP, and a member of Cuba's Parliament, as well as Leima Martinez, North American representative of ICAP. Such a visit would not have been possible without the newly normalized relations.

The Travel Triad

My three trips abroad were enlightening experiences where I gained personal knowledge, expanded my vision for workers, and made connections with people far and wide. I brought those lessons home to Richmond. The purpose of those trips was not vacation or personal gain, they were for building relationships, seeing first-hand how other people deal with similar troubles that we have here in Richmond, and sharing common struggles. I did not take those trips lightly, nor were they costly trips. For the record, the Praxis Peace Institute paid for my trip to Mondragon, and the Ecuadorian government paid for my trip to the rainforest. My fellow councilmembers took far more trips overseas, some quite luxurious, on Richmond's dime. The three trips I took comprised a total of twenty-two days out of my 3,000 days in office—less than *one percent* of my mayoral term. True to form, in 2014, Chevron, finding nothing else on which they could attack me, plastered the city with billboards portraying me as a globe-trotter. Their bill-boards posed the question, "have you seen your mayor lately?" followed by an exaggerated statement about my travels. Richmond voters were not swayed, they knew that ninety-nine percent of the time, their mayor was standing by their side. And if and when she was travelling, the purpose was for Richmond's betterment.

The Local is Global

GAZA. Global connections don't always require travel time or money, sometimes we simply give verbal support in hopes others will join the chorus. In 2010 I joined Jeff Ritterman in sponsoring a resolution in support of a human rights flotilla heading to Gaza loaded with medical supplies and food. We wanted to honor and thank the people who were risking their lives and safety traveling on this dangerous voyage. Two of those travelers were Richmond residents. We supported their dedication to the people of Gaza. Unfortunately the majority of the Council did not support the resolution, so we were stymied from making our public support official.

Yet the struggle in Gaza continues. The atrocities foisted upon the people who live in Gaza and the West Bank have not stopped. This situation persists at the heart of much of the conflict in that geographical region. On the plus side, many Palestinian-Americans who live in Richmond and other parts of the Bay Area were grateful that some elected officials were not afraid to speak about the injustices happening to their relatives and others living in those areas. Many peace and solidarity groups, including and especially Jewish Voice for Peace, became allies of our progressive Richmond.

These gestures, voices, and resolutions are not always about winning or getting our way. Sometimes we have be the first to take a stand; to plant seeds of peace and hope and water them over time. Democracy strengthens through numbers of people and we need to rally forth many voices to effect change. If this is something our people still stand for, in time we will rise up again with more voices and make sure our resolutions ring out loud and clear.

TIBETAN COMMUNITY. Another meaningful international

connection during my mayoral tenure came through the Tibetan Association of Northern California (TANC) when they moved their community center to Richmond. This group shared with me their history and struggle for self-determination, and they invited me to offer words of solidarity at many of their events. When His Holiness the Dalai Lama came to bless the community center in 2013, I presented a proclamation welcoming His Holiness to Richmond.

HAITI. Crises in other parts of the world are opportunities to build relationships with our brothers and sisters around the globe. When tragedy strikes, it is vital for us to respond. I am reminded of one beautiful connection during my mayoral years when Haiti was struck with a devastating earthquake in 2010. We worked with a wonderful organization, Haiti Action Committee, and we passed a City Council resolution of solidarity and commitment to help facilitate contributions to the Haiti relief effort. In 2004, Haiti had experienced a political earthquake, when a coup d'état backed by the U.S. overthrew their popular and democratically elected president Jean-Bertrand Aristide. As Mayor I had many occasions to express support for the resistance of the Haitian people against the oppressive coup regimes as well as their fight for dignity and empowerment. I wrote letters calling for the release of Haitian political prisoners during this time. Acts like this, however small, help bring communities closer to understanding hardships and they build bonds of support.

AFRICA. As an activist mayor, I had the privilege of learning from other activists directly involved in struggles in other global communities. The human rights struggles in Eritrea, as well as the shack dwellers movement in Durban, South Africa were projects among some Richmond residents. They shared with our community a broader understanding of the difficult and heroic efforts that are taking place in the African diaspora. From activist to activist, we build a chain of human solidarity.

MUSLIM SUPPORT. The war on terror continues to rage in our nation no matter who is in the White House. Xenophobia and hate have become fertile grounds across our country. Many of us have been shocked and stunned by the hate crimes and threats directed at our Arab-American and Muslim communities. In late 2015, a person who had serious mental health problems threatened a group of local Muslims. In response, on Christmas Eve, RPA member Zak Wear organized a solidarity event at a local mosque. Hundreds of people came together to show support for our Muslim community. At moments when international affairs intersect with municipal responsibility, it is crucial that we respond quickly and clearly to communicate what we stand for and what we stand against. On that Christmas Eve, communities of people who hold different religious faiths and no religious faith stood together outside that mosque as a vivid sign of solidarity and support.

Time Travel: Past and Future

When I was a teenager, I was deeply moved by a documentary film about the Vietnam War called "Winning Hearts and Minds." It was an epic film portraying the agony of war at home and abroad. Documenting the horrors of this long protracted war and the divisions that it created at home, "Hearts and Minds" was one of the first films produced and released before the war's end in 1975 that criticized government officials and policies. The film melded together the emotional and intellectual experience of that era. For me, it brought to light that being against war is more than taking a stand for peace—it is about preserving the human family and all that we stand for as a world community.

I have always held true to my antiwar activist roots, which is also foundational to the RPA from our founding during the initial years of the Iraq War. During my tenure we had a unified message opposing that and subsequent wars.

I took public stands with that antiwar spirit in the early days of the U.S. occupation of Iraq. In 2006 I joined Michael Berg, the father of Nick Berg, who had been beheaded in Iraq in 2004 when we spoke at the Unitarian Church in nearby Berkeley.[45] Michael took a non-retaliatory position and ran for congress in Delaware on the Green Party ticket. We championed a non-retaliatory position and tried to send this message to young people involved in street crime. We made the connections between those horrific acts committed by our country overseas as ones that actually send a message to our youth that violence and killing is a solution to problems. I tried to emphasize those links from the local to the global every chance I could, providing a consistent message of peace and collaboration. Our youth need to see better ways to exist in the world—war is not the answer.

I also allied with other elected officials who brought peace messages to their constituents by joining Mayors for Peace. I was even honored by our local Richmond Native American Health Center for being a part of that organization. I also affiliated with other U.S. mayors to co-sponsor resolutions against nuclear weapons and war, that was adopted at the U.S. Conference of Mayors.[46]

Not everyone in Richmond shared my antiwar views and values. I often found myself in heated dialogue with people who held different perspectives on peace and nonviolence (like on Veterans' Day referred to earlier). I was faced with how to relate the World War II history of Richmond, which is home to the Rosie the Riveter World War II Homefront Historical National Park. I felt a responsibility to use the bully pulpit for a peace message.

As the chief elected political official in the City, I was asked to speak at our Annual Homefront Festival. I tailored my remarks on two fronts. First, I proudly acknowledged the many Richmond residents who had worked in the shipyards and honored them as people working hard together to accomplish major feats in short turnaround times. For example, one story includes a Liberty ship that was built in less than five days! That kind of unity and work ethic led to great accomplishments. It is a testament to what we can accomplish in the present, with our own combination of mutual support for one another and purposefulness in overcoming today's local and national challenges.

But I also used those celebratory events to share non-triumphant war stories. I spoke about rounding up Japanese-Americans into internment camps, about the bombs that were dropped on Nagasaki and Hiroshima, and about large-scale discrimination, including segregation within the armed forces. Those were also the experiences of Richmond residents during that era.

We have an icon in Richmond: long-time resident Betty Reid

Soskin, who at ninety-five years old is the oldest National Park Ranger in the country. She works at the Rosie the Riveter World War II Homefront Historical National Park. Betty's experience goes back to the war era when she worked as a file clerk for the Black auxiliary at a segregated plumbers union hall. Richmond has the nation's largest concentration of intact civilian World War II structures. With her first-hand remembrances of many of these sites as historic places of racial segregation, Betty often speaks about the need to process that history in order to move into a better future.

Setting a new tone adding serious reflection for those Homefront events in my speeches and comments has been important to me. I talk about wars that continue to cause grave pain and sorrow, and how war must never be glorified. War includes mass destruction, death, and suffering to countless people and our planet. I remember meeting with Betty and Park Superintendent Martha Lee in my first year as mayor, when I shared with them my antiwar stance. I expressed with them my concerns about presenting only one side of Richmond's World War II story. Together we shared ideas on how to make sure we told a more complete interpretation of that history, forging a different narrative over the years.

Talking about the past as it really played out is essential for how we live in the present and move into the future. The history of World War II, as it was lived among our people in Richmond and throughout the world, should speak to the reality of war. The war ended by carving up the globe, paving the way for future geopolitical conflicts. Since 1945, our United States has been involved in countless military involvement in numerous countries, including the invasion of fifty nations since that time.[47]

Educating our community about global affairs, the good and the bad, whether through my travels or in the re-telling of events and proclaiming City Council resolutions, has also been a part of how I have governed. Local problems sometimes require global solutions. The global connections I have made have all been in pursuit of the liberty and justice for all that we assert in our nation's Pledge of Allegiance. That freedom will only happen when we see in each other, in every corner of the world, a sisterhood and brotherhood, one people, and one world.

Encore! Encore!

In 2014 I was ready to take my final bow. My second term as mayor would be up, and by city charter, two terms is the maximum. Recall that I had also served two years on the Council prior to being mayor, so that made a full decade in elected office. I had worked hard, had a good many scars, and though I still loved Richmond and knew I'd continue working on issues near and dear to my heart, it felt like time for me to make a change. At the same time, I needed to assure that new leadership would advance the work I had begun during my tenure that RPA had helped me set in motion.

The title of this chapter, "encore" has a number of meanings for the stories I recount in this chapter. The first encore is for my personal decision to run for another City Council seat. As I said above, a part of me was ready to waltz off, if only to delve more deeply into RPA work from a different vantage.

But the other meaning of "encore" had to do with more repeat performances. I knew we would still need to pay attention to Chevron, who would no doubt *again* fill political coffers with funds to smear RPA candidates, as well as use their own spin on issues we had been working on, including their modernization plan. I could imagine colleagues on the City Council engaging once *again* in back-door deals without considering the best interests of our Richmond residents. And RPA, too, needed to retool itself *again* in the spirit of a new race, a new mayor for our city. I wanted to do all that I could to keep RPA's values and progressive agenda alive and well in our city.

The last encores were beyond my knowledge: two incumbents would choose not to serve *again*; another would run for mayor *again* after having lost in 2010. And lastly, despite RPA's earnest efforts, an additional councilmember who had decided not to run for mayor would change his mind, which would create more trouble down the line.

This was the setting for my transition period. I would need to compose my new score, gather all the key players and cast members, and assemble a new production.

New Set Design

The 2014 transition can be traced back to early 2013 with a new project that I hoped would reignite our base and expand our progressive vision. RPA and I led a campaign we named the "I Love Richmond" campaign. As always we started with the grassroots community to recharge our local movement. This effort would re-inspire me as well. I held half-hour hour meetings in my home, meeting neighborhood and community activists, encouraging them to be a part of this community uplift. I asked them to commit to walking their own neighborhood precincts—going door to door, and handing out materials with the message that we love Richmond, and also reminding our residents of Chevron's business in our city—how they had polluted our air as well as our elections, and how untrustworthy the oil giant had been. Even the Chevron fire of several months earlier seemed to be fading in peoples' memories, and we hadn't even settled the lawsuit for damages. Even though this wasn't an election year, we felt that it was important to remind people of the obstacles we faced, and we wanted to prepare our neighbors to make informed choices in the upcoming election.

Dozens of activists participated in the "I Love Richmond" campaign. It was exhilarating. "I Love Richmond" signs showed up in residents' homes and car windows. People started coming to Council meetings holding "I Love Richmond" signs. This was not a high-profile campaign, but it kindled the impulse for change from below, where it really matters. "I love Richmond" laid a new set design for the upcoming electoral season.

My Next Role

Having weathered storm after storm over my last two terms, I was thankful to still be standing. But I had to answer some questions about what would come next for me as well as what I thought Richmond needed. I had learned so much over the past eight years. I was not the same person I had been when I started in these electoral roles. I had deepened my investment in an urban community that I loved, and did not want Richmond to lose ground.

My decision to run for City Council came slowly, born, ultimately, out of my desire to do more. I was fortunate to rely on ace RPA organizer Juan Reardon once again as my campaign manager. I wanted to keep doing all I could to make a difference, and I didn't want to let down the countless people of Richmond who had voiced confidence and support for my leadership and asked me to stay in office.

RPA candidates Jovanka Beckles and Eduardo Martinez also declared their intentions to run—Jovanka for re-election and Eduardo trying again for a seat. We were looking for a third Council candidate. When I decided to run, our voices were naturally increased. The final issue was the toughest. We needed to scout for a mayoral candidate to take my place.

A New Tenor

We needed a new voice. Someone with experience, passion, political savvy, vision, and some name recognition. Mike Parker soon emerged. I introduced Mike and his wife Margaret Jordon in the chapter on Measure T and taking on Chevron. They had brought their considerable talents and skills to RPA when they moved to Richmond in 2008. Their efforts helped RPA reach a new level of operation. Mike and Margaret pushed us to get our own office so we could have a place of our own to hold meetings and events, as well as run our electoral campaigns. The brick and mortar headquarters took us to a new level as an organization and gave us more standing in the community. Mike and Margaret spearheaded our becoming a membership organization and later promoted other structural changes that helped us transition to become stronger, more inclusive, and more diverse.

Mike started our *RPA Activist* e-newsletter, serving as editor for several years. He is an extraordinary debater. Anyone who has attended City Council meetings knows Mike will come up to the podium for public comment on a number of topics. He is well spoken, articulate, thorough, erudite, and has keen political acumen. That he was willing to be our mayoral candidate was a boon for us. Mike has an exceptional resume as an activist and successful career in the labor movement.[48]

Jovanka, Eduardo, Mike, and I came together as RPA candidates. We called ourselves "Team Richmond." This is from our first press release:

> Mayor Gayle McLaughlin (limited by City Charter to two terms as Mayor) will run for a City Council seat, along with Vice Mayor Jovanka Beckles, and Planning Commissioner Eduardo Martinez. Mike Parker will seek the office of Mayor.
>
> Nicknamed, "Team Richmond," the four candidates are united in their commitment to continue and expand Richmond's remarkable transformation during a decade of progressive policies spearheaded by McLaughlin. The team is also dedicated to standing strong for Richmond residents in the City's dealings with the Chevron Corporation, demanding safety, transparency and accountability from the oil giant as plans are negotiated for major repairs and a renewal project for the Chevron Richmond Refinery.

Mike had learned the art of political campaigning. He walked precincts throughout the city and campaigned at community events, engaging with residents. Margaret organized house parties for the Team where we mingled with neighbors, sharing RPA's values, speaking about what we had accomplished, and calling attention to ongoing challenges. With each house party, we picked up steam and gained new volunteers, increasing RPA's memberships along the way. I told people that while my mayoral years were coming to an end, my commitment to Richmond lived on. That was why I was running for City Council and passing the baton to Mike. We needed all of Team Richmond to continue the phenomenal work of transforming our city. People were enthusiastic and receptive. They had experienced the changes in our city and wanted to see more of the same. Incidentally, Mike sings tenor for the Contra Costa Chorale.

Chevron Billboards Everywhere

While we were busy with the "I Love Richmond" campaign and preparing for the approaching electoral season, Chevron geared up for another kind of performance. They launched a public relations extravaganza, buying up almost all the billboards in the city. Chevron aimed at putting a human and environmentally friendly face on their refinery, portraying Chevron as champions of our bay shoreline and our parks. Let me be clear: progressives—RPA and our allies—were the ones who advocated for the preservation of our bay trails and city parks. In the lead-up to the approval of the oil giant's billion-dollar retooling project, otherwise known as the "modernization" project, Chevron sported the faces of community members on their billboards as if to show Richmond citizens supporting their project.

To refresh: Chevron had an earlier expansion project that had been stopped by the courts in 2009, due to a lawsuit filed by environmental groups. A revised project had actually been in the works for quite some years. I served on an ad hoc committee reviewing that project. We wanted to make sure the revised one was better than the one that had been rejected. I was joined on the committee with current Mayor (then councilmember) Tom Butt. I also rallied representatives of some environmental justice groups so they could participate in some of the meetings. Together we made a transparent process, with a full series of community meetings when the Environmental Impact Report was released. We wanted the public to be informed and educated about this multi-billion dollar refinery project.

We pressed for strict regulations and a community benefits package. We gathered input from the community on the types of benefits they deemed necessary. Staff compiled two benefits proposals—one at $60 and one at $100 million. Chevron was reluctant, especially with the higher price tag, but city staff explored options.

Sidestepping the official committee, some councilmembers engaged Chevron unofficially just as we had seen years ago when negotiating with them on their prior expansion proposal. This back-door deal got the oil giant to agree to a $90-million pack-

Chevron cartoon

age that included a fair amount of the community's suggestions. But this approach did not help build relationships with the community, even if there were good aspects of the proposal. In fact, one snag included a significant amount of funds earmarked for a wasteful and ineffective transportation project that was a pet project of one councilmember. This isn't the way a democracy should work. It is opportunism.

The Modernization Project came to the Council for a vote in July 2014. We held the meeting in the city auditorium that was packed with members of the public interested in weighing in on the project. Ultimately we approved an alternative version that was both smaller and better with less footprint and less risk to the health and safety for our residents. We were successful in stopping further pollution, but we were not able to get the reduction in emissions.

Galley Cries for a Hospital

The outcome of the July vote was a credit to our environmental justice community that had spent years providing grassroots community pressure leading up to the project's approval. Many of us were quite disturbed about the way the community benefits got approved. The majority of councilmembers rammed through a vote on the benefits package without any discussion. Jovanka and I never even had an opportunity to discuss the package. Our expectation, along with innumerable Richmond activists who spoke on the issue at the public meeting, was to advocate for a benefits package that included money to keep open a local hospital. This was not frivolous. Doctors Hospital, the only full service hospital in close vicinity to Richmond residents, was on the verge of closing. RPA had joined the California Nurses Association, among others, seeking funds to keep it open. We knew that closing this public hospital would harm our community, especially our low-income residents. One idea was to have the community benefits package for Chevron's Modernization Project include money for the hospital. This made perfect sense to us, especially since Chevron's 2012 fire had sent thousands of Richmond residents to Doctors Hospital for treatment.

Based on our rules of procedure, the motion to end debate forced me, as mayor and chair of the meeting, to move to a vote without discussion. Our City Council rules of procedure—Rosenberg's Rules of Order—disallows any discussion once a motion to end debate is on the table and requires the motion to be brought immediately to a vote. Five members voted yes to end debate; Jovanka and I voted no. Following that vote, the Council majority voted to approve the $90 million package without any funds for Doctors Hospital. Chevron got its project and we got a community benefits package with some good perks, but not a penny for the hospital.

Cast Change at the Dress Rehearsal

Team Richmond continued our campaign heading into the 2014 election with our four-person slate. Just a few months before Election Day we were presented with an unexpected challenge. One of the first people we had asked to run for mayor back in 2013 was Tom Butt, a longtime councilmember. Butt had allied with the RPA on many issues over the years. At that time he was unwilling to run, but in August he had a change of heart. This presented a problem for RPA because it could result in a split of the progressive vote. Tom believed Mike would not likely win and feared that we would end up with the Chevron-endorsed candidate Nat Bates. Tom argued that his name recognition, having served on the council for many years, offered a better chance to win.

It was an agonizing decision for us. In the end, we agreed. Mike pulled out of the race, with RPA's support. This was a hard blow for us. It seemed so unfair. Mike's campaign had been in full swing for months. I was using my position as mayor to serve the people of Richmond in a strong and dynamic way, and at the same time I was introducing Mike, who would add to the work I had done. I was also learning the art of ending a monumental period of my life as mayor and simultaneously promoting myself as a candidate for City Council. It was a juggling act for me emotionally and practically. While losing Mike was a huge loss, there was no time to grieve. Team Richmond had to move on.

Jovanka, Eduardo, and I sharpened our focus and built the dynamics of our council races, while Mike gracefully slipped out of the race. With great aplomb, he then stepped into pulling together and coordinating our three separate, but overlapping, Council campaigns.

Team Richmond endorsed Tom Butt. Most active members of the RPA also supported him. The RPA only endorses candidates

Team Richmond

who vow not to take corporate donations, and since Tom wouldn't agree to this, RPA would not be an official endorser. Still most of us in the RPA provided mayoral candidate Butt with a lot of publicity and volunteer support. Team Richmond had already been on the campaign trail for several months building on our progressive base of support, as we had done previously. Once Tom jumped into the electoral arena in 2014, Team Richmond urged a vote for him, along with one other incumbent councilmember, Jael Myrick, who was running for the short-term seat.

While we hold true and strong to our values in the RPA, we also understand the bigger picture and the importance of forming alliances. We also believe in not being swept aside or diminished for the work we have spearheaded. Before Mike withdrew from the race, RPA forged an agreement with Tom that he would ally with the RPA in his vote for a councilmember to fill his vacant seat should he become mayor. Tom and the RPA remembered this agreement differently. We recalled his willingness to support a key RPA activist of our choosing. Tom claimed he just agreed to "work with us" on finding an appropriate replacement.

Over the campaign season we had high hopes for a new progressive coalition. We were not looking at potential future conflicts. Our focus was on winning an election and keeping Chevron from retaking our city once again.

Staging a Grand Finale

The 2014 election season turned into a flamboyant battle of operatic proportions. All that recent Chevron public relations work had served a purpose beyond their modernization project. That earlier marketing campaign allowed them to seamlessly change their billboards from new, environmentally friendly faces to feature their 2014 candidates. You might recall my mention of billboards fashioning me as the globetrotting mayor in the previous chapter. This was the same campaign. Chevron's advertising was mostly met with laughter from the community.

Chevron out spent RPA twenty to one, to the tune of $3 million. We pulled resources and sent our joint mailers with a simple message calling for continuing our transformation and making it clear who were Chevron's candidates. We rented the few billboards not snatched up by Chevron and posted photos of Jovanka, Eduardo, and me, with the message: "Join the Home Team. Vote Team Richmond." We also published our own newspaper during the election, *Richmond Sun*. In 2013, Juan Reardon had created a bi-lingual community newspaper called *La Voz de Richmond* (*Richmond's Voice*), which spoke to all in the community, but especially to the Latino community. *Richmond Sun* fashioned itself after *La Voz* and used newsprint to distinguish itself from Chevron's glossy mailers. We mailed *Richmond Sun* to all the voters, passed it out when canvassing, and distributed it at community events. The community seemed to really appreciate the paper, and we have continued regular publication since.

A month before our election, Bernie Sanders visited Richmond. He was exploring the presidential run, but hadn't made up his mind. Steve Early, local RPA member and avid supporter brought Bernie to Richmond. Steve had a long history with Bernie dating back to their earlier days in Vermont. (Read more about this visit in Early's book, *Refinery Town*.[49]) RPA organized a town

Bernie in Richmond

hall meeting in the Auditorium that filled it to capacity with early, eager supporters.

Sanders gave us a boost when he endorsed Team Richmond. We also gave him the same kind of hope and encouragement as he pondered whether or not to go forward with his presidential run. Bernie said it straight up when he spoke to the crowd in Richmond: "Whether you know it or not, the eyes of the country are on you. And if Chevron can roll over you, they and their buddies will roll over every community in America. If you can stand up and beat them with all of their money, you're going to give hope to people all over America that we can control our destinies."

And that is what we did. When Election Day rolled around, hundreds of Team Richmond volunteers went out on the streets, at the polling places, and on phones encouraging voters to get out and vote. Richmond voters were clear. It was either Team Richmond or Team Chevron. Our voters cast their votes enthusiastically. I came in first place, Jovanka second, and Eduardo placed third. We won the three open four-year seats. Tom won the mayor's race and Jael won the two-year seat.

All of Chevron's candidates lost.

Rave Reviews

Our 2014 victory brought us huge accolades. That a city the size of Richmond was able to defeat a major oil company's obscene influx of money into our elections was notable. We received national attention from *The Nation*, Bill Moyers' "Moyers and Company," Rachel Maddow of MSNBC, *Democracy Now!*, *Al Jazeera America* and other news outlets before, during, and after the campaign. Bernie politicked about our victories too: "The inspiring electoral victories in Richmond would not have been possible without the

Black Lives Matter

prior development of a multi-issue, diverse progressive organization. Our country obviously needs a great deal of change at the state and federal levels. But laying a solid local foundation, like activists in Richmond have done, is an important first step toward overcoming working-class alienation from politics and resulting low voter-turnout rates."[50] Richmond's success was a sign that progressive politics in America is alive and well.

Not long after the election, in the wake of Michael Brown's shooting in Ferguson, Missouri, our city drew national attention from a photo with Police Chief Chris Magnus holding a Black Lives Matter sign up at a local protest. It became a symbol of our city's community policing model. The RPA was also at that protest, but to have a police chief in uniform hold the sign made big news.

The Council Selects a Stand-In

In 2015 we were all sworn in and the new City Council was seated. When Tom took his mayor's seat, his former Council seat became vacant. Filling this seat became the first fallout. All vacant seats on the City Council must be filled by a majority vote of the sitting Council. This meant four votes of the body were needed for any nominee to be confirmed. Any Councilmember could make nominations. The RPA wanted Marilyn Langlois. She was the most qualified person to fill the seat, but Tom would have none of that. He lobbied hard against Marilyn, who had been a long-time activist in Richmond, a co-founder of RPA, and had served as a staffer in my office for four and a half years. She knew city issues inside and out. All Tom could see was Marilyn's connection to RPA. He claimed that having a fourth RPA voice on the Council would make him irrelevant. I disagreed. RPA has a long history of engagement with coalitions made up of people who don't agree with us on lots of issues. We have worked through many differences to establish and maintain good relationships. Tom was unyielding. Vinay Pimplé, a relative newcomer to Richmond politics was voted in for the vacant seat. Mike Parker recounts the final casting decision:[51]

Contrary to the understanding reached between RPA and Butt when he asked Parker to drop out of the mayor's race, Butt was unwilling to accept an RPA leader, arguing that he did not want a council with a majority of RPA members (four out of seven). Butt said he wanted council to appoint a person more like himself, a "moderate." The RPA and its allies then backed a Latina immigrant activist, Claudia Jimenez, who was not an RPA member but had led important community struggles, including the one to divert state funds from building prisons to providing reentry services. Butt opposed her, claiming she had insufficient experience. The debate stretched out more than a month and turned ugly. Butt and some of his supporters portrayed the RPA as a conspiratorial cabal making a power grab. They had no problem with a Democratic Party majority on council, in the legislature, or in Congress, but a majority of council identifying with the RPA was a threat to democracy. In a confusing vote, Martinez ended up providing the needed support to Butt, Myrick, and Bates to appoint "anyone but another RPA member." Vinay Pimplé, with little government experience, little community involvement, and unknown views on many issues, was appointed to the seat.

Tom ignored a basic principle about the RPA and the nature of our organization. We are a democratic structure, not a homogenous, one-voice chorus. We hold that every person has the right to his or her own perspective. In the RPA, we often disagree passionately among ourselves. The same holds true for RPA councilmembers who frequently vote differently. At the same time we share deep principles and stand strong together on the big issues that confront our community.

My personal relationship with Tom is that I have been able to work with him, even with a majority RPA councilmembers sitting at the dais, because I respect his expertise on a number of issues. Some of Tom's ideas and projects have and will continue to help move our city forward. The Mayor and I continue to work together on issues we share in common. Yet everyone knows that I won't surrender my politics and values that I share with the organization I helped found and have nurtured over the years. RPA has given me strength and has helped me do my part in bringing about a better Richmond.

Two New Voices Singing on Key

Two years later we have two more new RPA councilmembers,

Melvin Willis and Ben Choi. These men ran extraordinary campaigns linking themselves to our fight for rent control, outlined in chapter 15. With five members of the RPA now serving on the Council we have new possibilities for greater progress. We also have new responsibilities. When your progressive agenda is the majority vision of the elected body, people have higher expectations. We are up to the challenge. We know how to harmonize even when other voices scream off key. When the nation moved to the right in 2016, we swayed left. And we keep on singing.

Spin-Offs

RPA's grand performance in 2016 continues to get more publicity with requests for new productions. Communities up and down California and beyond have been clamoring for us to come speak with their groups. They want to start their own progressive alliances. RPA has formed an outreach team made up of Juan Reardon, me, Steve Early, and others to spread the word on progressive alliances. I have given presentations to various groups in many cities over the past year, and those groups are well on their way to creating their own progressive alliances. We don't offer how-to sessions for building progressive alliances, nor do we want people to simply copy with our star power. We tell our story and encourage others to write their own scripts, narrate what they see as problems facing their communities, and then build structures to work for their people and circumstances. The spin-offs for building progressive alliances are about *values* and *principles*. That begins with no corporate money or influence; find a few good people with whom you share progressive ideas and values; build an independent organization, and have corporate-free candidates run for office; educate and develop your community, and so on. Juan Reardon has written an eight-page document recounting RPA's origin, stories, and organizing principles that we offer communities for basic information.[52] We tell people to take what they want use from our playbook and use it. But the key is really in getting each community to write their own score and form alliances for strength in numbers and shared purpose.

Each community needs to stage their own progressive alliance.

Epilogue

I travelled across the country nearly twenty years ago and landed in California hoping to reach new horizons and to fine-tune my life to make a difference in the world. Richmond was fertile ground for me to set down new roots and work on some of the issues I had prepared for through my earlier activism. I landed in a city that beheld blinding contrasts—exquisite landscapes and terrific people, yet corporate greed whose stretch into local government arrested growth for the vast majority of poor and low-income people who live here. I encountered a city with deep urban problems facing its schools, environment, and safety, along with a rich assortment of activist groups who work against all odds to prevail over those difficulties.

We founded the RPA nearly fourteen years ago. Little did I know what a monumental turn my life would take when I joined with other activists to form such an awesome organization and run for electoral office. Building the RPA and working on the entrenched issues of our city was a massive task, but we made huge strides bringing our progressive agenda to the people. We recognized the pressing need for an independent progressive political structure in a city that had been dominated by a giant corporation for over a hundred years. The RPA became that structure. Our successes came from building a local movement. We created the capacity to take on big oil, big banks, big soda, big charters, and big landlords.

My experience in Richmond helped me become a better and stronger person; one with a deeper understanding of the troubles we face as a society. As I built relationships throughout Richmond, I saw personally the level of pain and suffering that people were dealing with in their daily lives. I also felt their yearnings for something better. It was a yearning I shared. That is what drove me day in and day out.

Challenges came our way and seemed insurmountable. Being in elected office has been the most difficult thing I have ever done, but the successes outweighed the hardships again and again. I can also vouch from my experience that the roles of elected official and activist are not contradictory. I went into public office as an activist, and my activist skills complimented and added positively to my work in elected office.

Democracy is key, of course. It takes an empowered community to define a just future. I played a leadership role as Richmond's mayor for eight years, helping to make space for that community involvement. I used my position to champion good policies and programs, appointing progressives to boards and commissions, and setting a new tone and direction from the mayor's seat. And I worked side by side with community members and groups—the RPA acted as the hub, bringing people and groups together. Democracy and collective action has helped make Richmond a more vibrant and progressive city.

The RPA itself has evolved over the years. From the beginning, our key leadership included people of color and individuals from diverse cultures—all of us working-class people. In 2015 we sought to improve our diversity and bring in younger people. We spent a year reaching out to individuals and allied groups, asking for their input on how we could develop the RPA and encouraging these activists to become RPA steering committee members. We wanted our leadership to reflect the demographics of our community, and within two years we were able shift the composition of our leadership. Today, people of color make up a majority of our steering committee members, and we're trying to get the larger membership to reflect this diversity as well.

Richmond progressive politics has become the spark for many cities ready to stand up for the rights of their community and take collective responsibility for making change. Since the 2016 election I have worked as part of the RPA Outreach Team, giving presentations to interested groups of activists in various cities. We have been sharing our experiences about creating progressive change on the local level and encouraging others to build their own progressive alliances.

While we continue to do this local organizing work, we are

also clear that we can only do so much on a local level. Statewide policies and lack of resources limit what we can do locally even with good democratic progressive forces in place.

So this brings me to my next chapter. As I end the telling of this story about my political life in Richmond, I feel much differently now after over a decade of service in elected office. I have seen people power in action, normal folks getting together, talking about their progressive values, and taking action little by little until big changes take hold in their city. I have seen people grieve and mourn together, and then rise together, creating something new out of those tragedies.

We are in a different political climate today; one that is very disturbing. These are shocking times for our nation and we need to reset our course. When I see fellow activists crouch and cry in anguish and hopelessness over our state of affairs, I respond that we cannot stop now. Now is the time to act. We need to re-group and organize around each and every issue that calls for redress.

The way we have made change in Richmond makes me think about movements in general. We have a rich history of successful movement building in our country. I find an unlimited source of inspiration from many movements that have changed our nation: for women's equality, Civil Rights, labor, antiwar, and the environment, to name a few. When people unite, we make social progress. More recently the fights for justice have birthed movements like Occupy, Black Lives Matter, and now #MeToo. We are living in daunting times, for sure. But I agree with Bernie Sanders' evaluation of the current era: "This country faces more serious problems today than at any time since the Great Depression and, if you include the planetary crisis of climate change, it may well be that the challenges we face now are more dire than at any time in our modern history."[53]

We all need to challenge ourselves to participate in reversing the current state of affairs and not listen to those who say that big picture systemic fixes, like single payer healthcare, are not practical or feasible. Bernie reminds us that now is not the time to think small. Now is the time to dream big, think big, and act big.

But there are no short cuts. We need to build grassroots change from the bottom up, resolving conflicts as we go, respecting different approaches and not getting caught up in theoretical arguments on how to make progressive change. We need action, and those actions need to come about in concert with people and groups who will do the work.

We must take our organizing work to larger scale and keep working with others to facilitate a network of progressive organizations, state unions, and community groups. We need to concentrate on issues that cannot be solved by local politics and that require statewide solutions. We need to address many issues in California at the state level: single-payer healthcare for all, free college, property tax reform (for Californians that means Proposition 13 reform to remove the corporate loophole); a ban on fracking, a progressive millionaires' tax, an oil severance tax, aid to cities for sustainable development, immigration rights and reform, affordable housing, quality public education, a state public bank, new incentives for union organizing, and, of course, campaign finance reform. California, the sixth largest economy in the world, can and must do better. Too many of our state elected officials are controlled by their corporate donors and lobbyists. There is a better way—a true democratic way—to serve the public. Richmond Progressive Alliance has succeeded in that better way on a local level by electing five corporate-free councilmembers (out of seven). This can be done in other cities too.

As we continue organizing locally, we also need to make our State of California government more independent from corporate influence. We must not waste time. Progressives up and down the state want a progressive program for our state.

We need leadership for that agenda. I have thrown my hat into the ring. I am running for the office of Lieutenant Governor of California. California has never had a corporate-free Lieutenant Governor or a woman in that office. It is time for that to change.

I am using this political race to spread our local progressive organizing message. In RPA fashion, I am both running for office and organizing. My campaign has two purposes. The first is to encourage others to build local political power in their own cities. Over the past several months, after hearing about the RPA model, several new progressive alliances have emerged and more are in the making. People are inspired by our accomplishments and are coming together to form their own alliances to bring about their own successes.

The second goal of my campaign, of course, is electoral. If I am elected Lieutenant Governor, I will continue to organize and network organizations throughout our state, so that collectively we have the political strength and power to address our statewide issues. I will educate our people on the corporate corruption in our state politics and keep an eye on Sacramento, where corporate interference undermines the interests of the people of California. Learn more about my campaign at GayleforCalifornia.org.

Join me as we bring corporate-free, progressive politics to the Golden State in 2018. We won many victories in Richmond. We can do the same for California. Let's build a powerful, independent network of progressive forces across the state from the grassroots. A better California is possible.

Acknowledgements

The people of Richmond have been central to this success story. While this book focuses primarily on the founding and energizing forces of the Richmond Progressive Alliance, without the resiliency and determination from generation to generation of Richmond's diverse population, this unique story would never have taken shape. For sure, the RPA successes stand on the shoulders of many great community leaders.

My appreciation goes to every activist who has played a role in bringing the RPA to where it is today. Countless people deserve mention, and I rest assured you all know who you are. I thank you for your tireless work and dedication to transforming our city. Winning Richmond is our collective achievement.

A special thank you to RPA leader Juan Reardon, who not only spearheaded the idea of building a progressive alliance back in 2003, for the purpose of gaining local political power, but who worked tirelessly to get the RPA off the ground and has helped our organization soar higher than imagined. I echo that gratitude to Marilyn Langlois as well. Marilyn's hard work and commitment to our progressive journey, including her key role as a mayoral advisor to me and as an RPA leader, also propelled our efforts. Both Juan and Marilyn also provided critical input and feedback as early readers of *Winning Richmond*.

Writing a book like this is an enormous undertaking. To my incredible editor and sometime scribe, Diana Wear, I give heartfelt thanks. Diana, a dedicated RPA leader and professional editor, has been with me in this book-writing enterprise every step of the way. Far more than providing her expert editing, she embraced this book, and me personally, with the tender loving care of someone who wanted to see the Richmond story, and all its sub-plots, come alive on the pages of this book. She guided me through iteration after iteration of each chapter, sharing ideas, suggestions, and feedback. As my schedule got busier, due to my current campaign for Lt. Governor, she played an even greater role with some of the latter chapters, taking them to completion from my rough drafts. My thanks also goes to my publisher, Tim Sheard of HardBall Press, for his belief in me and for his keen feedback on how to more effectively tell this story. Without Diana's and Tim's dedication to helping me bring this book to the finish line, there would be no book. I remain forever grateful for their hard work and encouragement along the way.

On a personal note, I thank my loving husband, Paul Kilkenny, for his steadfast support in helping me bring this book to fruition. Paul provided me with the space I needed to concentrate on issues big and small and to attend to the task of writing. Paul lived the Richmond story side by side with me as it unfolded in real time, and he relived the telling of this tale throughout my storytelling. His recollections, both as my partner and as a major RPA activist himself, his research, advice and staunch backing for me are embedded throughout this book.

Surroundings matter and most writers need a special place for recalling and penning their tales. Paul's extended family, the Kilkenny's, gave me that space and opportunity to write at their property, affectionately known as "Kilkenny Kamp" in the breathtaking beauty and serenity of the Mendocino National Forest. Co-founder and longtime RPA activist, Tarnel Abbott and her family allowed me use of their Foresta cabin in Yosemite National Park. To both families, I express my deep gratitude. There is nothing like the great outdoors for tapping into one's muse.

Lastly, I offer enormous gratitude to Praxis Peace, my fiscal sponsor, who helped administer the fundraising aspect of this project. I am grateful to Ralph Nader and to RPA leader Mike Parker for their help with fundraising outreach. And I send wholehearted thanks to all the generous donors who made financial contributions that allowed me to concentrate on writing. There is a reason we call many financial supporters "angels."

During the writing of this book, my oldest sister, Sharon McLaughlin Dumrauf, passed away under the throes of a fast-moving disease. Losing Sharon has left a hole in my heart. Yet I was comforted to have had the chance to share with her my chapter on my personal story and get her valuable feedback. Sharon's support and love for me over the course of my life is a treasure that I hold forever. Adding to that, I thank my entire family of origin, not only for their love and support, but for demonstrating that working-class families have what it takes to keep the struggle alive through our determination to rise above adversity.

And that is what I hope is the take home message of this book. Set out to build better tomorrows for our communities and no matter what obstacles you confront, keep on going and never turn back.

Ten Key Values Of The Green Party[1]

1. Grassroots Democracy

Every human being deserves a say in the decisions that affect his or her life and should not be subject to the will of another. Therefore, we will work to increase public participation at every level of government and to ensure that our public representatives are fully accountable to the people who elect them. We will also work to create new types of political organizations which expand the process of participatory democracy by directly including citizens in the decision-making process.

2. Social Justice and Equal Opportunity

All persons should have the rights and opportunity to benefit equally from the resources afforded us by society and the environment. We must consciously confront in ourselves, our organizations, and society at large, barriers such as racism and class oppression, sexism and homophobia, ageism and disability, which act to deny fair treatment and equal justice under the law.

3. Ecological Wisdom

Human societies must operate with the understanding that we are part of nature, not separate from nature. We must maintain an ecological balance and live within the ecological and resource limits of our communities and our planet. We support a sustainable society which utilizes resources in such a way that future generations will benefit and not suffer from the practices of our generation. To this end we must practice agriculture which replenishes the soil; move to an energy efficient economy; and live in ways that respect the integrity of natural systems.

1   http://www.gp.org/10kv (last accessed 25 February 2016).

4. Nonviolence
It is essential that we develop effective alternatives to society's current patterns of violence. We will work to demilitarize, and eliminate weapons of mass destruction, without being naive about the intentions of other governments. We recognize the need for self-defense and the defense of others who are in helpless situations. We promote nonviolent methods to oppose practices and policies with which we disagree, and will guide our actions toward lasting personal, community and global peace.

5. Decentralization
Centralization of wealth and power contributes to social and economic injustice, environmental destruction, and militarization. Therefore, we support a restructuring of social, political, and economic institutions away from a system which is controlled by and mostly benefits the powerful few, to a democratic, less bureaucratic system. Decision-making should, as much as possible, remain at the individual and local level, while assuring that civil rights are protected for all citizens.

6. Community-Based Economics
Re-design our work structures to encourage employee ownership and workplace democracy. Develop new economic activities and institutions that will allow us to use our new technologies in ways that are humane, freeing, ecological and accountable, and responsive to communities. Establish some form of basic economic security, open to all. Move beyond the narrow "job ethic" to new definitions of "work," "jobs" and "income" that reflect the changing economy. Restructure our patterns of income distribution to reflect the wealth created by those outside the formal monetary economy: those who take responsibility for parenting, housekeeping, home gardens, community volunteer work, etc. Restrict the size and concentrated power of corporations without discouraging superior efficiency or technological innovation.

7. Feminism and Gender Equity
We have inherited a social system based on male domination of

politics and economics. We call for the replacement of the cultural ethics of domination and control with more cooperative ways of interacting that respect differences of opinion and gender. Human values such as equity between the sexes, interpersonal responsibility, and honesty must be developed with moral conscience. We should remember that the process that determines our decisions and actions is just as important as achieving the outcome we want.

8. Respect for Diversity

We believe it is important to value cultural, ethnic, racial, sexual, religious and spiritual diversity, and to promote the development of respectful relationships across these lines. We believe that the many diverse elements of society should be reflected in our organizations and decision-making bodies, and we support the leadership of people who have been traditionally closed out of leadership roles. We acknowledge and encourage respect for other life forms than our own and the preservation of biodiversity.

9. Personal and Global Responsibility

We encourage individuals to act to improve their personal well-being and, at the same time, to enhance ecological balance and social harmony. We seek to join with people and organizations around the world to foster peace, economic justice, and the health of the planet.

10. Future Focus and Sustainability

Our actions and policies should be motivated by long-term goals. We seek to protect valuable natural resources, safely disposing of or "unmaking" all waste we create, while developing a sustainable economics that does not depend on continual expansion for survival. We must counterbalance the drive for short-term profits by assuring that economic development, new technologies, and fiscal policies are responsible to future generations who will inherit the results of our actions. Make the quality of life, rather than open-ended economic growth, the focus of future thinking.

RPA Public Official Candidate Endorsement Process

1. RPA Steering Committee (or a sub-committee of SC) holds an interview with an interested candidate for local public office to gain an understanding of the candidate's progressive values, stance on current issues, etc.

2. Candidates must support the mission of the RPA. As stated in the RPA bylaws:

> The RPA is an independent progressive organization that seeks to unite Richmond's diverse communities and form alliances with other community based organizations to promote actively social justice, economic equality, health, environmental protection and democracy. We work to elect government officials who share these progressive values, and who do not accept corporate donations.

3. Candidate must be willing to sign a pledge to take "no corporate donations," which includes no donations from any businesses, including small and medium-size businesses—business owners can contribute as individuals.

4. The pledge must clarify that the RPA can retract its endorsement if a candidate takes such a corporate/business donation, unless it is returned.

5. Candidates for Richmond City Council must be willing to run as part of a slate with other RPA-endorsed candidates.

6. Eighty percent of the Steering Committee must support the candidate.

Early RPA Members with brief background and party affiliation (at the time)

Gayle McLaughlin – Richmond resident, registered Green and City Council candidate, Chevron accountability activist

Andres Soto – Richmond resident, registered Democrat, and City Council candidate, police accountability activist

Juan Reardon – Richmond resident, registered Green, founder Richmond Greens, McLaughlin Campaign Manager, Latino rights activist

Susan Prather – Richmond resident and homeless advocate

Roberto Reyes – Richmond resident, registered Democrat and youth advocate

Kay Wallis – Richmond resident, registered Green and health educator

Alejandro Soto-Vigil – Richmond resident, registered Democrat, and UC Berkeley student activist

Whitney Dotson- Richmond resident, registered Democrat, and President of North Richmond Shoreline Open Space Alliance (NRSOSA)

Malia Everette – Richmond resident, registered Green, and Director of Global Exchange's Reality Tours

Paul Kilkenny – Richmond resident, registered Green and McLaughlin Treasurer **Tarnel Abbott** – Richmond resident, registered Green and City of Richmond librarian and union activist

Marilyn Langlois – Richmond resident, registered Green, past president of League of Women Voters of Diablo Valley and Just Cause Coalition activist

Soula Culver – Richmond resident, registered Green, health and environmental justice activist

Che Soto-Vigil – Richmond resident, registered Democrat, Laney College student activist

Henry Clark – born in North Richmond, environmental justice activist, and executive director for West County Toxics Coalition

Jerome Smith – Richmond resident, registered Green, animal rights and homeless advocate

Daniel Cabrera – Richmond resident, registered Green, Latino activist

Howard Sodja – El Sobrante resident, registered Green, RPA and McLaughlin campaign webmaster

Edgar Monk – Richmond resident, registered Green, labor and United Farm Workers activist

Tony Sustak – Richmond resident, registered Green, economic, social, and environmental activist

Kathy Guruwaya – Pinole resident, registered Green, campaign volunteer

Devin O'Keefe – Richmond resident, registered Green, Laney College student activist

Robby Block – El Cerrito resident, high school student, education activist

Millie Cleveland – Oakland resident, registered Democrat, SEIU 790 (now 1021) field representative

Susan Swift – El Sobrante resident, registered Green (switched to Democratic Party and ran for local Health Care Director)

Kim Stewart – Richmond resident, registered Democrat, union organizer for university employees

Evan Blickenstaff – El Cerrito resident, registered Green, co-founder El Cerrito Greens

Tony Martarella – former Richmond resident living in central Contra Costa County, registered Democrat, later founded Contra Costa Progressive Alliance

Barry Paperno – Richmond resident, registered Green, McLaughlin campaign volunteers

David Marin – El Cerrito resident, registered Green, UC Berkley graduate student activist, co-founded El Cerrito Greens

Speech at Democratic Presidential Candidate
Dennis Kucinich Panel

I welcome this opportunity to stand before you, my co-Richmond residents in this, our embattled but not embittered, city. Thank you all for coming out tonight. I am Gayle McLaughlin, registered with the Green Party and a candidate for the Richmond City Council. I am part of a long-needed local coalition of progressive Democrats, Greens, and Independents: The Richmond Progressive Alliance! I am running with the Richmond Progressive Alliance because we are running out of time: Democracy is running out of time, social and economic justice is running out of time, the environment is running out of time, and our children are running out time for a decent future.

The words of Fred Jackson's song Too Early Too Young resonate in our hearts because we know it is true. The loss of the precious young lives of Richmond, along with the loss of precious hopes and aspirations, is occurring way too early and way too young. The broken windows at Downer Elementary offer no protection against the toxic releases of the ChevronTexaco refinery. More kids are slated for joining "the asthma club" instead of the art club or the debate club. But these losses and problems are not unique to Richmond. They are common to many cities and communities. And we are not only losing the young of our cities, we are losing our whole republic. Most of the institutions of our democracy have suffered a corporate coup d'état. All the way from Washington DC to the Richmond City Council we have lost our representative institutions. These include, lamentably, those political parties that have historically played a role in our democracy.

That is why it is both an honor and a privilege, to meet and salute representative Dennis Kucinich and his campaign, along with all the people with whom his message resonates. We wish Kucinich and his campaign great success in their endeavor to bring forth a better America for us all. We salute them for their struggle to rescue the Democratic Party from corporate control.

And if some day they conclude that such a goal is not possible, they know already that we are here. We are willing to build with them, and with all our progressive sisters and brothers, an alternative political structure: one that will take our nation where it badly wants to go and painfully needs to go.

• We, the Richmond Progressive Alliance, say: Let's begin right here and now to build a progressive future for our polluted, our corrupted...our life-threatened city.
• We can build a Richmond where ChevronTexaco pays its fair share of taxes and we can build a Richmond where this giant polluter is seriously penalized for every polluting crime.
• We can build a city where democracy and public participation are encouraged and honored. We can create all around us an environment of justice, giving special protection to those most in need: our children, our elders, our homeless, our renters facing eviction, our sick, and newcomers to our city.
• We can transform this city into a place where small, clean businesses come knocking on our door.
• And more than that: we can promote that creativity and American entrepreneurial ingenuity that already exists in the people of Richmond. And we can make this creativity and ingenuity blossom into jobs for our citizens and revenue for our city.

But we cannot do any of this unless we work together. So let's commit to work together. Let's end the chaotic implosion of our city! Let's commit to building the nation we want by building the city we need! Let's rise up, let's stand together, and let's become progressive unity!

Roots of Richmond Violence Run Deep[2]

In the guest commentary of June 11th, Richmond Mayor Irma Anderson reflected on the June 4th Black on Black Crime Summit held in Richmond. This event was organized by African-American, Christian, and Muslim ministers to readdress the endemic problem of violent crime that has decimated Richmond for at least twenty-five years and cost hundreds of young lives. In her commentary, the mayor pledged to support youth programs, citing an upcoming initiative funded by private contributions that will give 200 young people part-time jobs for the summer.

More recently, other members of the council have called for a "state of emergency," insisting that only a larger police presence will solve the ongoing violence problem.

I respectfully disagree with my fellow city councilpersons. We are not currently going through a violence "crisis" in Richmond, but continuing to suffer from chronic violence, several decades in the making. Richmond's chronic street violence is largely drug- and/or gang- related. The availability of drugs to be traded and the use of guns to secure turfs are key causal factors.

Even deeper roots lie in our decimated educational system and lack of jobs, which create a giant surplus of desperate and angry unemployed young men. When young men in the drug trade are confronted, countless times they tell us: "You want my gun? Give me a job!"

I profoundly believe that most of our troubled young men would chose a better life if given the right opportunities and the appropriate guidance. How do we make significant and long-lasting opportunities for alienated and underserved young people?

---

2   Gayle McLaughlin, Guest Commentary, *West Contra Costa Times*, 25 June 2005.

Not through greater police repression.

Mayor Anderson's summer jobs program is certainly well intentioned, but it is insufficient, and the impact of such a small program on Richmond's street violence will be, I believe, minuscule. Mayor Anderson and many of my colleagues on the Richmond City Council would love to have the money to invest in youth employment and education-strengthening programs.

Let us be clear: the money is within reach, but most of my City Council colleagues are unwilling to pay the political price to access those funds. I refer to closing the corporate loopholes that allow multi-billion-dollar corporations like Chevron to get away without paying millions of dollars of taxes to the city every year. Repealing the utility users' tax cap granted to Chevron more than ten years ago would generate millions of dollars of revenue to support Richmond youth programs.

The cycle of violence in Richmond also has another difficult mechanism: the fewer resources we utilize to prevent violence with employment and education, the more dangerous is the job of repressing the local violence, and police and firefighter officers expect more compensation for the work they perform. The public safety unions swallow the bulk of the city's budget, and take the lion's share of any new initiative that the citizenry may vote into effect, such as Measure Q, the city's ½ cent sales tax on the November ballot.

Chevron and the public safety unions directly influence the decisions of the Richmond City Council. Chevron spent approximately $150,000 in the last election to support its candidates. The "Keep Richmond Safe" PAC of the Richmond Police Officers Association and the Richmond Firefighters Association spent close to $120,000. It is very hard for Richmond elected officials to ignore the weight these powerhouses exert on their political futures.

The special interests will attack anyone who questions their priorities and calls for a fairer distribution of resources. And so, youth programs are chronically under funded, and the cycle of violence continues.

The city of Richmond needs to remove the utility users' tax cap and collect the millions in additional dollars due to our city. The city of Richmond needs to allocate millions of dollars every year to a year long youth part-time employment program that hires, trains and educates several thousand young residents.

The life of one Richmond child is certainly more valuable than the profits of Chevron stockholders, and infinitely more valuable than the political careers of any city council member.

Casino at Point Molate is a Losing Bet for Richmond[3]

On April 30 the *Times* ran a commentary by Richmond Mayor Irma Anderson titled, "The Future of Point Molate is the Future of Richmond." In her article, Mayor Anderson tells us that the casino complex planned for Point Molate is a "world-class destination resort" and that it will bring jobs and prosperity to Richmond. In our Mayor's mind, the casino complex will be the miracle medicine, able to cure all of Richmond's woes in a single dose.

A single, easy solution to our problems would be nice, but let's look at reality here, and the real effects of urban gambling. Call it a "world-class destination resort" as much as you like, but remember that the proposed "resort" is totally dependent on urban gambling. A Point Molate resort without a casino is like a ship without water. It won't float.

I ran for, and was elected to, the Richmond City Council last November with a clearly stated position against bringing casinos to our West County communities. I continue to uphold my position. I do not see the proposed casino complex as the "golden opportunity" painted by Anderson. I believe that elected officials must bear the responsibility of making sure that any decision—regardless of good intent—has the actual ability to create more good than bad for our city.

The questions we must ask are: Will a casino at Point Molate sustain our economy, our environment and the social well being of Richmond? Will it make us a better community?

To answer these questions, we must take a hard look at the facts about urban casinos. Studies abound, and the data all point to one conclusion: casinos bring more problems to the cities that host

3   Gayle McLaughlin, Guest Commentary, *West Contra Costa Times*, 25 June 2005.

them than they solve. The exhaustive study "Casinos, Crime and Community Costs" which was conducted by Grinols and Mustard in the late 1990s and revised in September of 2004, examines the relationship between casinos and crime. The study shows that the opening of casinos creates new crimes (as opposed to moving crime from one neighborhood to another) and values the social cost of these crimes at $75 per adult. (This is based on costs in 1996; today's costs would be higher.)

Applying the findings of this study to our city of 100,000, we can project that a few years after the opening of a casino at Point Molate, we will suffer 60 additional robberies, 1,000 additional larcenies, 300 additional burglaries, 100 more auto thefts, 60 more rapes, and 100 more aggravated assaults every year than if there was no casino here. At a cost of $75 per adult, the casino will cost us over $6 million a year. And the crime gets worse over time. Any crime-reducing effects from the increase of new low-skilled jobs tend to occur before, and for only a short time after, a casino opens. Over time, the good effects are canceled out.

The number of problem gamblers in Richmond will also increase. Clinical research shows that problem gamblers and pathological gamblers typically take two to four years to complete the cycle of starting to gamble, to becoming addicted, and exhausting their financial resources. Casinos, by definition, make money from those who lose money. No product or benefit is exchanged in the process of gambling. Many, many people drop money that they can't afford to lose and are left with nothing at all in hand.

Yes, poor families in Richmond need jobs, but gambling disproportionately affects the poor. Gamblers with household incomes under $10,000 wager nearly three times more than those with household incomes over $50,000. The negative impact of casinos on financially strapped families will far outweigh the positive impact of new jobs. And as small wheels turn inside larger wheels, the plight of the individual gambler becomes the plight of the larger society. A casino is a regressive economic development. Much more money will leave Richmond than will stay. We will pay the costs, and the profits will go to Harrah's and the developers.

I was glad to read that Major Anderson acknowledges the existence of "public concerns" about the Point Molate proposal and about casinos in general. The people of Richmond have expressed their opposition to urban casinos in polls and votes and would tumble this irresponsible idea in the ballot box again if given a chance.

Has our mayor failed to notice that we voted no on Prop. 68 and 70 in the 2004 Statewide ballot? A casino at Point Molate is a direct undermining of the democratic process in which the voters have spoken. Casinos, tribal or non-tribal, simply don't belong in urban areas. As our cities struggle to regain their balance from failed local, state, and federal policies, we must search for real and viable methods to generate revenue and employment—and refrain from jumping on the shortsighted casino bandwagon that only causes more problems in the end.

How about modifying the application of Proposition 13 to corporate property and ending corporate tax perks and giveaways? How about requiring Chevron to pay their fair share of utility taxes? Putting naive visions of easy money aside, what can Richmond families realistically expect from a casino complex at Point Molate?

Rather than a vision of international tourists and high rollers flocking to Richmond to leave their money with us, the more realistic image is one of casinos filled with local older adults, women and people of color, leaving their hard earned money at the slots in an "easy fix" effort to break the cycle of poverty and misery in which many find themselves.

To add pain to this suffering, other problems associated with casinos are sure to emerge or expand: prostitution, drug trafficking, substance abuse, domestic violence, depression, suicide, and increased poverty. On a different level, but with serious and far-reaching consequences, an increase in traffic and its pollution are sure to aggravate a situation already among the worst in the country. The need to handle all of these problems will result in the redirecting of city resources to serve the casino rather than the needs of our community.

A casino at Point Molate is a losing bet for Richmond. It will bring more problems than solutions. Let's not gamble Richmond's future.

About the Author and Editor

Gayle McLaughlin is the former two-term mayor and councilmember (2005-2017) of Richmond, California (population 110,000). In 2003, she co-founded the Richmond Progressive Alliance and, as mayor, Gayle led Richmond into a significant progressive transformation.

Gayle McLaughlin

Under her leadership, Richmond increased the minimum wage to $15 an hour by 2018, reduced homicides 75%, forced the Chevron Richmond refinery to pay millions in additional taxes, sued the oil giant for its harm to the community, and passed many cutting-edge environmental initiatives. Gayle also led the fight against foreclosures advocating for the use of city eminent domain powers to reduce underwater mortgage principals and keep homeowners in their homes.

Gayle has never taken a dime of corporate money, and has triumphed repeatedly over Chevron's millions of dollars thrown into the local elections. In 2016, with Gayle as a leading proponent, Richmond passed the first new rent control law in California in 30 years, and elected two additional corporate-free progressives to the local city council for a corporate-free super-majority of five councilmembers out of seven.

Over her twelve and a half years of elected service, Gayle has won many awards for her leadership.

Diana Wear, editor. Diana is a member of RPA and she has been an activist in the Bay Area for over thirty years. She has worked in faith, social justice, and political arenas, including worker justice, the Sanctuary Movement, nonviolence, antiwar activism, and women's ordination in the Roman Catholic Church. She has a BA from UC San Diego, a Master

Diana Wear

of Divinity from the Jesuit School of Theology, and a Master of Public Health from UC Berkeley. She was a managing editor for an academic journal and served as Assistant Director for the Office for History of Science and Technology at UC Berkeley for nearly three decades.

Unless otherwise noted, all photos are printed courtesy of the Richmond Progressive Alliance Photo Archive.

Page 8: "Contrasting Images of Richmond." Top: Chevron refinery pumping toxins into our air. Bottom: The Richmond's beautiful shoreline at sunset. Photo 1b. courtesy of Rita Gardner.

Page 42: "Speaking at First RPA Forum." Gayle speaking at "A Dialogue on Richmond," 2004.

Page 50: "People's Convention." Gayle and West County Toxics Coalition Director Henry Clark at Richmond's People's Convention in 2004.

Page 80: "Swearing in as Mayor." Gayle being sworn-in for her first term as mayor, with Councilmembers John Marquez and Nat Bates sitting on dais, 2006.

Page 110: "Fair Taxation Campaign." RPA member Michael Beer dressed as "Chevron Man" at a rally demanding fair taxation from Chevron, 2011.

Page 113: "Pt Molate." View of Pt. Molate's scenic waterfront beauty with historic Winehaven buildings.

Page 126: "No Casino." Packed Richmond auditorium demanding that the City Council adhere to the advisory vote of the 2010 electorate and reject a casino development at Pt. Molate, 2011.

Page 131: "Cap the Crude Banner." March to Richmond refinery demanding Chevron cap crude production at the refinery, provide safe jobs, and a call for climate justice. Photo courtesy of Joseph Woodard, 2009.

Page 134: "North Shoreline." The open space beauty of Dotson Marsh, one of the last intact wetlands along the San Francisco Bay, on Richmond's scenic north shoreline.

Page 147: "Solar Richmond." Gayle with Solar Richmond and others rallying for green jobs and solar energy at Atchison Village neighborhood event.

Page 151: "Reelection Kickoff." Mayoral reelection kick-off with the theme, "Building a Better Richmond Together," 2010.

Page 154: "Mayor Listens to Us." Competing campaign signs: Top: Police Union attacks Gayle saying she won't listen to them, while

Bottom: Disability Brigade counters with their own handmade sign saying "The Mayor Listens to Us," 2010.

Page 170: "City Council Disruption." Mayor McLaughlin with Councilmember Beckles sitting to her right on the dais, gives warning to disruptive audience member.

Page 175: "Chevron Fire." August 6, 2012 fire at Chevron Richmond refinery.

Page 183: "3,000 Strong March." Three thousand people marched from Richmond BART to the refinery on the first year anniversary of the 2012 fire, August 2013.

Page 190: "Guerilla Art Mural." Repainted Gompers High School Mural welcoming people to the Richmond Greenway.

Page 295: "Immigration Municipal IDs." Packed Council Chambers supporting Richmond Municipal ID for all residents, regardless of immigration status.

Page 215: "Eminent Domain." Protesters stage a skit called "How the Wall Street Grinch Stole Our Homes" outside Richmond City Hall in support of Richmond CARES (eminent domain program). Photo courtesy of Brant Ward, SF Chronicle, December 18, 2013.

Page 221: "Rent Control." Richmond renters mobilize at a City Council meeting, sharing their testimonies about skyrocketing rents and the need for rent control.

Page 233: "Ecuardorian Newspaper Ad." On stage with Andres Soto at the start of the 2013 march to the Richmond refinery, Gayle displays the full-page newspaper ad from the Contra Costa Times expressing the solidarity of the people of Ecuador with the people of Richmond, 2013.

Page 234: "Three Mayors in Ecuador." Mayor McLaughlin with Mayors of Lago Agrio and Shushufindi, 2013.

Page 248: "Chevron Cartoon." RPA member David Moore's cartoon illustrates Chevron-funded candidates singing Chevron's tune, 2014.

Page 250: "Team Richmond." Team Richmond billboard with Gayle, Jovanka, and Eduardo, 2014.

Page 252: "Bernie Sanders in Richmond." Bernie Sanders speaks to a full house at town hall meeting in Richmond auditorium, 2014.

Page 253: "Black Lives Matter." Mayor McLaughlin, Richmond Police Chief Chris Magnus, and Vice-Mayor Beckles hold Black Lives Matter sign at demonstration organized by the RYSE Center, 2014.

1 Edgar Cervano-Soto, "Richmond and Chevron: A Story of Love and Hate," Richmond Pulse 6 Aug 2013; http://richmondpulse. org/2013/08/06/richmond-and-chevron-a-story-of-love-and-hate/ (accessed 10 April 2016).

2 See http://www.ci.richmond.ca.us/112/History-of-Richmond (accessed 9 May 2016).

3 Wilbur Gary's comments can be found at www.jovankabeckles. net/GARYSTORY.pdf, p. 4 (accessed 8 December 2017).

4 For Jovanka Beckles report, see www.jovankabeckles.net/GAR-YSTORY.pdf, p. 12 (accessed 8 December 2017).

5 See http://www.bayareacensus.ca.gov/cities/Richmond.htm (accessed 9 May 2016).

6 http://www.endcorporalpunishment.org/assets/pdfs/reference-documents/Durrant-GenerationwithoutSmacking-2000. pdf (accessed 15 September 2016).

7 Frederick Douglass. BrainyQuote.com, Xplore Inc, 2016. http:// www.brainyquote.com/quotes/quotes/f/frederickd107360.html (accessed 1 Jun 2016).

8 Evelyn Reed, *Women's Evolution: From Matriarchal Clan to Patriarchal Family* (New York: Pathfinder Press, 1975), and Is Biology Women's Destiny? (New York: Pathfinder Press, 1972).

9 Thomas Paine, *Rights of Man*, 1791.

10 See http://www.contracostatimes.com/ci_23394901/chevron-announces-change-leadership-at-richmond-refinery (accessed on 24 May 2016).

11 RPA's mission statement was updated in 2015. It now reads: The RPA is an independent progressive organization that seeks

to unite Richmond's diverse communities and form alliances with other community based organizations to promote actively social justice, economic equality, health, environmental protection and democracy. We work to elect government officials who share these progressive values, and who do not accept corporate donations.

[12] For more on Argentina's Dirty War, see http://www.britannica.com/event/Dirty-War.

[13] Langston Hughes, "Dream Deferred (Harlem)," in *101 Great American Poems*, ed. Andrew Carroll, et al. (Mineola, New York: Dover, 1998), 75.

[14] Maya Cooper was a severely disabled young person who used music to participate most fully in the world around her. Maya's parents created Maya's Music Therapy Fund to remember Maya and to allow others to continue the joy she experienced through music." See www.mayasmusic.org.

[15] Peter Camejo, *California: Under Corporate Control* (Canada: Transcontinental Printing Imprimerie Gagné, 2006), 27.

[16] See Jeff Kilbreth, http://richmondprogressivealliance.net/issues/Chevron-Tax.html (accessed 1 August 2016).

[17] David Helvarg, *The Golden Shore* (New York: St. Martin's Press, 2013), 309.

[18] On Mary Swift-Swan's article, see http://www.baycrossings.com/Archives/2003/05-June/the_last_whaling_station.htm (accessed 30 September 2016).

[19] Earl L. Grinols, David B. Mustard, and Cynthia Hunt Dilley, "Casinos, Crime and Community Costs" (June 2000). See SSRN: http://ssrn.com/abstract=233792 - http://dx.doi.org/10.2139/ssrn.233792 (accessed 30 September 2016).

[20] Gayle McLaughlin, "Casino Benefit Still Doesn't Add Up for Richmond, op ed, *Contra Costa Times*, 25 July 2009.

[21] See http://www.cfspm.org/Ltr_of_1-30-12_toUpstream.pdf (accessed 18 September 2016).

[22] See Kathryn Gillick, "Parchester's Marsh," Ecology Center, 15

November 2004, see also http://ecologycenter.org/terrainmagazine/fall-2005/parchesters-marsh/ (accessed 23 August 2016).

23 Tim Holt, "Reclaiming Richmond," *San Francisco Chronicle* Magazine (22 July 2007), 10-15, 27, on 12.

24 Denny Larson, "Breathing Fire: In their Own Words," Global Community Monitor and its National Refinery Reform Campaign; for the report, see http://www.gcmonitor.org/wp-content/uploads/2013/06-/GCMFlareReport.pdf and http://www.gcmonitor.org/-communities/resources/gcm-reports/

25 Ibid.

26 Editorial, *Contra Costa Times,* 22 August 2008.

27 Ibid.

28 Van Jones, 17 April 2010. From Van Jones speech at my mayoral reelection kick-off. See https://www.youtube.com/watch?v=iofd5-dIckwand https://www.youtube.com-/watch?v=2DfdOBEWDEM (parts 1 and 2).

29 Rev. Alvin C. Bernstine, "The Politics of Dis-Ease; A Pastoral Comment on Richmond's Mayoral Campaign," *Richmond Globe*, 27 October 2010.

30 Three and a half years later, about a month before the 2014 election, Rogers finally agreed to time limits. And during his reelection campaign, Rogers had the nerve to claim he spearheaded such a change in the rules to help create decorum in the Chambers. Rogers would go on to lose his bid for re-election in both 2014 and 2016.

31 BK Williams received the American INSIGHT award as an Official Selection for her documentary Against Hate and for her tackling of this important intersection of hate speech and free speech.

32 See http://caselaw.findlaw.com/us-supreme-court/315/568.html.

33 See http://www.csb.gov/chevron-refinery-fire/.

34 See http://www.csb.gov/videos/chevron-richmond-refinery-fire-animation/.

35 See http://4cleanair.org/Documents/EPA-Letter-to-Chevron-12-17-13.pdf.

36 Bakken crude is a highly flammable crude oil extracted from the Bakken region of North Dakota and Canada, using hydraulic fracking and other dangerous technologies. A train carrying Bakken Crude derailed and exploded in Lac-Magentic, Canada, killing forty-seven people in 2013. In March 2014, RPA hosted a community forum that featured Marilaine Savard from the Citizens Committee of Lac-Mégantic and Antonia Juhasz, writer and researcher about oil-related hazards.

37 Don Adams and Arlene Goldbard, "Community, Culture, and Globalization" (The Rockefeller Foundation, 2002), 9.

38 Arlene Goldbard, *New Creative Community: The Art of Cultural Development*" (Oakland, CA: New Village Press, 2006), 20.

39 Fred Davis Jackson, "Thoughts Set Free on the Wings of Expression" (Richmond, CA: Magnolia Tree Books, 2011), 155. Listen also to his musical production, "Bouquet According to Fredology."

40 Lynda Carson, "How Big Money Stole Richmond Renters' Protections in Less than a Month," *San Francisco Bay View*, September 2015.

41 See http://caselaw.findlaw.com/us-9th-circuit/1490887.html.

42 Tyler Osburn, "Richmond Homeless Vigil a Beacon of Light for those on the Street," *Richmond Confidential*, May 2012.

43 Don José María Arizmendiarriet, *Reflections of Don José María Arizmendiarriet* (Otalara: Mondragón Corporacion Cooperativa, c. 1978), on 29-30.

44 The latest chapter includes a filing in the U.S. Supreme Court by the rainforest communities to overturn the lower court's ruling in Chevron's favor in this 'racketeering' case. See https://thechevronpit-.blogspot.com/2017/03/chevrons-false-evidence-in-ecuador-now.html (Last accessed 15 March 2017).

45 See https://www.indybay.org/newsitems/2006/08/04/18294778.php

46 See http://www.mayorsforpeace.org/english/index.html.

47 See http://academic.evergreen.edu/g/grossmaz/interventions.html.

48 See http://mikeparkerforrichmond.net/aboutmike.html

49 Steve Early, *Refinery Town: Big Oil, Big Money, and the Remaking of an American City* (Boston, MA: Beacon Press, 2016). This book chronicles many of the stories you've read here, more from an investigative perspective—a must read for progressive organizers.

50 Ibid., ix.

51 Mike Parker, "A Social Policy Case Study and Follow-Up on Richmond Progressive Alliance Two Years Later: Richmond Progressive Alliance: Defeating Big Money in Politics," *Social Policy* (2016).

52 Juan Reardon, with contributions by Mike Parker and Gayle McLaughlin, "Sharing Our Experience: The Richmond Progressive Alliance," 2016, http://www.richmondprogressive-alliance.net/about_rpa.

53 Bernie Sanders, *Our Revolution: A Future to Believe In* (New York: St. Martin's Press, 2016), 118.

A Great Vision – A Militant Family's Journey Through the Twentieth Century – by Richard March

Caring – 1199 Nursing Home Workers Tell Their Story

Fight For Your Long Day – Classroom Edition, by Alex Kudera

Love Dies, a thriller, by Timothy Sheard

Murder of a Post Office Manager, A Legal Thriller, by Paul Felton

New York Hustle – Pool Rooms, School Rooms and Street Corners, a memoir, Stan Maron

Passion's Pride – Return to the Dawning, Cathie Wright- Lewis

The Secrets of the Snow, a book of poetry, Hiva Panahi

Sixteen Tons, a Novel, by Kevin Corley

Throw Out the Water, the sequel to Sixteen Tons, by Kevin Corley

We Are One – Stories of Work, Life & Love, Elizabeth Gottieb (editor)

What Did You Learn at Work Today? The Forbidden Lessons of Labor Education, by Helena Worthen

With Our Loving Hands – 1199 Nursing Home Workers Tell Their Story

Winning Richmond – How a Progressive Alliance Won City Hall, by Gayle McLaughlin

Woman Missing, A Mill Town Mystery, by Linda Nordquist

THE LENNY MOSS MYSTERIES by Timothy Sheard

This Won't Hurt A Bit

Some Cuts Never Heal

A Race Against Death

No Place To Be Sick

Slim To None

A Bitter Pill

Someone Has To Die

CHILDREN'S BOOKS

The Cabbage That Came Back, Stephen Pearl (author), Rafael Pearl (Illustrator), Sara Pearl (translator)

Good Guy Jake, Mark Torres (author), Yana Podrieez (Illustrator), Madelin Arroyo (translator)

Hats Off For Gabbie, Marivir Montebon (author), Yana Podriez (illustrator), Madelin Arroyo (translator)

Jimmy's Carwash Adventure, Victor Narro (author & translator), Yana Podriez (illustrator)

Joelito's Big Decision, Ann Berlak (author), Daniel Camacho (Illustrator), José Antonio Galloso (Translator)

Manny & The Mango Tree, Ali R. Bustamante (author), Monica Lunot-Kuker (illustrator), Mauricio Niebla (translator)

Margarito's Forest, Andy Carter (author), Allison Havens (illustrator), Omar Mejia (Translator)

Polar Bear Pete's Ice is Melting! – Timothy Sheard (author), Madelin Arroyo (translator), A FALL 2018 RELEASE

Trailer Park – Jennifer Dillard (author), Madelin Arroyo (translator), Rafael Pearl (illustrator) A SUMMER